BETWEEN MARKET ECONOMY AND STATE CAPITALISM

One major issue facing the world trading system today is how to deal with the challenge of China's state capitalism. Many commentators believe that the existing WTO rules are insufficient and, thus, new rules are needed. This book challenges this conventional wisdom. Through meticulous studies and fresh analysis of the commitments in China's WTO accession package, existing rules on state capitalism in WTO agreements and recent attempts to make new rules on these issues at bilateral, regional and multilateral levels, this book argues that existing WTO rules, especially those on subsidies, coupled with China-specific rules in its accession protocol, do provide feasible tools to counter China's state capitalism. This book also discusses the reasons for the lack of usage of these rules and provides concrete policy suggestions on how the rules may be better utilized, as well as how to conduct constructive negotiations on new rules in the WTO and beyond.

HENRY GAO is a senior fellow at the Centre for International Governance Innovation and Professor of Law at Singapore Management University. He sits on the Advisory Board of the WTO Chairs Program and the editorial boards of the *Journal of International Economic Law* and *Journal of Financial Regulation*.

WEIHUAN ZHOU is Associate Professor and Director of Research at the Faculty of Law and Justice, UNSW Sydney and a member of the Faculty's HSF CIBEL Centre. He is the author of *China's Implementation of the Rulings of the World Trade Organization* (2019), co-Secretary of the Society of International Economic Law (SIEL) and editorial board member of the *Journal of International Trade Law and Policy*.

CAMBRIDGE INTERNATIONAL TRADE
AND ECONOMIC LAW

Series Editors

Professor Lorand Bartels
University of Cambridge
Professor Thomas Cottier
University of Berne
Professor Tomer Broude
Hebrew University of Jerusalem
Professor Andrea K. Bjorklund
McGill University, Montréal

Processes of economic regionalisation and globalisation have intensified over the last decades, accompanied by increases in the regulation of international trade and economics at the levels of international, regional and national laws. At the same time, significant challenges have arisen with respect to economic liberalization, rule-based systems of trade and investment, and their political and social impacts. The subject matter of this series is international economic law, in this contemporary context. Its core is the regulation of international trade, investment, finance and cognate areas such as intellectual property and competition policy. The series publishes books on related regulatory areas, in particular human rights, labour, environment and culture, as well as sustainable development. These areas are horizontally interconnected and vertically linked at the international, regional and national levels. The series also includes works on governance, dealing with the structure and operation of international organisations related to the field of international economic law and the way they interact with other subjects of international and national law. The series aims to include excellent legal doctrinal treatises, as well as cutting-edge interdisciplinary works that engage law and the social sciences and humanities.

Books in the Series

Capital Controls and International Economic Law
Bryan Mercurio

The Law and Practice of Global ICT Standardization
Olia Kanevskaia Whitaker

New Asian Regionalism in International Economic Law
Pasha L. Hsieh

Essential Interoperability Standards:
Interfacing Intellectual Property and Competition in International Economic Law
Simon Brinsmead

Digital Services in International Trade Law
Ines Willemyns

Law and Politics on Export Restrictions:
WTO and Beyond
Chien-Huei Wu

Energy in International Trade Law:
Concepts, Regulation and Changing Markets
Anna-Alexandra Marhold

Shareholders' Claims for Reflective Loss in International Investment Law
Lukas Vanhonnaeker

Transparency in the WTO SPS and TBT Agreements:
The Real Jewel in the Crown
Marianna B. Karttunen

Preferential Services Liberalization:
The Case of the European Union and Federal States
Johanna Jacobsson

Emerging Powers in International Economic Law:
Cooperation, Competition and Transformation
Sonia E. Rolland and David M. Trubek

Commitments and Flexibilities in the WTO Agreement on Subsidies and
Countervailing Measures
José Guilherme Moreno Caiado

The Return of the Home State to Investor-State Disputes:
Bringing Back Diplomatic Protection?
Rodrigo Polanco

Industrial Policy and the World Trade Organization:
Between Legal Constraints and Flexibilities
Sherzod Shadikhodjaev

The Public International Law of Trade in Legal Services
David Collins

The Prudential Carve-Out for Financial Services:
Rationale and Practice in the GATS and Preferential Trade Agreements
Carlo Maria Cantore

Preferential Services Liberalization:
The Case of the European Union and Federal States
Johanna Jacobsson

Judicial Acts and Investment Treaty Arbitration
Berk Demirkol

Distributive Justice and World Trade Law:
A Political Theory of International Trade Regulation
Oisin Suttle

Freedom of Transit and Access to Gas Pipeline Networks under WTO Law
Vitalily Pogoretskyy

Reclaiming Development in the World Trading System, 2nd edition
Yong-Shik Lee

Developing Countries and Preferential Services Trade
Charlotte Sieber-Gasser

Establishing Judicial Authority in International Economic Law
Edited by Joanna Jemielniak, Laura Nielsen and Henrik Palmer Olsen

WTO Dispute Settlement and the TRIPS Agreement:
Applying Intellectual Property Standards in a Trade Law Framework
Matthew Kennedy

Trade, Investment, Innovation and their Impact on Access to Medicines:
An Asian Perspective
Locknie Hsu

The WTO and International Investment Law:
Converging Systems
Jürgen Kurtz

The Law, Economics and Politics of International Standardisation
Edited by Panagiotis Delimatsis

Export Restrictions on Critical Minerals and Metals:
Testing the Adequacy of WTO Disciplines
Ilaria Espa

Optimal Regulation and the Law of International Trade:
The Interface between the Right to Regulate and WTO Law
Boris Rigod

The Social Foundations of World Trade:
Norms, Community, and Constitution
Sungjoon Cho

Public Participation and Legitimacy in the WTO
Yves Bonzon

The Challenge of Safeguards in the WTO
Fernando Piérola

General Interests of Host States in International Investment Law
Edited by Giorgio Sacerdoti, with Pia Acconci, Mara Valenti and Anna De Luca

WTO Disciplines on Subsidies and Countervailing Measures:
Balancing Policy Space and Legal Constraints
Dominic Coppens

The Law of Development Cooperation:
A Comparative Analysis of the World Bank, the EU and Germany
Philipp Dann

Liberalizing International Trade after Doha:
Multilateral, Plurilateral, Regional, and Unilateral Initiatives
David A. Gantz

Domestic Judicial Review of Trade Remedies:
Experiences of the Most Active WTO Members
Edited by Müslüm Yilmaz

The Relevant Market in International Economic Law:
A Comparative Antitrust and GATT Analysis
Christian A. Melischek

International Organizations in WTO Dispute Settlement:
How Much Institutional Sensitivity?
Marina Foltea

Public Services and International Trade Liberalization:
Human Rights and Gender Implications
Barnali Choudhury

The Law and Politics of WTO Waivers:
Stability and Flexibility in Public International Law
Isabel Feichtner

African Regional Trade Agreements as Legal Regimes
James Thuo Gathii

Processes and Production Methods (PPMs) in WTO Law:
Interfacing Trade and Social Goals
Christiane R. Conrad

Non-Discrimination in International Trade in Services:
'Likeness' in WTO/GATS
Nicolas F. Diebold

The Law, Economics and Politics of Retaliation in WTO Dispute Settlement
Edited by Chad P. Bown and Joost Pauwelyn

The Multilateralization of International Investment Law
Stephan W. Schill

Trade Policy Flexibility and Enforcement in the WTO:
A Law and Economics Analysis
Simon A. B. Schropp

BETWEEN MARKET ECONOMY AND STATE CAPITALISM

China's State-Owned Enterprises and the World Trading System

HENRY GAO
Singapore Management University

WEIHUAN ZHOU
University of New South Wales

Shaftesbury Road, Cambridge CB2 8EA, United Kingdom

One Liberty Plaza, 20th Floor, New York, NY 10006, USA

477 Williamstown Road, Port Melbourne, VIC 3207, Australia

314–321, 3rd Floor, Plot 3, Splendor Forum, Jasola District Centre, New Delhi – 110025, India

103 Penang Road, #05–06/07, Visioncrest Commercial, Singapore 238467

Cambridge University Press is part of Cambridge University Press & Assessment, a department of the University of Cambridge.

We share the University's mission to contribute to society through the pursuit of education, learning and research at the highest international levels of excellence.

www.cambridge.org
Information on this title: www.cambridge.org/9781108828499

DOI: 10.1017/9781108908795

© Cambridge University Press & Assessment 2023

This publication is in copyright. Subject to statutory exception and to the provisions of relevant collective licensing agreements, no reproduction of any part may take place without the written permission of Cambridge University Press & Assessment.

First published 2023
First paperback edition 2024

A catalogue record for this publication is available from the British Library

ISBN 978-1-108-83006-5 Hardback
ISBN 978-1-108-82849-9 Paperback

Cambridge University Press & Assessment has no responsibility for the persistence or accuracy of URLs for external or third-party internet websites referred to in this publication and does not guarantee that any content on such websites is, or will remain, accurate or appropriate.

CONTENTS

List of Figures and Tables   xii
Foreword   xiii
GREGORY SHAFFER
Preface and Acknowledgements   xv
Table of Cases   xvii
List of Abbreviations   xxii

1 **China, State Capitalism and the World Trading System**   1
  1.1 Introduction   1
  1.2 State Capitalism, State-Owned Enterprises and China   4
  1.3 International Regulation of State-Owned Enterprises   7
  1.4 The Structure of This Book   9

2 **The Evolution of China's Reforms of State-Owned Enterprises (1978–2020)**   13
  2.1 Introduction   13
  2.2 SOE Reform in China: 1978–2012   13
    2.2.1 Phase 1 (1978–1986) and Phase 2 (1987–1992): Devolution of Corporate Power   15
    2.2.2 Phase 3 (1993–2002): Privatisation, Corporatisation and Modernisation   17
    2.2.3 Phase 4 (2003–2012): Creation of National Champions   19
  2.3 The Current Reform: Elements, Progress and Issues   23
    2.3.1 Classification of SOEs   24
    2.3.2 Corporate Governance   26
    2.3.3 Ownership Diversification   29
    2.3.4 Restructuring and Reorganisation   34
    2.3.5 State Asset Management System   38
  2.4 A Summary of Current Status and Future Reform   39
  2.5 Conclusion   41

3 State Capitalism in China's Accession to the WTO: Concerns and Solutions 42
3.1 Introduction 42
3.2 China and the GATT 42
3.3 Resumption of GATT Contracting Party Status 46
3.4 WTO Accession 52
3.5 Concerns and Solutions on China's State Capitalism Model 53
    3.5.1 The Role of SOEs 54
    3.5.2 Pricing Policies and Distortions 57
    3.5.3 Industrial Policies and Subsidies 61
    3.5.4 Trading Rights 64
3.6 Conclusion 67

4 The Limits of General WTO Rules 69
4.1 Introduction 69
4.2 The Limitations of GATT/WTO Rules in Challenging State Capitalism 69
    4.2.1 Non-discrimination and State Trading Enterprises 71
    4.2.2 Tariffs and Import Monopoly 77
    4.2.3 Quantitative Restrictions and State Trading Enterprises 79
    4.2.4 Transparency 80
    4.2.5 Anti-dumping 87
4.3 Conclusion 95

5 The Potential of WTO Rules on Industrial Subsidies and China-Specific Obligations 97
5.1 Introduction 97
5.2 China's WTO-Plus Obligations on State-Owned Enterprises 97
5.3 WTO Subsidy Rules and China-Specific Obligations 102
    5.3.1 Covered Types of Subsidies: Financial Contributions and Income/Price Support 102
    5.3.2 Public Body 111
    5.3.3 Benefits Conferred 114
    5.3.4 Specificity 119
    5.3.5 Concluding Remarks 125
5.4 Conclusion 125

6 Emerging Approaches to Regulating State-Owned Enterprises: The Comprehensive and Progressive Agreement for Trans-Pacific Partnership (CPTPP) and Post-CPTPP Free Trade Agreements 127
6.1 Introduction 127
6.2 An Overview of SOE Rules in Free Trade Agreements 128

6.3 The CPTPP SOE Chapter   133
   6.3.1 Definition of SOE   133
   6.3.2 Substantive Obligations: Non-discrimination and Commercial Considerations   137
   6.3.3 Non-commercial Assistance   139
   6.3.4 Transparency   141
   6.3.5 Exceptions and Non-conforming Measures   145

6.4 Development of SOE Rules in Post-CPTPP Free Trade Agreements   148

6.5 Conclusion   153

7 Tackling China's State Capitalism: WTO Litigation and Trade Negotiation   154

7.1 Introduction   154

7.2 WTO Litigation   154
   7.2.1 Does WTO Litigation Work?   156
   7.2.2 Which Cases?   158
   7.2.3 Is There Enough Evidence?   166
   7.2.4 How to Bring Them?   167

7.3 Trade Negotiation   170
   7.3.1 Bilateral Negotiation   170
   7.3.2 Multilateral Negotiation   172

7.4 Conclusion   183

8 Conclusion: The Potential of Multilateralism   185

Index   192

FIGURES AND TABLES

Figure

2.1 SOE classifications   26

Tables

2.1 List of industries and State ownership   31
2.2 List of central SOE mergers between January 2013 and December 2020   35

FOREWORD

This book is sorely needed. A single vision regarding China and the trading system has become the norm in Washington, in which the US–China trade relationship is viewed in zero-sum terms. That is dangerous.

Not long ago, many powerful figures promoted a single vision for trade that focused on squeezing efficiency out of the global economy to reduce consumer costs. When workers' wages were squeezed, and their jobs became more precarious, that vision emboldened populist, nativist politicians. They helped trigger a new singular vision, one where security specialists dominate trade policy and governments increasingly invoke national security exceptions, including as pretexts. Countries have legitimate national security concerns regarding trade in certain sectors. But aggressive attempts to block China's rise through generalised trade protectionism on national security grounds will not only fail, it will exacerbate conflict and thus reduce security. When security exceptions become the norm, the rule of law is undermined – nationally and internationally.

The world is messier than captured in single visions. China engaged in major economic reforms. Even though it has since backtracked, there are divisions within China as to how to proceed on economic policy, just as there are in the United States. Viewing China reductively and only as a 'threat' is counterproductive; it simply will empower nativist, reactionary forces in China.

This book helps to explode the myth that the challenges of the world trading system can be reduced to China and its economic system, on the one hand, and the failure of the World Trade Organization to discipline China, on the other. Among the central challenges that the world faces today – if we are not to blow or burn up this earth – is how to manage the US–China economic and trade relationship. To do that, we need trade rules that govern the interface between the US and Chinese economic systems.[1] This book shows how the multilateral trading system already offers tools that can be used to challenge China's practices when they contravene agreed rules and thus manage the interface. Unilateral protectionist policies in the United States neither changed China nor helped the United States. This book proposes a different approach where the United States and others engage with the multilateral trading system and the dispute settlement mechanism that they helped forge. It offers hope. That hope, however, depends on enhancing trust between the United States, China and others, which, in turn, will inform the policy choices they make. Our future lies in the balance.

Gregory Shaffer
Chancellor's Professor of Law and Political Science
University of California, Irvine

---

[1] Gregory Shaffer, "Governing the Interface of U.S.–China Trade Relations" (2021) 115(4) *American Journal of International Law* 622.

PREFACE AND ACKNOWLEDGEMENTS

This book is a milestone of our ongoing research project which explores the ways to address the longstanding and mounting challenges posed by China's state capitalism to the multilateral trading system and its trading partners. We started the project in 2017 and have published several articles to ensure timely engagement in the academic and policy debate over the relevant issues, including (1) 'Building a Market Economy through WTO-Inspired Reform of State-Owned Enterprises in China', published in the *International & Comparative Law Quarterly*, (2) 'Subsidizing Technology Competition: China's Evolving Practices and International Trade Regulation', published in the *Washington International Law Journal*, (3) 'WTO Reform and China: Defining or Defiling the Multilateral Trading System', published in the *Harvard International Law Journal*, (4) 'Rethinking the (CP)TPP as a Model for Regulation of Chinese State-Owned Enterprises', published in the *Journal of International Economic Law*, and (5) 'China's Changing Perspective on the WTO: From Aspiration, Assimilation to Alienation', published in the *World Trade Review*. Chapters 2, 3, 4, 5 and 6 of this book have used materials published in these articles.

Due to the outbreak of the COVID-19 pandemic, we were significantly delayed in delivering this book. However, compared with five years ago, China's state-led economic model has become an even more important and controversial issue and will remain central to international trade policymaking at bilateral, plurilateral and multilateral fora in the years to come. From this perspective, we believe this book arrives at a better time.

Colin Picker, Andrew Mitchell and Junji Nakagawa encouraged us to turn the project into a book. With their encouragement, we submitted a book proposal to Cambridge University Press. Joe Ng, Acquisition Editor (Social Science), has since provided tremendous guidance and assistance in various matters from the review of the book proposal to the completion, promotion and publication of this book. Three anonymous reviewers provided valuable and constructive comments and suggestions on the book proposal, allowing us to improve the structure and content of this book. Over the years, we have benefited enormously from intellectual dialogues with many experts and friends in the international trade law community, especially those with Gregory Shaffer, Mark Wu, Robert Howse, Joost Pauwelyn, Jennifer Hillman, James Bacchus and Simon Lester on topics relating to this book.

This research is supported by the National Research Foundation, Singapore under its Emerging Areas Research Projects (EARP) Funding Initiative. Any opinions, findings and conclusions or recommendations expressed in this material are those of the authors and do not reflect the views of the National Research Foundation, Singapore.

We are also grateful for the funding support of the Lee Kong Chian Fellowship at Singapore Management University, the IEEM Academy Research Grant 2020 and the Herbert Smith Freehills China International Business and Economic Law (CIBEL) Centre of the Faculty of Law and Justice, UNSW Sydney.

Our sincere gratitude must also go to Dr Xue Bai for her excellent research assistance throughout this project and Carley Bartlett for her editorial comments on each chapter of this book.

Last, but not least at all, we are deeply indebted to our respective families. Without their generosity, patience and tireless support, it would have been impossible for us to devote time to this book.

TABLE OF CASES

Short Title	Full Citation
Australia – A4 Copy Paper	Panel Report, *Australia – Anti-Dumping Measures on A4 Copy Paper*, WT/DS/529/R, adopted 27 January 2020.
Australia – Automotive Leather II	Panel Report, *Australia – Subsidies Provided to Producers and Exporters of Automotive Leather*, WT/DS126/R, adopted 16 June 1999.
Australia – Tobacco Plain Packaging	Panel Report, *Australia – Certain Measures Concerning Trademarks, Geographical Indications and Other Plain Packaging Requirements Applicable to Tobacco Products and Packaging*, WT/DS435/R, WT/DS441/R, WT/DS458/R, WT/DS467/R, adopted 29 June 2020.
Brazil – Taxation	Appellate Body Report, *Brazil – Certain Measures Concerning Taxation and Charges*, WT/DS472/AB/R, WT/DS497/AB/R, adopted 11 January 2019.
Canada – Aircraft	Appellate Body Report, *Canada – Measures Affecting the Export of Civilian Aircraft*, WT/DS70/AB/R, adopted 20 August 1999.
Canada – Autos	Appellate Body Report, *Canada – Certain Measures Affecting the Automotive Industry*, WT/DS139/AB/R, WT/DS142/AB/R, adopted 19 June 2000.
Canada – FIRA	GATT Panel Report, *Canada – Administration of the Foreign Investment Review Act*, L/5504–30s/140, adopted 7 February 1984.

Canada – Provincial Liquor Boards (EEC)	GATT Panel Report, *Import, Distribution and Sale of Alcoholic Drinks by Canadian Provincial Marketing Agencies*, L/6304-35S/37, adopted 22 March 1988.
Canada – Provincial Liquor Boards (US)	GATT Panel Report, *Canada – Import, Distribution and Sale of Certain Alcoholic Drinks by Provincial Marketing Agencies*, DS17/R-39S/27, adopted 18 February 1992.
Canada – Renewable Energy/Feed-in Tariff Program	Panel Report, *Canada – Certain Measures Affecting the Renewable Energy Generation Sector/Measures Relating to the Feed-in Tariff Program*, WT/DS412/R, WT/DS426/R, adopted 24 May 2013.
	Appellate Body Report, *Canada – Certain Measures Affecting the Renewable Energy Generation Sector/Measures Relating to the Feed-in Tariff Program*, WT/DS412/AB/R, WT/DS426/AB/R, adopted 24 May 2013.
Canada – Wheat	Panel Report, *Canada – Measures Relating to Exports of Wheat and Treatment of Imported Grain*, WT/DS276/R, adopted 27 September 2004.
	Appellate Body Report, *Canada – Measures Relating to Exports of Wheat and Treatment of Imported Grain*, WT/DS276/AB/R, adopted 27 September 2004.
China – Auto Parts	Panel Report, *China – Measures Affecting Imports of Automobile Parts*, WT/DS339/R, WT/DS340/R, WT/DS342/R, adopted 12 January 2009.
	Appellate Body Report, *China – Measures Affecting Imports of Automobile Parts*, WT/DS339/AB/R, WT/DS340/AB/R, WT/DS342/AB/R, adopted 12 January 2009.
China – GOES	Panel Report, *China – Countervailing and Anti-Dumping Duties on Grain Oriented Flat-rolled Electrical Steel from the United States*, WT/DS414/R, adopted 16 November 2012.

China – Publications and Audiovisual Products	Appellate Body Report, *China – Measures Affecting Trading Rights and Distribution Services for Certain Publications and Audiovisual Entertainment Products*, WT/DS363/AB/R, adopted 19 January 2010.
China – Rare Earths	Panel Report, *China – Measures Related to the Exportation of Rare Earths, Tungsten and Molybdenum*, WT/DS431/R, WT/DS432/R, WT/DS433/R, adopted 29 August 2014.
	Appellate Body Report, *China – Measures Related to the Exportation of Rare Earths, Tungsten and Molybdenum*, WT/DS431/AB/R, WT/DS432/AB/R, WT/DS433/AB/R, adopted 29 August 2014.
China – Raw Materials	Panel Report, *China – Measures Related to the Exportation of Various Raw Materials*, WT/DS394/R, WT/DS395/R, WT/DS398/R, adopted 22 February 2012.
	Appellate Body Report, *China – Measures Related to the Exportation of Various Raw Materials*, WT/DS394/AB/R, WT/DS395/AB/R, WT/DS398/AB/R, adopted 22 February 2012.
EC – Aircraft	Panel Report, *European Communities and Certain Member States – Measures Affecting Trade in Large Civil Aircraft*, WT/DS316/R, adopted 1 June 2011.
	Appellate Body Report, *European Communities and Certain Member States – Measures Affecting Trade in Large Civil Aircraft*, WT/DS316/AB/R, adopted 1 June 2011.
EC – Fasteners	Appellate Body Report, *European Communities – Definitive Anti-Dumping Measures on Certain Iron or Steel Fasteners from China*, WT/DS397/AB/R, adopted 28 July 2011.
EEC – Apples	GATT Panel Report, *European Economic Community – Restrictions on Imports of Apples – Complaint by the United States*, L/6513 – 36S/135, adopted 22 June 1989.

EU – Biodiesel	Appellate Body Report, *European Union – Anti-Dumping Measures on Biodiesel from Argentina*, WT/DS473/AB/R, adopted 26 October 2016.
EU – PET (Pakistan)	Panel Report, *European Union – Countervailing Measures on Certain Polyethylene Terephthalate from Pakistan*, WT/DS486/R, adopted 25 May 2018.
	Appellate Body Report, *European Union – Countervailing Measures on Certain Polyethylene Terephthalate from Pakistan*, WT/DS486/AB/R, adopted 25 May 2018.
Japan – DRAMs (Korea)	Appellate Body Report, *Japan – Countervailing Duties on Dynamic Random Access Memories from Korea*, WT/DS336/AB/R, adopted 17 December 2007.
Korea – Beef	Panel Report, *Korea – Measures Affecting Imports of Fresh, Chilled and Frozen Beef*, WT/DS161/R, WT/DS169/R, adopted 10 January 2001.
Korea – Beef (Australia)	GATT Panel Report, *Republic of Korea – Restrictions on Imports of Beef – Complaint by Australia*, L/6504 – 36S/202, adopted 7 November 1989.
Korea – Commercial Vessels	Panel Report, *Korea – Measures Affecting Trade in Commercial Vessels*, WT/DS273/R, adopted 11 Apr. 2005.
India – Quantitative Restrictions	Panel Report, *India – Quantitative Restrictions on Imports of Agricultural Textile and Industrial Products*, WT/DS90/R, adopted on 22 September 1999.
US – Aircraft (2nd complaint)	Appellate Body Report, *United States – Measures Affecting Trade in Large Civil Aircraft (Second Complaint)*, WT/DS353/AB/R, adopted 23 March 2012.
US – Anti-Dumping and Countervailing Duties (China)	Panel Report, *United States – Definitive Anti-Dumping and Countervailing Duties on Certain Products from China*, WT/DS379/R, adopted 25 March 2011.
	Appellate Body Report, *United States – Definitive Anti-Dumping and Countervailing Duties on Certain Products from China*, WT/DS379/AB/R, adopted 25 March 2011.

US – Carbon Steel (India)	Appellate Body Report, *United States – Countervailing Measures on Certain Hot-Rolled Carbon Steel Flat Products from India*, WT/DS436/AB/R, adopted 19 December 2014.
US – Countervailing Measures (China)	Panel Report, *United States – Countervailing Duty Measures on Certain Products from China*, WT/DS437/R, adopted 16 January 2015.
	Appellate Body Report, *United States – Countervailing Duty Measures on Certain Products from China*, WT/DS437/AB/R, adopted 16 January 2015.
US – Countervailing Measures (China) (Article 21.5)	Appellate Body Report, *United States – Countervailing Duty Measures on Certain Products from China – Resources to Article 21.5 of the DSU by China*, WT/DS437/AB/RW, adopted 15 August 2019.
US – Export Restraints	Panel Report, *United States – Measures Treating Exports Restraints as Subsidies*, WT/DS194/R, adopted 23 August 2001.
US – Hot-Rolled Steel	Appellate Body Report, *United States – Anti-Dumping Measures on Certain Hot-Rolled Steel Products from Japan*, WT/DS184/AB/R, adopted 23 August 2001.
US – Safeguard Measure on PV Products	Panel Report, *United States – Safeguard Measure on Imports of Crystalline Silicon Photovoltaic Products*, WT/DS562, circulated 2 September 2021.
US – Section 301 Trade Act	Panel Report, *United States – Sections 301–310 of the Trade Act of 1974*, WT/DS152/R, adopted 27 January 2000.
US – Softwood Lumber IV	Appellate Body Report, *United States – Final Countervailing Duty Determination with Respect to Certain Softwood Lumber from Canada*, WT/DS257/AB/R, adopted 17 February 2004.
US – Upland Cotton	WTO Panel Report, *United States – Subsidies on Upland Cotton*, WT/DS267/R, adopted 21 March 2005.

ABBREVIATIONS

AB	Appellate Body
AD	anti-dumping
AD Agreement	Anti-Dumping Agreement
AP	Protocol on the Accession of China
APA	Administrative Procedure Act
Baosteel	Baosteel Group Corporation
CAI	China–EU Comprehensive Agreement on Investment
Caihong	Caihong Group Corporation
CETC	China Electronics Technology Group Corporation
Chengtong	China Chengtong Holdings Group Limited
China Grain	China Grain and Logistics Corporation
China Hi-Tech	China Hi-Tech Group Corporation Limited
China Shipping	China Shipping (Group) Company
Chinatex	Chinatex Corporation Limited
CICT	China Information and Communication Technologies Group Corporation
CITS	China International Travel Service Group Corporation
CNACGC	China National Arts and Crafts (Group) Corporation
CNBM	China National Building Materials Group Corporation
CNEC	China Nuclear Engineering and Construction Corporation
CNNC	China National Nuclear Corporation
CNR	China CNR Corporation Limited
CNV	Constructed Normal Value
COFCO	China National Cereals, Oils and Foodstuffs Corporation
COSCO	China Ocean Shipping (Group) Company
COSCOCS	China COSCO Shipping Corporation Limited
CPC/Party	Communist Party of China
CPI	China Power Investment Corporation
CPTPP	Comprehensive and Progressive Agreement for Trans-Pacific Partnership
CSIC	China Shipbuilding Industry Company
CSR	CSR Corporation Limited

CSSC	China State Shipbuilding Corporation
CWB	Canadian Wheat Board
EC	European Communities
Erzhong	China National Erzhong Group Corporation
EU	European Union
FIEs	foreign-invested enterprises
FTAs	free trade agreements
GATS	General Agreement on Trade in Services
GATT	General Agreement on Tariffs and Trade
Guodian	China Guodian Corporation
HKCTS	China Travel Service (HK) Group Corporation
Huafu	China Huafu Trade and Development Corporation
IAs	investigating authorities
IPO	Initial Public Offering
IPR	intellectual property rights
ITO	International Trade Organization
LPMO	Livestock Products Marketing Organisation
MCC	China Metallurgical Group Corporation
MFN	most-favoured-nation
MIC 2025	made in China 2025
Minmentals	China Minmetals Corporation
MOFCOM	Ministry of Commerce
MOFET	Ministry of Foreign Economic and Trade
MPIA	multi-party interim appeal arbitration arrangement
Nam Kwong	Nam Kwong (Group) Company Limited
National Cotton	China National Cotton Reserves Corporation
NCA	non-commercial assistance
NCMs	non-conforming measures
NDRC	National Development and Reform Commission
NEVs	new energy vehicles
NME	non-market economy
NT	national treatment
OCT	ordinary course of trade
OECD	Organization for Economic Co-operation and Development
PMS	particular market situation
POEs	privately-owned enterprises
Poly Group	China Poly Group Corporation
PRC	People's Republic of China
R&D	research and development
RCEP	Regional Comprehensive Economic Partnership
ROC	Republic of China

SASAC	State-Owned Assets Supervision and Administration Commission
SCICs	State capital investment companies
SCIOs	State capital investment and operation companies
SCM Agreement	Agreement on Subsidies and Countervailing Measures
SCOCs	State capital operation companies
Shenhua	Shenhua Group Corporation Limited
Sinograin	China Grain Reserves Corporation
Sinolight	Sinolight Corporation
Sinoma	China National Materials Group Corporation Limited
Sinomach	China National Machinery Industry Corporation
Sinotrans Group	Sinotrans Group Limited
SNPTC	State Nuclear Power Technology Corporation Limited
SOEs	State owned enterprises
SPS	sanitary and phytosanitary
STEs	State trading enterprises
TBT	technical barriers to trade
TPP	trans-Pacific partnership
TPRM	trade policy review mechanism
TRIPs	Agreement on Trade-Related Aspects of Intellectual Property Rights
US	United States
USMCA	United States–Mexico–Canada agreement
USSR	Union of Soviet Socialist Republics
USTR	United States trade representative
VAT	value-added tax
WISCO	Wuhan Iron and Steel (Group) Corporation
WPR	report of the Working Party on the Accession of China
WTO	World Trade Organization
Zhen Rong	Zhuhai Zhen Rong Company

1

China, State Capitalism and the World Trading System

1.1 Introduction

On 10 November 2001, China finally joined the World Trade Organization (WTO) after a marathon accession negotiation stretching 15 years.[1] Fast forwarding 20 years, China has emerged as the largest trader in the world, yet the world trading system is in crisis, with its dispute settlement system in paralysis and its latest negotiation round – the Doha Round – languishing for most of the past decade. Some observers argue that the triumph of China and the decline of the WTO are not mere coincidence but deeply correlated. According to them, China manipulated its trade practices through its state capitalism model to get where it is today, and this is exactly what precipitated the crisis at the WTO, because its rules are ill-equipped to deal with China's practices which violate the spirit but not necessarily the letter of the world trade law, thus leading to the collapse of its dispute settlement and negotiation functions.

As we write this book, this narrative remains the most popular in the trade law circle, with some key WTO Members, particularly the United States, pushing for reforms of the multilateral trade rules. The United States, under the Trump administration, vehemently criticised the WTO for being 'incapable of fundamentally changing [China's] trade regime that broadly conflicts with the fundamental underpinnings of the WTO system'.[2] The Biden administration has largely maintained this position. In a recent speech, the United States Trade Representative (USTR) Katherine Tai criticised 'China's lack of adherence to global trading rules'

---

[1] World Trade Organization, 'WTO Ministerial Conference Approves China's Accession', 10 November 2001, available at: www.wto.org/english/news_e/pres01_e/pr252_e.htm. The last accessed date for all websites within this title is 1 March 2022.
[2] United States Trade Representative, '2019 Report to Congress on China's WTO Compliance', March 2020, available at: https://ustr.gov/sites/default/files/2019_Report_on_China%E2%80%99s_WTO_Compliance.pdf.

and failure to make 'meaningful reforms to address the concerns' about 'its state-centered economic system'.³ The European Union (EU) shared the United States' concerns by labelling China's 'state-capitalist model' and associated 'unfair trade practices' as the fundamental challenge for the world trading system.⁴ To address these concerns, the two Members, along with Japan, issued a series of joint statements calling for the strengthening of the WTO rules on state owned enterprises (SOEs) and industrial subsidies.⁵

The popularity of this narrative is not hard to understand as it combines all of the right elements: the economic rise of China, its practice of state capitalism and the decline of the world trading system. Yet, having the right elements can only guarantee a nice story, not the correct answer. The biggest flaw of the narrative is that it mistakes correlation with causation. As we will unpack in this book, the full story of the interactions between China's state capitalism and the world trading system is much more nuanced than this simplistic narrative. As a matter of fact, concerns over the potential incompatibilities between China's unique economic system and the rules of the multilateral trading system are not new. As soon as China applied to return to the General Agreement on Tariffs and Trade (GATT),⁶ the predecessor of the WTO, the Members noticed the problems and carefully crafted China-specific rules to tackle them in the final accession package. Upon its accession, China initially made a conscientious effort to reform its economic system, especially its SOEs, in the direction of more market-orientation

---

³ Centre for Strategic and International Studies, 'A Conversation with Ambassador Katherine Tai, U.S. Trade Representative', 4 October 2021, available at: www.csis.org/analysis/conversation-ambassador-katherine-tai-us-trade-representative.
⁴ European Commission, 'Trade Policy Review – An Open, Sustainable and Assertive Trade Policy', COM(2021)66 Final, 18 February 2021, 2, 9–14, available at: https://ec.europa.eu/transparency/regdoc/rep/1/2021/EN/COM-2021-66-F1-ENMAIN-PART-1.PDF.
⁵ Office of the United States Trade Representative, 'Joint Statement on Trilateral Meeting of the Trade Ministers of the United States, Japan, and the European Union', 31 May 2018, available at: https://ustr.gov/about-us/policy-offices/press-office/press-releases/2018/may/joint-statement-trilateral-meeting; Office of the United States Trade Representative, 'Joint Statement of the Trilateral Meeting of the Trade Ministers of the United States, European Union, and Japan', 23 May 2019, available at: https://ustr.gov/about-us/policy-offices/press-office/press-releases/2019/may/joint-statement-trilateral-meeting; European Commission, 'Joint Statement of the Trilateral Meeting of the Trade Ministers of Japan, the United States and the European Union', 14 January 2020, available at: https://trade.ec.europa.eu/doclib/docs/2020/january/tradoc_158567.pdf.
⁶ General Agreement on Tariffs and Trade, Geneva, 30 October 1947, in force 1 January 1948, 61 Stat A-11, 55 UNTS 194 (GATT).

as aligned with the requirements of WTO rules. However, as time went by, China's reform process stalled and even went into reverse gear over the past decade. But this does not necessarily mean that the existing WTO rules are useless in dealing with China's state capitalism. If anything, the degree of marketisation in China today is certainly much higher than it was 20 years ago, when China first joined the WTO, and even more so than 36 years ago, when China sought its return to the multilateral trading system. Thus, the extensive discussions on China's state capitalism that took place during the accession negotiation, including the problems with state control of the economy and the solutions worked out by existing WTO Members and China together, are highly relevant today.

This book challenges the conventional wisdom that the existing WTO rules are inadequate to address China's state capitalism, particularly the market-distortive conduct of Chinese SOEs supported by industrial policies and subsidies. Our key argument is that China's WTO-plus obligations, coupled with the general rules on subsidies, can be applied to tackle these problems. This argument is advanced not only through a detailed analysis of the relevant general WTO rules, but also a thorough examination of the evolution of China's SOE reforms, especially fresh insights from the latest phase, and a critical review of the WTO-plus obligations in China's WTO accession package. The latter review shows that these China-specific rules were not intended to mandate a systemic change of China's economic model, but merely to tackle select aspects of the Chinese system. Thus, the concerns with China's state capitalism model were more specific than systemic, contrary to the above-mentioned narrative that has dominated the debate about China and the world trading system. Through these discussions, this book also expounds the challenges posed by state intervention, SOEs and non-market economies (NMEs) to the multilateral trading system and the relationship between WTO rules and state intervention, the nature of rules on subsidies and other market-distortive practices. Moreover, to strengthen our argument, this book critically examines the efficacy of new sets of rules advanced in recent free trade agreements (FTAs), particularly the Comprehensive and Progressive Agreement for Trans-Pacific Partnership (CPTPP) and some major post-CPTPP agreements such as the China–EU Comprehensive Agreement on Investment (CAI). We argue that, compared with these new rules, China's WTO-plus obligations remain more rigorous in many substantive aspects.

Based on the above analyses, a major policy recommendation of this book is that WTO Members should continue to resort to the WTO dispute settlement system to challenge China's state capitalism using existing rules. This book provides detailed guidelines on how to make this litigation strategy more fruitful. New WTO rules, if needed, can be developed only via multilateral negotiations. Here, the ongoing discussion on WTO reform provides a good opportunity to engage China, especially in view of President Xi's recent announcement that China would be willing to engage in discussions on issues relating to SOEs and subsidies, which are the key elements in its state capitalism model. While the details for such discussions are still being worked out, the negotiations can only be successful if certain rules of engagement, as outlined in this book, are followed. Of course, as it takes time to negotiate the new rules, WTO litigation based on existing rules remains the best option, at least for now and for some time to come.

Finally, while this book focuses on China (for good reasons), most of its analysis is not limited to China alone. Instead, issues such as the challenges of SOEs for global trade and governance, the applicability of WTO rules to SOEs and the development of multilateral and regional approaches to tackling SOE-related issues are all systemic problems in international trade regulation. Accordingly, this book offers a valuable source for future studies, policymaking and trade law practice not only in relation to China but also the development of the world trade rules more generally.

1.2 State Capitalism, State-Owned Enterprises and China

As an evolving concept, 'state capitalism' has developed new meanings in the globalised world. Nowadays, it is no longer accurate to equate state capitalism with purely planned or command economies, or bluntly contrast it with free market capitalism.[7] Most economies have undergone some degree of market opening and domestic reforms in pursuit of economic growth. A more nuanced definition of state capitalism, thus, refers to the magnitude of government involvement in business activities depending on 'state ownership stake in or significant influence over' the

---

[7] See e.g. Aldo Musacchio and Sérgio G. Lazzarini, 'Leviathan in Business: Varieties of State Capitalism and Their Implications for Economic Performance', Harvard Business School Working Paper No 12–108, June 2012, 9–10.

business sector.⁸ While state capitalism takes different forms in different economies,⁹ a common feature pertains to the extensive role that SOEs have been playing in consolidating and expanding state capitalism.

The mounting challenges posed by SOEs to the world economy are widely documented. The Organization for Economic Co-operation and Development (OECD), in particular, has taken a range of initiatives to explore these challenges and the regulatory approaches to address them.[10] The starting point is to treat SOEs as a global issue because many economies other than China maintain a significant state sector.[11] As observed by the OECD, the underlying problem arises from the non-commercial behaviour and conduct of SOEs driven by political or policy motives rather than commercial interests.[12] Such behaviour and conduct is typically enabled by a wide spectrum of unfair competitive advantages given to SOEs, ranging from subsidies and preferential financing to privileged access to information, regulatory advantages, protected monopolistic positions and other forms of government support.[13] As SOEs increasingly compete with privately-owned enterprises (POEs) in home and foreign markets, their privileged position and anti-competitive practices lead to significant market distortions and undermine the interests of POEs, particularly those of trading partners.

When it comes to China, it is widely observed that, despite the rapid growth of the private sector and the progressive liberalisation in China,[14] SOEs remain one of the principal mechanisms of Chinese state capitalism.[15] In fact, China's ongoing SOE reform has strengthened rather than weakened state capitalism through the growing influence of the state and

---

[8] See Joshua Kurlantzick, *State Capitalism: How the Return of Statism Is Transforming the World* (New York: Oxford University Press, 2016), 13–14; Musacchio and Lazzarini, 'Leviathan in Business', n. 7, 3–4.

[9] See generally Kurlantzick, *State Capitalism*, n. 8, 29–47.

[10] See e.g. Antonio Capobianco and Hans Christiansen, 'Competitive Neutrality and State-Owned Enterprises: Challenges and Policy Options', OECD Corporate Governance Working Papers No 1, 1 May 2011; OECD, *Guidelines on Corporate Governance of State-Owned Enterprises* (Paris: OECD Publishing, 2015); OECD, *State-Owned Enterprises as Global Competitors: A Challenge or an Opportunity?* (Paris: OECD Publishing, 2016).

[11] See OECD, *State-Owned Enterprises as Global Competitors*, n. 10, 21–6.

[12] Ibid., 27.

[13] Ibid., 28–30.

[14] See Nicholas R. Lardy, *Markets over Mao: The Rise of Private Business in China* (Washington, DC: Peterson Institute for International Economics, 2014).

[15] See Benjamin L. Liebman and Curtis J. Milhaupt, 'Introduction: The Institutional Implications of China's Economic Development', in Benjamin L. Liebman and Curtis J.

the Communist Party of China (CPC or Party) on Chinese firms, especially SOEs.[16] The control of SOEs by the state/Party is not necessarily problematic, at least not under the rules of the WTO. However, combined with other factors, such control could and often does result in anti-competitive effects. One such factor concerns a range of state support conferring significant competitive advantages on Chinese SOEs through direct and indirect subsidies, preferential regulatory treatment and exemptions, etc. These problems are further exacerbated by China's unique economic model, which treats SOEs as the primary economic agents of the state and the main instrument for implementing industrial and other national policies.[17] Frequently, the state combines large SOEs that are already market leaders individually to create behemoth national champions in disregard of antitrust concerns.[18] In addition to squeezing competitors out of the relevant Chinese market,[19] SOEs have also been used as a vehicle to restrict market access to China by foreign competitors and expand China's presence in foreign markets through aggressive bids and other means, often with the financial backing of the Chinese government.[20] Moreover, state/Party controls not only create such anti-competitive effects but also tend to sustain those effects by preventing markets from self-correcting through the confluence of factors such as vertical policy actions, administrative monopoly and preferential support for SOEs.[21] Accordingly, these practices not only raise concerns about competition in general but also pose mounting challenges to the multilateral trading system, as they undermine the conditions of competition

---

Milhaupt (eds.), *Regulating the Visible Hand? The Institutional Implications of Chinese State Capitalism* (New York: Oxford University Press, 2016), xiii, xv.

[16] See also Nicholas R. Lardy, *The State Strikes Back: The End of Economic Reform in China?* (Washington, DC: Peterson Institute for International Economics, 2019).

[17] See William Kovacic, 'Competition Policy and State-Owned Enterprises in China' (2017) 16(4) *World Trade Review* 693, 704.

[18] See Li-Wen Lin, 'A Network Anatomy of Chinese State-Owned Enterprises' (2017) 16(4) *World Trade Review* 583, 587.

[19] See Peter Harrell, Elizabeth Rosenberg and Edoardo Saravalle, 'China's Use of Coercive Economic Measures', Center for a New American Security, June 2018, 1, 22, available at: https://s3.amazonaws.com/files.cnas.org/documents/China_Use_FINAL-1.pdf?mtime=20180604161240.

[20] See e.g. Kanupriya Kapoor and Hidayat Setiaji, 'Indonesia Favouring China over Japan in Railway Bid – Govt Sources', Thomson Reuters, 31 August 2015, available at: www.reuters.com/article/indonesia-infrastructureidUSL4N1162WK20150831. Also see Angela Huyue Zhang, 'The Antitrust Paradox of China, Inc.' (2017) 50 *New York University Journal of International Law and Politics* 159, 166.

[21] See Kovacic, 'Competition Policy and State-Owned Enterprises in China', n. 17, 705.

that the WTO is designed to maintain. Therefore, they put to the test the adequacy and efficacy of WTO rules in coping with Chinese state capitalism.

1.3 International Regulation of State-Owned Enterprises

The challenges posed by SOEs entail two essential policy responses. Competitive neutrality, as the first response, seeks to constrain preferential treatment or the privileged position of SOEs so as to remove their competitive advantages and level the playing field vis-à-vis POEs.[22] This approach requires not only rules to deal with subsidies and other preferential treatment enjoyed by SOEs but also rigorous competition laws and enforcement more broadly.[23] Competition policies and enforcement, including competitive neutrality, vary considerably across jurisdictions, and harmonisation among different economic, political and social systems can hardly be achieved in any near future.[24] In the case of China, its competition law and enforcement have largely failed to constrain the competitive advantages and anti-competitive practices of Chinese SOEs.[25] Therefore, while competitive neutrality is a key element to address the 'SOE problems', it is also imperative to discipline the market-distortive behaviour and conduct of SOEs directly.

The second response tackles the market-distortive behaviour and conduct of SOEs, especially when engaged in commercial activities that harm the interests of foreign competitors.[26] The scope of these disciplines hinges on how SOEs are defined and enforcement requires access to detailed information about SOEs, the support they receive from

---

[22] See Capobianco and Christiansen, 'Competitive Neutrality and State-Owned Enterprises', n. 10; Alicia García-Herrero and Gary Ng, 'China's State-Owned Enterprises and Competitive Neutrality', Bruegel Policy Contribution Issue No 05/21, February 2021.
[23] See García-Herrero and Ng, 'China's State-Owned Enterprises and Competitive Neutrality', n. 22.
[24] Robert Anderson, William Kovacic, Anna Caroline Muller and Nadezhda Sporysheva, 'Competition Policy, Trade and the Global Economy: Existing WTO Elements, Commitments in Regional Trade Agreements, Current Challenges and Issues for Reflection', WTO Staff Working Paper ERSD-2018-12, 31 October 2018.
[25] See García-Herrero and Ng, 'China's State-Owned Enterprises and Competitive Neutrality', n. 22, 11–16; Kovacic, 'Competition Policy and State-Owned Enterprises in China', n. 17, 706–11.
[26] See OECD, *State-Owned Enterprises as Global Competitors*, n. 10, 83–95.

governments, etc., which in turn calls for rules on transparency and disclosure.²⁷ At the same time, however, the legitimate needs of governments to use SOEs for public policy objectives are also generally recognised.²⁸ This means that international disciplines on SOEs are necessarily subject to exceptions and exemptions so as to save the policy space needed by governments.

This book does not discuss competition rules in trade agreements but focuses on disciplines on the behaviour and conduct of SOEs. The general WTO rules that apply to all Members do not define SOEs and provide only limited disciplines. While we acknowledge that the existing WTO rules are not perfect in this regard, especially the general agreements of the WTO, we do believe in the potential of several China-specific rules in its accession package which have been strikingly underutilised to date. Given the broad coverage of these rules, they can be applied to address the major problems associated with China's state capitalism such as non-commercial behaviour of Chinese SOEs, the supportive industrial policies and subsidies they receive and state intervention in the market more broadly. However, to unleash the full potential of these rules, WTO Members need to invoke these rules to challenge the relevant Chinese laws and practices via litigation. As shown in past cases, WTO litigation can not only build a body of jurisprudence that clarifies the scope of the China-specific obligations but also push China to undertake systemic adjustments.²⁹ Without recourse to the dispute settlement system, the potential of these obligations and their impact on China will only remain tenuous. It follows that the conventional narrative about the inadequacy or ineffectiveness of the existing WTO rules is untenable and misleading.

As noted in the Introduction, we are aware of the efforts by some WTO Members to explore new approaches to regulate SOEs in FTAs such as the CPTPP and the CAI. However, these rules do not add much new to the existing rules in China's WTO accession package. While China's engagement with the EU on the negotiations of the CAI and its recent request for entry into the CPTPP are a good sign of its

---

[27] See OECD, *State-Owned Enterprises as Global Competitors*, n. 10, 18–19; OECD, *Guidelines on Corporate Governance of State-Owned Enterprises*, n. 10, 24–5.
[28] See e.g. OECD, *State-Owned Enterprises as Global Competitors*, n. 10, 19; OECD, *Guidelines on Corporate Governance of State-Owned Enterprises*, n. 10, 12–13.
[29] Weihuan Zhou, *China's Implementation of the Rulings of the World Trade Organization* (Oxford: Hart Publishing, 2019).

willingness to accept more international disciplines on SOEs, trade negotiators will need to rethink the efficacy of the CPTPP/CAI rules on SOEs.

1.4 The Structure of This Book

The summary provided in this chapter not only provides a background for our detailed discussions in this book but also maps our core arguments, which will be unfolded in the subsequent chapters as follows:

In Chapter 2, we trace the contours of China's SOE reform since 1978, when the reform and opening up policy was first adopted. We divided the four decades of reform into five phases, where the first two phases focused on ensuring the survival of SOEs by granting them operational autonomies, first at the firm level and then at the managerial level. China did not have much choice for the initial phases of the reform, as the old system of central planning was obviously not working, as proven by the dilapidated state most SOEs were in as they emerged from the Cultural Revolution before Deng Xiaoping took power in 1978. The third phase of the reform was premised on the philosophy that SOEs should be made profitable, which saw the adoption of corporatisation strategies for the ones deemed promising and privatisation of the ones deemed unviable. It is interesting to note that this wave of privatisation took place in the decade after Deng's famous Southern Tour and also coincided with the final stretch of China's WTO accession. It could be argued that the privatisation efforts helped to dispel potential concerns over the sincerity of China's economic reform and paved the way for China's final accession. The fourth phase of the reform covered the first decade after China's accession to the WTO, where the earlier trajectories were continued, as we can see in the efforts to continue the market-oriented reform for SOEs with plans of commercialisation and modernisation. At the same time, a worrying trend also started to emerge during this period, when the government launched various campaigns to create national champions. This trend was not only inherited but also amplified as we enter the new era of 'Socialism with Chinese Characteristics', where SOEs, strengthened by the previous rounds of reforms, started to squeeze out private firms in various forms. At the same time, the CPC has also stepped up its efforts to enhance its influence in SOEs by launching aggressive drives to build Party cells in these entities to enhance Party control in the current round/phase of SOE reform. This goes against the direction of market-oriented reform in previous phases, and it is no wonder that this phase also saw the rise of the narrative that WTO rules are ill-equipped to handle China's state capitalism, a claim that we debunk in Chapter 3.

In Chapter 3, we deflate the myth that China's state capitalism is a new problem, with an extensive review of how such concerns were discussed and addressed during China's WTO accession. Drawing from the negotiation records in the Report of the Working Party on China's accession, we demonstrate that WTO Members were well aware of the potential clashes between WTO rules and China's state capitalism since the very beginning. Yet, contrary to those who argue that state capitalism is inherently incompatible with the WTO, the Members believed that practical solutions could be found to minimise the inconsistencies between WTO rules and China's trade practices. Thus, they meticulously identified specific aspects of the Chinese system that might undermine its WTO commitments and carefully crafted surgical solutions to address these problems in WTO-consistent ways. Such an approach is much better than the one demanding a complete overhaul of China's economic system, as it not only minimises the resistance of China but also ensures that the problematic areas are fully addressed. Thus, the theory that the accession negotiation failed to address the problems presented by China's state capitalism is unconvincing. Instead, the practical approach adopted in the negotiation demonstrates the faith among WTO Members in the ability of the WTO to act as a neutral forum for countries with different economic systems to interact with each other, which is the topic that we explore further in Chapters 4 and 5.

In Chapters 4 and 5, we explore the utility of different WTO rules in disciplining market-distortive behaviours of SOEs and subsidies that enhance their competitive advantages, with some being more promising and others less so. The less promising ones are discussed in Chapter 4, including GATT rules on import monopolies, state trading enterprises (STEs), transparency, and anti-dumping (AD) measures. In our view, these rules are all of limited utility, albeit for different reasons: the rules on import monopolies and STEs are quite narrow in terms of the coverage of policy instruments and the prescribed obligations, the transparency obligation is rather toothless, while the ability to use AD measures to deal with market distortions due to state intervention has been curtailed by the Appellate Body (AB) in recent cases. Of course, this does not mean that all WTO rules are useless. Instead, as discussed in Chapter 5, great potential can be found in China-specific rules on pricing and the commercial behaviour of SOEs, coupled with WTO rules on subsidies both in the original Agreement on Subsidies and Countervailing Measures (SCM Agreement) and further elaborated in China's WTO Accession Protocol. In particular, in response to the argument that WTO subsidy rules have been rendered ineffective by the AB's interpretation of the term 'public body', we argue that the utility of the provision has been rehabilitated by the AB's subsequent decision in *US – Countervailing Measures (China) (Article 21.5)*. Moreover, even the original 'authority-based' test is no longer an insurmountable hurdle due to the backtracking of China's SOE reform in recent years, which resulted in more micro-management by the Party and state in the management of SOEs. Thus, the best way to tackle China's state capitalism is through WTO litigation based on existing rules discussed in this chapter. That said, we are aware of the different views and proposals of some key Members in favour of the development of new rules on SOEs. Their approaches to advancing such new rules, particularly through various regional initiatives such as the CPTPP, are discussed in Chapter 6.

Chapter 6 provides a critical evaluation of the new rules on SOEs developed in international trade and investment agreements, with the CPTPP as the leading example. Despite its reputation as a 'twenty-first century high-standard trade agreement', we argue that the SOE rules in the CPTPP do not add much to the existing rules in the WTO and are less rigorous than China's WTO-plus obligations discussed in Chapter 5. In particular, the scope of the covered entities under the CPTPP tends to be narrower, while its rules on commercial considerations, non-discrimination, and subsidies do not go beyond the obligations crafted for China in its accession package. Moreover, the rigour of these CPTPP rules is further reduced by the inclusion of extensive exemptions and exceptions that allow CPTPP governments to carve out sub-central SOEs and schedule non-conforming measures. This chapter then examines some major post-CPTPP trade and investment agreements with significant rules on SOEs including the EU–Japan FTA, the EU–Vietnam FTA, the United States–Mexico–Canada Agreement (USMCA) and the CAI. As one of China's latest international agreements, the CAI is also the first treaty where China agreed to SOE rules outside the WTO. Again, the main substantive obligation here – the one on commercial considerations – simply repeats the existing obligation in China's WTO accession package. While all of the FTAs discussed in this chapter should be praised for setting new and higher standards of transparency, they do not resolve the longstanding problem of enforcement – the most challenging issue under the WTO's transparency regime. By the end of this chapter, we have set out all the materials and analysis to support our core policy recommendations focusing on litigation and negotiation in the WTO, which are elaborated in Chapter 7.

Drawing on our analysis in the previous chapters, Chapter 7 is dedicated to a more focused discussion on how to tackle China's state capitalism in the WTO. The first option is utilising existing WTO rules, especially those China-specific provisions, to bring cases against China, which so far has not happened. This is partly due to the perception that WTO litigation does not work against China, an argument which we refute by referring to China's good compliance record with WTO decisions. At the same time, we do agree that a more strategic approach should be taken in bringing such cases and proceed to suggest the types of cases that should be brought and how the evidentiary burden could be met. The second option is through trade negotiations. While bilateral negotiations such as the US–China Phase One deal do not really work, there is great potential in multilateral negotiations. Here, we caution against those advocating the exclusion of China in such rule-making efforts and argue that China should be engaged to make the negotiation fruitful. To make the discussions more productive, we also suggest certain guidelines to make sure that China will be more constructively engaged. Hopefully, with President Xi's recent statement that China would be willing to engage in WTO reform discussions on SOEs and subsidies, coupled with the more widespread use of subsidies by Western governments during the COVID-19 pandemic, more common ground can be found between China and the other major players in the system in the pursuit of more advanced rules on SOEs and subsidies.

In the conclusion, Chapter 8 sets out the main findings and suggestions from the preceding chapters, and tries to gaze into the future even though we do not have a crystal ball. Only time will tell which of our predictions turn out to be true but, regardless of the outcome, we hope that our book has made some modest contribution towards the understanding of the multi-faceted challenges presented by China's state capitalism to the multilateral trading system and in turn helps strengthen the WTO, an institution that we have both served and deeply believe in.

2

The Evolution of China's Reforms of State-Owned Enterprises (1978–2020)

2.1 Introduction

This chapter reviews the four decades of state-owned enterprise (SOE) reform in China since 1978. It divides China's SOE reform between 1978 and 2012 into four phases and discusses the achievements and limitations of the reform in each phase. It then provides a detailed analysis of the current round of reform commenced in 2013. We argue that, while China's SOE reform has achieved many positive and significant changes, the more recent reforms have led to a remarkable resurrection of state capitalism. The reform in the current round has been designed (and implemented) to ensure that the market-based transformation of SOEs serves China's industrial policies and economic goals and does not undermine the effective control of the Party/state. As market liberalisation and market-oriented economic reforms continue to progress in China, the SOE reform is becoming increasingly sophisticated, creating new challenges for the multilateral trading system.

2.2 SOE Reform in China: 1978–2012

SOE reform was one of the central elements of China's landmark economic reforms launched in 1978–1979, alongside and intertwined with the 'Opening-Up' policy, reform of the price system and reform of the financial sector, amongst others.[1] Under China's purely central-planning system before 1978, SOEs were essentially 'state-run enterprises' completely owned and managed by the government without any autonomy.[2] They took orders from the state on all important corporate and

---

[1] See generally Gregory Chow, 'Economic Reform and Growth in China' (2004) 5 *Annals of Economics and Finance* 127.
[2] See Qunhui Huang, 'How "New SOEs" Come of Age: Four Decades of China's SOE Reform' (2018) 13(1) *China Economist* 58, 60.

commercial matters in relation to, for instance, production (e.g. products and outputs), sales (e.g. customers, targets and prices), appointment of senior management and personnel and employment and benefits.[3] In addition, they were also expected to assume certain social functions such as running schools and hospitals.[4] As SOEs were fully funded by the state, they were not allowed to retain profits. Instead, their profits were remitted to the government while their losses were subsidised.[5] As an extension of the government, SOEs were overwhelmingly inefficient and uncompetitive. As China kicked off the economic reforms and undertook a gradual transition to a more market-oriented economy, the SOE reform was carried out on an experimental and incremental basis, with an aim to eventually transform SOEs to market-oriented commercial entities. The incremental approach was necessary given the dominant role of SOEs in the economy, the complexities in the state sector and the non-existence of a private sector at the outset of the reform.[6] More importantly, it reflected the need to strike a balance between the decentralisation, commercialisation and modernisation of SOEs on the one hand and the maintenance of political and social stability on the other,[7] which remains the core challenge facing China's reformers.

Prior to the current round of reform, China's SOE reform between 1978 and 2012 can be divided into four phases. While the first two phases focused on the devolution of corporate power or decentralisation of SOEs, the third phase sought to commercialise and modernise SOEs through privatisation and corporatisation. However, the last phase of reform shifted to the creation of 'national champions' of large SOEs, especially in strategic sectors.

---

[3] See Dong Zhang and Owen Freestone, 'China's Unfinished State-Owned Enterprise Reforms' (2013) 2 *Economic Roundup* 77, 8.; Hongfei Zhong, 'Where Is the Future: China's SOEs Reform' (2006) 1(1) *Journal of the Washington Institute of China Studies* 105.

[4] See Xin Li and Kjeld Erik Brodsgaard, 'SOE Reform in China: Past, Present and Future' (2013) 31(2) *The Copenhagen Journal of Asian Studies* 54, 56.

[5] Ibid., 55.

[6] See e.g. Nicholas Lardy, *China's Unfinished Economic Revolution* (Washington, DC: The Brookings Institution, 1998) 25–30; Zhang and Freestone, 'China's Unfinished State-Owned Enterprise Reforms', n. 3, 80.

[7] See Zhang and Freestone, 'China's Unfinished State-Owned Enterprise Reforms', n. 3, 78–9; OECD, 'State Owned Enterprises in China: Reviewing the Evidence', OECD Working Group on Privatisation and Corporate Governance of State Owned Assets, 26 January 2009, 1, 3.

2.2.1 Phase 1 (1978–1986) and Phase 2 (1987–1992): Devolution of Corporate Power

The first phase (1978–1986) focused on the devolution of corporate power by increasing the operational autonomy of SOEs so as to incentivise managers and employees to pursue profit and growth.[8] A series of policy documents were published, seeking to gradually increase the autonomy of SOEs in a range of corporate activities such as production and sales, profit distribution, human resources, procurement, etc.[9] The reform mandated that government agencies share some of their operational functions with the managers of SOEs, based on the view that managers have a better knowledge of the operation of the enterprises. Despite these efforts, the reform was merely the beginning of the 'devolution' process and the operational autonomy granted was largely limited to allowing enterprises to sell surplus products at market prices (after the state-planned production targets were met) and then to keep profits from such sales.[10] The state remained the owner of SOEs, in charge of a dominant proportion of their activities.[11] Consequently, the reform did not change the ownership or management structure of SOEs. Furthermore, the reform failed to provide sufficient incentives to SOEs due to, *inter alia*, the lack of an effective mechanism to enforce the repayment of state bank loans by unprofitable SOEs and the unclear allocation of responsibilities of SOEs under the so-called profit and loss contract responsibility system introduced in 1982.[12] Nevertheless, the steps taken in this phase laid the groundwork for the subsequent stages of reform.

The second phase (1987–1992) carried on the initiatives developed in the first phase. It sought to overcome the various obstacles to the

---

[8] See Yiping Huang, 'State-Owned Enterprises Reform' in Yiping Huang and Ronald Duncan (eds.), *Reform of State-Owned Enterprises in China: Autonomy, Incentive and Competition* (Canberra: Asia Pacific Press, 1998) 95, 9.; Huang, 'Four Decades of China's SOE Reform', n. 2, 60–4; Xiao Geng, Xiuke Yang and Anna Janus, 'State-Owned Enterprises in China: Reform Dynamics and Impacts' in Garnaut, Song and Woo (eds.) *China's New Place in a World in Crisis* (Canberra: ANU Press, 2009) 155, 157; Li and Brodsgaard, 'SOE Reform in China', n. 4, 56.

[9] See Huang, 'State-Owned Enterprises Reform', n. 8, 99; Huang, 'Four Decades of China's SOE Reform', n. 2, 62–4.

[10] See generally Jinglian Wu and Guochuan Ma, *Whither China?: Restarting the Reform Agenda*, Xiaofeng Hua and Nancy Hearst trans. (Oxford: Oxford University Press, 2016) 120–34.

[11] See Huang, 'State-Owned Enterprises Reform', n. 8, 100.

[12] Ibid., 100–1; Huang, 'Four Decades of China's SOE Reform', n. 2, 64.

expansion of managerial autonomy of SOEs and the separation between ownership and management.[13] Among the reform measures, the *Law on Industrial Enterprises Owned by the Whole People* of 1988[14] (Industrial Enterprises Law) endorsed the contract responsibility system and further regulated its implementation.[15] For example, Article 2 of the Law provided that the property of an SOE 'shall be operated and managed by the enterprise ... in line with the principle of the separation of ownership and managerial authority'. It further provided that the enterprise 'shall obtain the status of a legal person' and 'may ... adopt contract, leasing or other forms of the system of managerial responsibility'. Article 7 mandated the managers of SOEs to assume 'overall responsibility for the work' of the enterprises. Chapter III of the Law granted operational autonomy to SOEs in relation to production, sale, budget, lease and transfer of fixed assets, wages and bonuses, employment, organisational structure and joint operation. In practice, the delegation of managerial power on these matters was achieved through contracts between enterprise managers and the government.[16]

However, like in the first phase, the second phase failed to affect the ownership of and the government's control over SOEs. As Wu Jinglian, a leading proponent of economic reform in China, observed, 'The [contract responsibility] system did not turn enterprises into independent entities responsible for their own profits and losses, nor did it realize the separation of government from enterprises or equal competition among enterprises.'[17] Despite the attempt to pursue the separation of ownership and management, the Industrial Enterprises Law maintained the ownership structure of SOEs and the decision-making power of the state and required the enterprises to comply with state plans (e.g. Articles 2 and 3). In practice, decisions of SOEs were often overturned by the

---

[13] See Jinglian Wu, 《当代中国经济改革教程》 [*Understanding and Interpreting China's Economic Reform*], 2nd ed. (上海远东出版社 [Shanghai Far East Publishers], 2016) 152–3; Huang, 'Four Decades of China's SOE Reform', n. 2, 64.

[14] 《中华人民共和国全民所有制工业企业法》 [Law of People's Republic of China on Industrial Enterprises Owned by the Whole People], Order of the President of the People's Public of China No 3, adopted at the 1st Session of the 7th National People's Congress on 13 April 1988; amended on 27 August 2009, effective on the same date.

[15] For a more detailed discussion, see Huang, 'Four Decades of China's SOE Reform', n. 2, 64; Huang, 'State-Owned Enterprises Reform', n. 8, 101–2.

[16] See Huang, 'State-Owned Enterprises Reform', n. 8, 101–3; Huang, 'Four Decades of China's SOE Reform', n. 2, 64–6.

[17] See Wu and Ma, *Whither China?*, n. 10, 70.

state, particularly with respect to investment and employment.[18] Furthermore, while SOEs were entitled to retain certain profits, they were not generally held responsible for losses.[19] This led to the pursuit of short-term benefits by managers and employees at the expense of the firms' long-term interests. Eventually, the contract responsibility system became hard to implement, calling for more fundamental reform of ownership and institution. Further reform was also necessitated as China began negotiations for resumption of GATT membership in 1986 and subsequently for accession to the WTO.

2.2.2 Phase 3 (1993–2002): Privatisation, Corporatisation and Modernisation

More radical reform was introduced in the third phase (1993–2002) following the ideological breakthrough brought by Deng Xiao Ping's 'Southern Tour' in 1992 and the Third Plenum of the fourteenth Party Congress in 1993. The Plenum adopted the *Decision on Matters Concerning the Creation of a Socialist Market Economic System* (Decision 1993),[20] which marked a major turning point in China's transition from a centrally-planned to a market-oriented economy.[21] The Decision laid a blueprint for the establishment of a 'Socialist Market Economy', allowing the market to play a fundamental role in the allocation of resources under state macro-control. Based on this overarching principle, the Decision mandated the creation of a 'modern enterprise system' to transform SOEs into economic entities suitable for the new economic structure. The core elements of the reform included (1) clarification of property rights, (2) clarification of rights and

---

[18] See Huang, 'State-Owned Enterprises Reform', n. 8, 103.
[19] Ibid.; Lardy, *China's Unfinished Economic Revolution*, n. 6, 23; Daniel Ho and Angus Young, 'China's Experience in Reforming Its State-Owned Enterprises: Something New, Something Old and Something Chinese?' (2013) 2(4) *International Journal of Economy, Management and Social Sciences* 84, 85.
[20] 《中共中央关于建立社会主义市场经济体制若干问题的决定》 [Decision of the Central Committee of the Communist Party of China on Matters Concerning the Creation of a Socialist Market Economic System], 17 November 1993, available at: http://cpc.people.com.cn/GB/64162/134902/8092314.html.
[21] For a more detailed discussion of SOE reform in this phase, see Yingyi Qian and Jinglian Wu, 'China's Transition to a Market Economy: How Far across the River?' in Nicholas Hope, Dennis Tao Yang and Mu Yang Li (eds.), *How Far across the River?: Chinese Policy Reform at the Millennium* (Stanford, CA: Stanford University Press, 2003) 31, 35–8; OECD, 'State Owned Enterprises in China', n. 7, 4–5.

responsibilities of SOEs, (3) separation of regulatory and business functions, and (4) professional management. Significantly, the Decision endorsed the importance of private ownership to the economy (which was subsequently codified in China's Constitution in 1999)[22] and, for the first time, the privatisation of SOEs.[23] This created an environment for non-state firms to enter the market and resulted in phenomenal growth of the private sector while SOEs were gradually downsized.[24] In a practical sense, the reform pursued the 'corporatisation' of SOEs in accordance with the Chinese *Company Law* enacted in 1994.[25] This led to the recognition of companies as distinct legal entities (separate from their owners/shareholders), the recognition of limited liability of shareholders, the introduction of mixed ownership, and the development of a modern corporate structure and corporate governance system.[26] The goal was to transform SOEs into independent commercial entities and create a level playing field for state and non-state sectors to compete in the market.[27] The ambitious SOE reform in this period, combined with the other elements of the economic reforms, facilitated China's accession to the WTO in 2001.

However, it must be noted that the SOE reform was carried out based on the principle of 'grasping the large, releasing the small', which resulted in different forms and degrees of privatisation according to the size of SOEs.[28] While small and medium sized SOEs were typically converted into stock cooperative companies through the sale of shares to employees, large SOEs were converted into joint stock companies or limited

---

[22] Amendment to the Constitution of the People's Public of China, National People's Congress, 15 March 1999, Article 16. That private sector may play a role in China's economy was recognised for the first time in China's Constitution in 1988. See Amendment to the Constitution of the People's Public of China, National People's Congress, 12 April 1988, Article 1.
[23] See Nicholas Lardy, *Markets over Mao: The Rise of Private Business in China* (Washington, DC: Peterson Institute for International Economics, 2014) 45.
[24] Ibid., 45–6; See also OECD, *OECD Reviews of Regulatory Reform – China: Defining the Boundary between the Market and the State* (Paris: OECD Publishing, 2009) 42–3.
[25] 《中华人民共和国公司法》 [Company Law of the People's Republic of China], Order of the President of the People's Republic of China No 8, adopted at the 5th Session of the 8th National People's Congress on 29 December 1993; amended on 25 December 1999; 28 August 2004; 27 October 2005; and 28 December 2013, effective on 1 March 2014.
[26] See Lardy, *China's Unfinished Economic Revolution*, n. 6, 24.
[27] See OECD, *OECD Reviews of Regulatory Reform – China*, n. 24, 18.
[28] See Lardy, *Rise of Private Business in China*, n. 23, 45.

liability companies through public listing.[29] Although the scale of the privatisation and corporatisation was massive across all SOEs, the depth of reform of large SOEs was limited as the state remained the dominant shareholder and continued to control these entities.[30] Furthermore, the influence of the Party was not reduced in large SOEs as it retained the power to appoint various agencies to supervise the operation of these entities.[31] As a result, the role of the Party in the operation of large SOEs remained unclear, to say the least. Another issue that emerged in this period of reform concerned the loss of state assets when some SOEs were sold at undervalued prices due to corruption in the privatisation process.[32] This problem became one of the key elements of the subsequent reform.

2.2.3 Phase 4 (2003–2012): Creation of National Champions

The establishment of the State-Owned Assets Supervision and Administration Commission (SASAC) in March 2003 opened the fourth phase of SOE reform (2003–2012). The priority of the reform shifted from the commercialisation and modernisation of SOEs to the preservation and expansion of state assets and the creation of 'national champions' of large SOEs, especially in strategic sectors.[33] On 27 May 2003, the State Council issued the *Interim Regulations on the Supervision and Administration of State-Owned Assets of Enterprises* (Regulation) to set forth the mandates of the SASAC and its local branches in managing state-owned assets and supervising the operation of SOEs.[34] It authorised the SASAC and its local branches to invest and expand state assets and to

---

[29] Ibid., 56. See also Huang, 'State-Owned Enterprises Reform', n. 8, 106; Mark Williams, 'China', in Mark Williams (ed.), *The Political Economy of Competition Law in Asia* (Cheltenham; Edward Elgar, 2013) 88, 99.

[30] See Lardy, *Rise of Private Business in China*, n. 23, 45–6.

[31] See Huang, 'Four Decades of China's SOE Reform', n. 2, 70; OECD, 'State Owned Enterprises in China', n. 7, 5; Qian and Wu, 'China's Transition to a Market Economy', n. 21, 46.

[32] For a more detailed discussion of the problems at this stage of reform, see Wu and Ma, *Whither China?*, n. 10, 158–9.

[33] See Lardy, *Rise of Private Business in China*, n. 23, 48–9; Li and Brodsgaard, 'SOE Reform in China', n. 4, 57; Zhang and Freestone, 'China's Unfinished State-Owned Enterprise Reforms', n. 3, 83.

[34] See e.g. 《企业国有资产监督管理暂行条例》 [Interim Regulations on the Supervision and Administration of State-Owned Assets of Enterprises], Order No. 378 of the State Council, 27 May 2003; amended on 8 January 2011, effective on the same date.

hold shares in the invested entities on behalf of the central or local governments.[35] While these institutions were required to defer to the operational autonomy of the invested entities, they had the power to guide and push forward the reform and restructuring of SOEs, supervise their activities and appoint or remove senior management personnel.[36] With the entry into force of the *State-Owned Asset Law* in 2009, the role of the SASAC was further strengthened.[37] The Law clarified the division of labour between the SASAC and its local branches, mandating the former to focus on industries critical to national security or the lifeline of the national economy (Article 4).[38] It classified state-invested enterprises (SIEs) into wholly-SIEs, state-invested holding companies, and state-invested joint stock companies (Article 5). It confirmed that the SASAC and its local branches not only had ownership rights but also the rights to participate in the decision-making of these entities (e.g. Articles 12 and 13). The assignment of multiple roles to the SASAC and its local branches increased the likelihood of government intervention in the business activities of SIEs and further blurred the role of government in the management and operation of these entities.[39] It has also been

---

[35] Ibid., Article 5.
[36] Ibid., Articles 7, 10, 13 and 17.
[37] 《中华人民共和国企业国有资产法》[Law of the People's Republic of China on State-Owned Assets of Enterprises], Standing Committee of the National People's Congress, Decree No. 5 of the President of the People's Republic of China, 1 May 2009. For a discussion of the issues relating to the legal status of the SASAC, see Mikael Mattlin, 'Chinese Strategic State-Owned Enterprises and Ownership Control' (2009) 4(6) *BICCS Asia Paper* 1, 9–10.
[38] According to Li Rongrong, the then Chairman of the SASAC, the state needs to maintain 'absolute control' in seven sectors, including military industries, power grids and power generation, the oil and petrochemical sectors, telecommunications, the coal industry, civil aviation and shipping. The state also needs to maintain 'comparatively strong control' in nine pillar industries, namely equipment manufacturing, automobile manufacturing, electronics and information technology, construction, iron and steel, ferrous metals, chemical products, survey and design and science and technology. See Ren Fang and Liu Bing, 国资委：国有经济应保持对七个行业的绝对控制力 [*SASAC: the State Should Keep Absolute Control Over Seven Industries*], 新华社 [Xinhua News Agency], 18 December 2006, available at: www.gov.cn/jrzg/2006-12/18/content_472256.htm.
[39] For a detailed discussion of SASAC's multiple roles, see Barry Naughton, 'Top-Down Control: SASAC and the Persistence of State Ownership in China', paper presented at the 'China and the World Economy' conference, Leverhulme Centre for Research on Globalisation and Economic Policy, University of Nottingham, 23 June 2006, 1–21. For a detailed discussion of how the SASAC can be influential on SOEs, see Fei Du, Guliang Tang and Mark Young, 'Influence Activities and Favoritism in Subjective Performance Evaluation: Evidence from Chinese State-Owned Enterprises' (2012) 87(5) *The Accounting Review* 1555–88.

observed that the Party played an important role in SASAC-controlled entities, maintaining a high level of influence on their operation.⁴⁰ In practice, large SOEs underwent significant restructuring through overseas listing, separation of core business from non-core business and mergers and acquisitions. These activities led to increasing concentration of central SOEs in key economic sectors, which reduced their number but created some of the world's largest companies.⁴¹ This led some to characterise the SASAC as the world's largest controlling shareholder and most powerful holding company.⁴² Meanwhile, the National Development and Reform Commission (NDRC) rolled out a host of industrial policies to promote the development of strategic and emerging industries, expanding state influence beyond public utilities.⁴³

However, it must be noted that, while the reform efforts in this period were predominantly dedicated to bolstering the state sector, the *Decision on Matters Concerning the Improvement of The Socialist Market Economic System*,⁴⁴ passed by the Third Plenum of the Sixteenth Party Congress in October 2003, endorsed the 'modern enterprise system' and the associated initiatives advanced in the previous phase of reform, such as mixed ownership, property rights and the growth of the private sector. This ensured that the commercialisation and modernisation of SOEs remained on the reform agenda and progressed in the meantime. SOEs ceded considerable space to private firms in almost all industrial product lines, including some of the pillar industries.⁴⁵ One compelling piece of evidence of this is the unprecedented expansion of private firms from 443,000 in 1996 to 5,918,000 in 2012, accounting for over seven-tenths of all firms.⁴⁶ Last but not least, China's entry into the WTO generated significant pressure on the government to accelerate, expand and deepen

---

⁴⁰ See Lardy, *Rise of Private Business in China*, n. 23, 51.
⁴¹ See Geng et al., 'State-Owned Enterprises in China', n. 8, 158–61; Lardy, *Rise of Private Business in China*, n. 23, 50.
⁴² See e.g. United States–China Economic and Security Review Commission, '2012 Report to Congress', November 2012, 48, available at: www.uscc.gov/sites/default/files/annual_reports/2012-Report-to-Congress.pdf.
⁴³ See Lardy, *Rise of Private Business in China*, n. 23, 52–5, 57–8.
⁴⁴ 《中共中央关于完善社会主义市场经济体制若干问题的决定》 [Decision of the Central Committee of the Communist Party of China on Matters Concerning the Improvement of The Socialist Market Economic System], 14 October 2003, available at: http://cpc.people.com.cn/GB/64162/64168/64569/65411/4429165.html.
⁴⁵ See Lardy, *Rise of Private Business in China*, n. 23, 76–9.
⁴⁶ Ibid., 66.

the economic reforms towards a market-oriented economy.[47] Among China's ambitious WTO commitments,[48] a number of WTO-plus obligations on the reform of the state sector were undertaken to minimise state influence on commercial activities. These commitments have the potential to drive the SOE reform and 'could have substantial economic effects on the Chinese economy'.[49] In reality, however, the market-based reform of SOEs progressed slowly due to the provision of a variety of financial support and preferential treatment to SOEs, entrenched state intervention in business decisions and activities and increasingly powerful SOEs, despite the shrinking state sector as a whole.[50] These issues provoked robust debates, internationally and domestically, over the needs and approaches to push forward the SOE reform.[51]

Prior to the launch of the current SOE reform, the number of SOEs and of their employees had shrunk, as had their market share in many sectors.[52] However, they had also become even more significant and influential in the economy. For example, in 2013, the 110 central SOEs (under the supervision of the SASAC) held 38,423 subsidiaries (compared with 16,290 subsidiaries in 2005) and controlled state assets worth a total of RMB 9.3 trillion (compared to RMB 3.7 trillion in 2005).[53] The

---

[47] For a discussion of how China used the WTO accession to promote domestic reforms, see Yongtu Long 'Negotiating Entry: Key Lessons Learned' in Carlos A. Magarinos, Long Yongtu and Francisco Sercovich (eds.), *China in the WTO: The Birth of a New Catching-Up Strategy* (New York: Palgrave Macmillan, 2002) 25–35; Ligang Song, 'The State of the Chinese Economy – Structural Changes, Impacts and Implications' in Deborah Z. Cass, Brett Williams and George Barker (eds.), *China and the World Trading System: Entering the New Millennium* (Cambridge: Cambridge University Press, 2003) 83–92.

[48] For an overview of China's WTO commitments, see Nicholas Lardy, *Integrating China into the Global Economy* (Washington, DC: Brookings Institution Press, 2002) 65–105.

[49] See e.g. Claustre Bajona and Tianshu Chu, 'Reforming State Owned Enterprises in China: Effects of WTO Accession' (2010) 13 *Review of Economic Dynamics* 800; Shanshan Li and Ningxiang Xu, 'The Influence of WTO Accession on China's State-Owned Enterprises' (2015) 3 *Open Journal of Business and Management* 192.

[50] See Zhang and Freestone, 'China's Unfinished State-Owned Enterprise Reforms', n. 3, 85–93.

[51] Ibid., 93. The World Bank and the Development Research Centre of the State Council of China, *China 2030: Building a Modern, Harmonious, and Creative Society* (Washington, DC: The World Bank, 2013) 109–15.

[52] Barry Naughton, 'The Current Wave of State Enterprise Reform in China: A Preliminary Appraisal' (2017) 12(2) *Asian Economic Policy Review* 282, 284–5.

[53] For 2013 data, see '中国国有资产监督管理年鉴编委会 [Editorial]' in 《中国国有资产监督管理年鉴 2014》 *[China's State-owned Assets Supervision and Administration Yearbook 2014]* (中国经济出版社 [Beijing: China Economic Publishing House], 2014) 687. For 2005 data, see '中国国有资产监督管理年鉴编委会 [Editorial]' in 《中国国有

efforts to create national champions had remarkable results, with eighty-five mainland Chinese companies (the majority of which were SOEs) included in the Fortune Global 500 list of the world's largest corporations in 2013, whereas there had only been eleven in 2003.[54] Notably, all of the 11 Chinese companies in the top 100 list in 2013 were central SOEs.

2.3 The Current Reform: Elements, Progress and Issues

The current phase of SOE reform was launched by the Third Plenum of the eighteenth Party Congress in November 2013, which adopted the *Decision on Matters on Comprehensively Deepening Reform* (Decision 2013).[55] The Decision seeks to further comprehensive economic reforms, focusing on enabling the market to play a decisive role in the allocation of resources and managing government intervention in a way that enhances fair competition. It reiterates the significance of pursuing a 'modern enterprise system' through the further severing of regulatory and business functions, improving corporate management and governance, and exposing SOEs to market competition. The Decision contemplates several important initiatives, including the classification of SOEs, the creation of state assets management entities, and the introduction of private ownership to industries or projects that were previously reserved for SOEs. At the same time, however, the Decision envisages that the economic reforms must be carried out under the Party's leadership. To implement the Decision, the Central Committee of the Party and the State Council jointly issued the *Guiding Opinions on Deepening the*

资产监督管理年鉴 2006》 *[China's State-Owned Assets Supervision and Administration Yearbook 2006]* (中国经济出版社 [Beijing: China Economic Publishing House], 2014) 597. See also Naughton, 'The Current Wave of State Enterprise Reform in China', n. 52, 285–6.

[54] For the full list of Fortune 500 companies 2003, see 财富 [Fortune], 2003年世界500强按国别和地区排名 [Fortune 500 company 2003], 1 October 2003, available at: www.fortunechina.com/fortune500/c/2003-10/01/content_9594.htm. For the full list of ninety-five Chinese companies that made the Fortune 500 2013, see 财富 [Fortune], 2013 年世界500强95家中国公司完整名单 [Full list of 95 Chinese Companies available on the 2013 Fortune 500], 8 July 2013, available at: www.fortunechina.com/fortune500/c/2013-07/08/content_164367.htm.

[55] 《中共中央关于全面深化改革若干重大问题的决定》[Decision of the Central Committee of the Communist Party of China on Matters on Comprehensively Deepening Reform], 12 November 2013, available at: www.gov.cn/jrzg/2013-11/15/content_2528179.htm.

Reform of State-Owned Enterprises[56] (Guiding Opinions) in August 2015, which was followed by numerous implementing regulations at both central and local levels.[57] After over five years of implementation, it has become clear that the reform has been conducted in ways that seek to create more powerful and globally competitive SOEs in the pursuit of industrial policies and economic development goals under the leadership of the Party.[58] Accordingly, the reform has led to growing state investment and influence in strategic sectors as contemplated in China's national policies, such as Made in China 2025[59] (MIC 2025) and its Thirteenth Five Year Plan (2016–2020).[60] Overall, the current reform is likely to strengthen rather than cause any fundamental change of China's state capitalism.

2.3.1 Classification of SOEs

The first element of the current reform concerns the classification of SOEs into 'General Commercial SOEs', 'Special Commercial SOEs' and

---

[56] 《中共中央、国务院关于深化国有企业改革的指导意见》[Guiding Opinions of the Communist Party of China Central Committee and the State Council on Deepening the Reform of State-Owned Enterprises], promulgated by Central Committee of the Communist Party of China and the State Council, Zhong Fa [2015] No. 22, effective on 24 August 2015 (Guiding Opinions).

[57] Liu Qingshan, 《攻坚克难 浴火重生——国企国资5年改革掠影》[A Glimpse of the Five years Reform of State-Owned Enterprises] (2017) No. 9, *State-Owned Assets Report* [国资报告] 10, 11.

[58] For an official summary of the major achievements in the SOE reform between 2015–2020, see SASAC, 'SOE in Past 5 Years', 22 December 2020, available at: http://en.sasac.gov.cn/2020/12/22/c_6394.htm.

[59] 《国务院关于印发<中国制造2025>的通知》(2015) [Notice on the Printing and Release of 'Made in China 2025' (2015)], issued by the State Council on 8 May 2015, effective on the same date. This ambitious ten-year action plan sets out ten strategic industries: information technology; numerical control tools and robotics; aerospace equipment; ocean engineering equipment and high-tech ships; railway equipment; energy saving and new energy vehicles (NEVs); power or renewable energy equipment; new materials; medicines and medical devices; and agricultural machinery.

[60] 《中华人民共和国国民经济和社会发展第十三个五年规划纲要(2016–2020)》[Thirteenth Five-Year Plan for National Economic and Social Development of the People's Republic of China (2016–2020)], promulgated on 17 March 2016, effective on the same date, available at: www.gov.cn/xinwen/2016-03/17/content_5054992.htm. This policy document further refined the priority sectors to seven strategic industries: energy-saving and environmental protection; new-generation information technology; biology; high-end equipment manufacturing; new energy; new materials; and new-energy automobile.

'Public Welfare SOEs'.[61] This classification is aimed at further integrating SOEs into market-based economic reforms and promoting both their commercial and social functions. Generally speaking, General Commercial SOEs are expected to operate independently in the market and continue to pursue corporatisation and ownership diversification with majority private shareholding allowed. Their performance is evaluated against three key criteria, including general financial indicators (e.g. revenue and profits), returns on state asset investment and market competitiveness. Special Commercial SOEs have their core businesses in industries or fields related to national security and essential to the national economy and undertake projects or tasks designated by the state. While they are also open to private capital and mixed ownership, the state must remain the controlling shareholder. In addition to the performance criteria applicable to General Commercial SOEs, Special Commercial SOEs are also required to contribute to the implementation of national strategies, the protection of national security and the development of strategic industries. Public Welfare SOEs, which exercise social functions and provide public goods and services, can decide themselves whether to remain wholly state-owned or to diversify ownership. The performance criteria for such SOEs concern their capacity to make social contributions, such as cost control, quality of services and efficiency. The classifications of SOEs are summarised in Figure 2.1.

General Commercial SOEs are most likely to operate as privately-owned enterprises (POEs). In contrast, Special Commercial SOEs and Public Welfare SOEs largely remain under the control of the state and are likely to be shielded from market competition. In practice, the process of classification has been implemented by the SASAC and its local branches. Due to the large number of local SASAC departments,[62] the reform has

---

[61] Guiding Opinions, n. 56, section 2. The implementing regulation for the SOE classification: 《关于国有企业功能界定与分类的指导意见》 [Guiding Opinions on the Functional Definition and Classification of State-Owned Enterprises], promulgated by SASAC, Ministry of Finance and NDRC, Guozifayanjiu [2015] No. 170, effective on 30 December 2015. In a recent conference, SASAC confirmed and clarified the classification and the major functions of the three types of SOEs, see Wang Xi, '深化国有企业分类改革 国资委明确三类企业改革发展主攻方向 [Deepening the Classification of SOEs and Major Functions of the Three Types of SOEs]', Xinhua News Agency, 29 April 2021, available at: www.sasac.gov.cn/n2588025/n2588139/c18295694/content.html.

[62] There are more than 300 local SASAC departments at provincial, municipal, county and town levels. See Liu Qingshan, '《特别策划 下篇: 那些已经"消失"的地方国资委》 [The "Disappeared" Local State-owned Assets Supervision and Administration Commission]' (2016) No. 8 *State-Owned Assets Report* [国资报告] 59, 44.

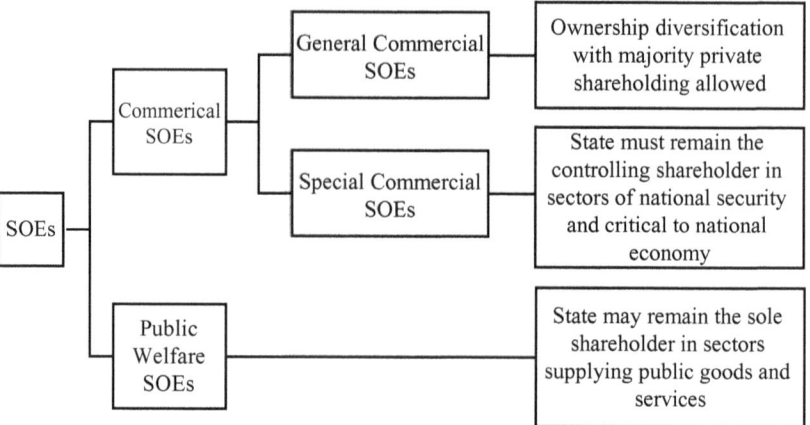

Figure 2.1 SOE classifications

had mixed results, with uncertain and fragmented classifications.[63] For instance, Shanghai SASAC, Chongqing SASAC and Shanxi SASAC have classified their SOEs into three groups, namely, competitive, functional and public service.[64] In contrast, Sichuan SASAC has defined all of its SOEs as commercial SOEs.[65] These inconsistent practices suggest that the classification of SOEs, by itself, may not provide clear guidance on whether an SOE is more market-oriented, policy-oriented, or whether it operates and competes according to market forces. Therefore, it is necessary to consider other elements of the reform or other features of SOEs when assessing their function and conduct.

2.3.2 Corporate Governance

The second element focuses on furthering the corporatisation and modernisation of SOEs.[66] The reform seeks to promote the restructuring of SOEs and

---

[63] Paul Hubbard, '"Fragmented Authoritarianism" and State Ownership', *East Asia Forum Quarterly*, 23 January 2017, available at: www.eastasiaforum.org/2017/01/23/fragmented-authoritarianism-and-state-ownership/.

[64] Yuan Shimeng, 《共性与差异 地方国企分类改革分析报告》[Similarities and Differences: An Analysis of the Classification of Local State-Owned Enterprises] (2016) No. 12 *State-Owned Assets Report* [国资报告] 71.

[65] 《关于印发《关于省属企业功能界定与分类监管的指导意见（试行）》的通知》 [Notice on the Printing and Distributing the Guiding Opinions on the Classifications of Provincial SOEs (Trial Implementation)], issued by Sichuan SASAC No. 115, 7 June 2016.

[66] See Guiding Opinions, n. 56, section 3.

group companies for public listing, ownership diversification, and regulation of shareholders' conduct, as well as to enhance the decision-making role of boards of directors and the autonomy of management. Accordingly, this element can be further broken down into three key components: corporate governance (which is discussed here), mixed ownership (discussed in Section 2.3.3) and restructuring and reorganisation (is discussed in Section 2.3.4).

The implementation regulation on corporate governance reform, released in April 2017, set the deadline for the corporatisation of central SOEs by the end of 2020.[67] This regulation required clarification of the rights and responsibilities of all organs and individuals central to the corporate governance system of SOEs, including shareholders, boards of directors, management, boards of supervisors, the Party and employee representatives (Section 2.2). The reform started by focusing on establishing a board of directors in central SOEs[68] before it is gradually implemented at sub-central levels. By the end of 2020, ninety-five (out of ninety-seven) central SOEs and over 90 per cent of provincial SOEs had established a board.[69]

However, it remains uncertain how government intervention in business decision-making can be effectively reduced. Despite the broad coverage of the reform, the Guiding Opinions stress that the Party will play a leadership role in SOEs through a representative committee created within enterprises (hereinafter Party Committee).[70] The constitutions of SOEs shall specify the functions of the Party Committee and the processes by which senior committee members will undertake executive roles in the firm and firm executives will undertake senior committee positions. In principle, the Party secretary of the committee will also serve as the chairman of the board. By 2017, all central SOEs had incorporated

---

[67] 《国务院办公厅关于进一步完善国有企业法人治理结构的指导意见》[Guiding Opinions of the General Office of the State Council on Further Improving the Corporate Governance Structure of State-Owned Enterprises], General Office of the State Council, Guo Ban Fa [2017] No. 36, 24 April 2017, section 1.3.

[68] OECD, 'OECD Economic Surveys: China 2017', 21 March 2017, 44, available at: www.oecd-ilibrary.org/economics/oecd-economic-surveys-china-2017_eco_surveys-chn-2017-en.

[69] Liu Qianshan, 《央企公司制改革取得历史性突破》[Historical Achievements of Corporatisation Reform of Central SOEs] (2020) No. 12 *State-Owned Assets Report* [国资报告], available at: www.sasac.gov.cn/n2588025/n4423279/n4517386/n16521178/c16522969/content.html; Yin Fengshou, 《坚持"两个一以贯之" 中国特色现代国有企业制度更加健全》[Improving the System for State-Owned Enterprises with Chinese Characteristics], (2020) No 9 *State-Owned Assets Report* [国资报告], available at: www.sasac.gov.cn/n2588025/n4423279/n4517386/n16018252/c16018578/content.html.

[70] See Guiding Opinions, n. 56, section 7.

provisions on Party Committees into their articles of association,[71] and over 30 HK-listed SOEs had established Party Committees through amendments of their articles of association.[72] For example, the amended Articles of Association for Datang International Power Generation Co., Ltd, a HK-listed central SOE, includes the following clauses:

> Article 10 In accordance with the requirements of the Constitution of the Communist Party of China, an organization of the Communist Party of China shall be established and play the core leadership role, functioning as the political core of the Company, providing direction, managing the overall situation and ensuring implementation …
>
> Article 139 (Item 20) The opinions of the Party Committee shall be heard before the board of directors decides on material issues of the Company.[73]

By June 2020, 1,036 SOEs had established a Party Committee.[74] On 31 December 2020, the Ministry of Finance and SASAC issued further guidance for how state entities should amend their articles of association to ensure that no major decisions are made by the board or senior executives without prior discussions with the Party Committee.[75]

In the past, the involvement of the Party in the corporate governance of SOEs was typically linked to the appointment of senior executives, a practice that generated concerns about state intervention in SOE management and decision-making. As Lin observed, '[i]n 53 central enterprises, the occupants of top positions, including the board chairman, CEOs, and party secretaries, are appointed and evaluated by the Central Organization

---

[71] Wang Qianqian, 《国务院国资委党委推进中央企业党建工作纪实》 [SASAC Promotes the Establishment of Party Committee in Central SOEs], 10 October 2017, available at: www.sasac.gov.cn/n2588030/n2588919/c7979758/content.html.

[72] Jennifer Hughes, 'Communist Party Control Written into Law at China's Big Companies', *The Financial Times*, 15 August 2017, available at: www.ft.com/content/a4b28218-80db-11e7-94e2-c5b903247afd; Naughton, 'The Current Wave of State Enterprise Reform in China', n. 52, 292.

[73] See Proposed Amendments to Articles of Association and Notice of EGM, Datang International Power Generation Co., Ltd, 29 June 2017, available at: www.hkexnews.hk/listedco/listconews/SEHK/2017/0630/LTN201706301016.pdf.

[74] See Yin Fengshou, '《坚持"两个一以贯之" 中国特色现代国有企业制度更加健全》 [Improving the System for State-Owned Enterprises with Chinese Characteristics]', n. 69.

[75] China's Ministry of Finance and SASAC issued a guideline for Chinese SOE corporate charters on 31 December 2020: 《关于印发《国有企业公司章程制定管理办法》的通知》 [Administrative Measures for the Establishment of Articles of Association of State-Owned Enterprises], promulgated by SASAC and Ministry of Finance, Guozi Fagaihui [2002] No 86, effective on 31 December 2020, available at: www.sasac.gov.cn/n2588035/c17288822/content.html.

Department of the Chinese Communist Party. This appointment practice predates the establishment of SASAC and persists until today.'[76] Under the current reform, the role of the Party is enhanced through explicit power to directly participate in the decision-making of the board beyond personnel appointments.[77] It leaves considerable room and flexibility for the Party to exert influence over the boards of directors, thereby creating clear tension between the pursuit of corporatisation and modern corporate governance. Thus, despite the classifications of SOEs, it remains possible that the commercial decisions of all types of SOEs will be affected by the Party. This possibility tends to be higher in Special Commercial SOEs and Public Welfare SOEs than in General Commercial SOEs, which are expected to optimise their commercial performance and competitiveness.

2.3.3 Ownership Diversification

The second component of corporatisation and modernisation is ownership diversification.[78] On the one hand, ownership diversification allows the injection of private capital in SOEs in various ways and the involvement of private investors in the restructuring and management of SOEs. In sensitive sectors such as oil, natural gas, electricity, railway, telecommunications, resources and public utilities, non-state capital is only allowed limited access to investment, subject to security reviews in accordance with relevant laws and regulations. In theory, the introduction of non-state interests to SOEs should contribute to the corporate governance reform, as it would introduce additional checks and balances and improve transparency in their decision-making.[79] In practice, the reform has led to the sale of either a majority (i.e. General Commercial SOEs) or minority interest (e.g. Special Commercial SOEs) in SOEs to

---

[76] Li-Wen Lin, 'A Network Anatomy of Chinese State-Owned Enterprises' (2017) 16(4) *World Trade Review* 583, 588.

[77] Hughes, 'Communist Party Control Written into Law at China's Big Companies', n. 72; Naughton, 'The Current Wave of State Enterprise Reform in China', n. 52, 292.

[78] See Guiding Opinions, n. 56, section 5. The implementing regulations: 《国务院关于国有企业发展混合所有制经济的意见》[Opinions of the State Council on the Development of Mixed Ownership Economy by State-Owned Enterprises], promulgated by the State Council, Guo Fa [2015] No. 54, effective 23 September 2015; 《国资委关于印发《中央企业混合所有制改革操作指引》的通知》[Operating Guidelines for the Mixed Ownership Reform of Central Enterprises], promulgated by SASAC, Guozi Chanquan [2019] No. 653, effective 21 October 2019, available at: www.sasac.gov.cn/n2588035/n2588320/n2588335/c12591910/content.html.

[79] OECD, 'OECD Economic Surveys: China 2017', n. 68, 36.

private investors. A typical example of the former is the diversification of ownership in Yunnan Baiyao Holdings, a provincial SOE that was initially 100 per cent owned by Yunnan SASAC. The state interest was diluted to 50 per cent with the injection of private capital by New Huadu Industrial Group in 2016, and then to 45 per cent with the introduction of another private investor, Yuyue Technology Development Co., Ltd., in 2017.[80]

With respect to Special Commercial SOEs, the mixed ownership reform is restricted to a list of industries specified in the *Opinions of the State Council on the Development of Mixed Ownership Economy by State-Owned Enterprises*[81] (Mixed Ownership Reform Opinions). In these industries, the participation of private capital is limited to certain activities, while the state retains the role of sole or controlling shareholder. These industries and the permitted ownership diversification are summarised in Table 2.1.

The mixed ownership reform of China United Network Communications Group Co., Ltd. (China Unicom), a central SOE, offers a good illustration of how the reform of Special Commercial SOEs may proceed. As one of six candidates selected for a pilot mixed ownership reform in 2016,[82] China Unicom reduced its shareholdings in China United Network Communications Co., Ltd. – a Shanghai-listed subsidiary company – from 62.74 per cent to 36.67 per cent in 2017.[83] The other major shareholders included state-owned China Life Insurance Company (10.22 per cent) and China Structural Reform Fund Co., Ltd.

---

[80] 云南白药：2016年年度报告 [Yunnan Baiyao Group Co Ltd Annual Report 2016], April 2017, 56, available at: http://file.finance.sina.com.cn/211.154.219.97:9494/MRGG/CNSESZ_STOCK/2017/2017-4/2017-04-22/3280103.PDF; 云南白药：2017年半年度报告摘要 [Yunnan Baiyao Group Co., Ltd. First Half Year 2017 Report Summary], 24 August 2017, 3, available at: https://pdf.dfcfw.com/pdf/H2_AN201708230822696802_1.pdf?1503510531000.pdf.

[81] 《国务院关于国有企业发展混合所有制经济的意见》[Opinions of the State Council on the Development of Mixed Ownership Economy by State-Owned Enterprises], promulgated by the State Council, Guo Fa [2015] No. 54, effective 23 September 2015.

[82] National Development and Reform Commission, '以混合所有制改革试点作为深化国企改革的突破口 实现完善治理强化激励突出主业提高效率的改革试点目标—国家发展改革委召开国有企业混合所有制改革试点专题会' [Press Conference on Pilot Programs of Mixed-Ownership Reform of SOEs], 30 September 2016, available at: www.ndrc.gov.cn/xwdt/xwfb/201609/t20160930_955188.html.

[83] Annual report of China Unicom (HONG KONG) Limited (2016), 20, available at: www.chinaunicom.com.hk/en/ir/reports/2016_20f.pdf. For an official announcement of the reform, see 中国联通关于混合所有制改革有关情况的专项公告 [China United Network Communications Limited, Special Announcement by China Unicom on Mixed Ownership Reform] (2017), available at: www.chinaunicom-a.com/wcm/1/papers/2017/8/21/preview1209.html.

Table 2.1. *List of industries and State ownership*

Industry	State ownership
(1) Important communications infrastructure, (2) transportation infrastructure hubs, (3) controlled water conservancy, (4) hydropower and avionics hubs along major river basins, and (5) inter-basin water diversion projects.	Sole or controlling shareholder (POEs may be permitted to participate in construction and operation)
(1) Development and utilization of important water resources, (2) forest resources, and (3) strategic mineral resources.	Sole or absolute controlling shareholder (POEs may be permitted to participate in construction and operation)
(1) Trunk river channels, (2) main oil and natural gas pipelines and networks, and (3) power grids.	Sole or absolute controlling shareholder in pipelines and networks of natural monopoly (Private capital is allowed in businesses already in competition)
(1) Basic data collection and utilisation of nuclear power, (2) basic data collection and utilisation of key public technology platforms, and (3) basic data collection and utilisation of meteorological mapping and hydrology.	Sole or controlling shareholder (POEs are encouraged to invest and participate in operation and government procurement)
(1) National reserves of grains, oil, natural gas and other strategic supplies.	Sole or controlling shareholder
(1) Special industries such as national defence and military industry, (2) scientific research and production of strategic weapons and equipment, and (3) fields of core military capabilities that concern national strategic security and core state secrets.	Sole or absolute controlling shareholder

Table 2.1. (cont.)

Industry	State ownership
(1) Important industries and key fields such as those serving national strategic goals, (2) important cutting-edge industries, (3) ecological and environmental protection fields, and (4) common technology platforms, etc.	Increase the investment by state-owned capital and use state-owned capital to guide and promote the development of the industries

(6.11 per cent), along with private investors Tencent (5.18 per cent), Baidu (3.30 per cent), JD.com (2.36per cent), Alibaba (2.04 per cent), Suning Commerce Group (1.88 per cent), Kuang-Chi Group (1.88 per cent) and Shenzhen Huaihai Ark Information Fund (1.88 per cent). Thus, the reform maintained the majority state ownership (i.e. 53 per cent) in the subsidiary SOE to maintain the state's control over the entity.

As far as Public Welfare SOEs are concerned, the Mixed Ownership Reform Opinions largely reproduces the relevant section of the Guiding Opinions and merely adds several examples of industries and fields supplying public goods and services, including utilities (i.e. water, electricity, natural gas, heat), public transportation, and infrastructure. In these sectors, ownership diversification is to be *guided* (e.g. not encouraged) according to the condition of SOEs.

The other important aspect of the mixed ownership reform pertains to the encouragement of state capital investment in POEs with a focus on public services, advanced technology, ecological and environmental protection, and other strategic industries. Article 4(13) of the Mixed Ownership Reform Opinions clarifies that state-owned capital investment and operating companies (which are discussed in Section 2.3.5) should play a major role in such investment. As Naughton observed, the reform 'may actually encourage the extension of SOEs into competitive markets where they do not currently have a presence ... [by] encouraging state capital to expand its investment in, and control of, private firms'.[84]

---

[84] Barry Naughton, 'Restructuring and Reform: China 2016', in Reserve Bank of Australia (eds.), *Structural Change in China: Implications for Australia and the World* (Sydney: Reserve Bank of Australia, 2016) 69, available at: www.rba.gov.au/publications/confs/2016/pdf/rba-conference-volume-2016.pdf.

Between 2013 and 2020, the mixed ownership reform of central SOEs alone had completed over 4,000 transactions, attracting investment of RMB 1.5 trillion mainly in the form of private placement and initial public offerings (IPOs).[85] By the end of 2020, over 70 per cent of central SOEs had a mixed ownership.[86] At the same time, the investment of state capital in POEs has also been on the rise, particularly in strategic industries. In 2020, central SOEs invested in over 6,000 POEs through more than RMB 400 billion of equity infusion.[87] One notable example is the high-tech sector which has become increasingly prominent in China's national policies like MIC 2025. SOEs are critical to the pursuit of the strategic goals in the high-tech sector, and China's massive government investment funds, for instance, have injected billions of dollars in the sector by way of equity infusion.[88] Thus, future SOE reform, particularly the mixed ownership reform, will most likely lead to more state capital and influence in the sector.[89] Overall, the mixed ownership reform is likely to lead to a concentration of state capital in strategic industries and consequently a change of major POEs in these industries to state entities. Given the existence of Party Committees in state entities, the reform maintains the Party/state's leadership in these industries.

---

[85] Xi Wang, '2013年以来央企累计实施混改超4000项 [Mixed Ownership Reform Led to over 4000 transactions since 2013]', Xinhua News Agency, 12 October 2020, available at: www.gov.cn/xinwen/2020-10/12/content_5550733.htm.

[86] PWC, 'A Review of China SOE Reform 2020 – Reform and Development of Central SOEs', *SOE Reform Blog*, March 2021, available at: www.pwccn.com/zh/blog/state-owned-enterprise-soe/reform-and-development-of-central-enterprises-mar2021.html.

[87] Ibid.; Deloitte, 'White Paper on the New Stage of Mixed Ownership Reform', March 2021, available at: www2.deloitte.com/content/dam/Deloitte/cn/Documents/ser-soe-br/deloitte-cn-soe-white-paper-on-thenew-stage-of-mixed-reform-zh-210322.pdf.

[88] See e.g. 'The Establishment of the National Integrated Circuit Investment Fund', Ministry of Industry and Information Technology (14 October 2014); 'The Establishment of the Advanced Manufacturing Industry Investment Fund', *SASAC* (12 June 2016); GF Securities, '国家集成电路产业基金一期投资解析(附股) [The Analysis of China's National Integrated Circuit Investment Fund First Tranche's Investment]', *Sina Finance*, 13 March 2019, available at: https://finance.sina.com.cn/stock/hyyj/2019-03-13/doc-ihsxncvh2157328.shtml; Sarah Dai, 'China Completes Second Round of US$29 Billion Big Fund Aimed at Investing in Domestic Chip Industry', *South China Morning Post*, 26 July 2019, available at: www.scmp.com/tech/science-research/article/3020172/china-said-complete-second-round-us29-billion-fund-will.

[89] See e.g. 《关于加快推进国有企业数字化转型工作的通知》[Notice on Accelerating Digital Transformation of State-Owned Enterprises], promulgated by SASAC, effective 21 August 2020, available at: www.sasac.gov.cn/n2588020/n2588072/n2591148/n2591150/c15517908/content.html.

2.3.4 Restructuring and Reorganisation

The third component of corporatisation and modernisation involves the restructuring and reorganisation of SOEs. The *Guiding Opinions on Promoting the Restructuring and Reorganisation of Central SOEs*[90] (Restructuring Opinions), released by the State Council in 2016, set out three key objectives of the reform. The first is to enhance the central SOEs' capability to protect and stabilise sectors of national security, their control in sectors of critical importance to the national economy, and their influence and leadership in strategic sectors. The second goal is to improve the efficiency and allocation of resources through mergers and acquisitions, institutional innovation and cooperation, the reduction of overcapacity and the disposal of inefficient and non-performing assets. The third is to boost the growth and internationalisation of the central SOEs. Overall, the reform seeks to establish a group of world-class multinational companies with innovative capacity and international competitiveness by 2020.

Between January 2013 and 31 December 2020, forty-one central SOEs were restructured through twenty-two horizontal or vertical mergers, as summarised in Table 2.2. Typical examples of horizontal mergers include the mergers of two rival companies in select industries, such as the railway equipment industry (i.e. the two largest railway equipment groups – China CNR Corporation Limited (CNR) and CSR Corporation Limited (CSR)) in 2015, the shipping industry (i.e. the two largest shipping groups – China Ocean Shipping (Group) Company and China Shipping Group) in 2016, the nuclear energy industry (i.e. China Nuclear Engineering and Construction Corp. (CNEC) and China National Nuclear Corp. (CNNC)) in 2018, and the shipbuilding industry (i.e. China State Shipbuilding Corporation (CSSC) and China Shipbuilding Industry Company (CSIC)) in 2019. This last merger reduced the number of central SOEs to ninety-seven[91] and created the world's largest shipbuilder, with total assets of RMB 790 billion

---

[90] 《国务院办公厅关于推动中央企业结构调整与重组的指导意见》 [Guiding Opinions on Promoting the Restructuring and Reorganization of Central State-Owned Enterprises State Council], promulgated by the State Council, Guo Ban Fa [2016] No. 56, effective 17 July 2016.

[91] A current list of central SOEs is published on SASAC's official website. See央企名录 [Directory of Central SOEs], 24 June 2021, available at: www.sasac.gov.cn/n4422011/n14158800/n14158998/c14159097/content.html.

Table 2.2. *List of central SOE mergers between January 2013 and December 2020*[*]

No.	Year	Central SOEs	Outcome
1	2019	CSSC and CSIC	Established a new company, China State Shipbuilding Corporation Ltd.
2	2019	China Poly Group Corporation (Poly Group) and China Silk Corporation	China Silk Corp. merged into Poly Group as a subsidiary
3	2018	FiberHome Technologies Group and Datang Telecom Technology and Industry Group	Established a new company, China Information and Communication Technologies Group Corporation (CICT)
4	2018	CNNC and CNEC	CNEC merged into CNNC as a subsidiary
5	2017	Guodian and Shenhua	Established a new company, China Energy Investment Corporation
6	2017	Sinolight Corporation (Sinolight) and China National Arts and Crafts (Group) Corporation (CNACGC) and Poly Group	Sinolight and CNACGC merged into Poly Group as a subsidiary
7	2017	China National Machinery Industry Corporation (Sinomach) and China Hi-Tech Group Corporation Limited (China Hi-Tech)	China Hi-Tech merged into Sinomach as a subsidiary
8	2016	China Grain Reserves Corporation (Sinograin) and China National Cotton Reserves Corporation (National Cotton)	National Cotton merged into Sinograin as a subsidiary
9	2016	Baosteel Group Corporation (Baosteel) and Wuhan Iron and Steel (Group) Corporation (WISCO)	Established a new company, China BaoWu Steel Group Corporation Limited
10	2016	China National Building Materials Group Corporation (CNBM) and China National Materials Group Corporation Limited (Sinoma)	Sinoma merged into CNBM as a subsidiary

Table 2.2. (cont.)

No.	Year	Central SOEs	Outcome
11	2016	China National Cereals, Oils and Foodstuffs Corporation (COFCO) and Chinatex Corporation Limited (Chinatex)	Chinatex merged into COFCO as a subsidiary
12	2016	China Travel Service (HK) Group Corporation (HKCTS) and China International Travel Service Group Corporation (CITS)	CITS merged into HKCTS as a subsidiary
13	2015	China Merchants Group Company Limited and Sinotrans and CSC Holdings, Corporation Limited (Sinotrans Group)	Sinotrans Group merged into China Merchants Group as a subsidiary
14	2015	China Ocean Shipping (Group) Company (COSCO) and China Shipping (Group) Company (China Shipping)	Established a new company, China COSCO Shipping Corporation Limited (COSCOCS)
15	2015	China Minmetals Corporation (Minmetals) and China Metallurgical Group Corporation (MCC)	MCC merged into Minmetals as a subsidiary
16	2015	Nam Kwong (Group) Company Limited (Nam Kwong) and Zhuhai Zhen Rong Company (Zhen Rong)	Zhen Rong merged into Nam Kwong as a subsidiary
17	2015	CNR and CSR	Established a new company, China Railway Rolling Stock Corporation Limited
18	2015	China Power Investment Corporation (CPI) and State Nuclear Power Technology Corporation Limited (SNPTC)	Established a new company, State Power Investment Corporation Limited
19	2014	China Huafu Trade and Development Corporation (Huafu) and COFCO	Huafu merged into COFCO as a subsidiary

Table 2.2. (cont.)

No.	Year	Central SOEs	Outcome
20	2013	China National Erzhong Group Corporation (Erzhong) and Sinomach	Erzhong merged into Sinomach as a subsidiary
21	2013	China Grain and Logistics Corporation (China Grain) and COFCO	China Grain merged into COFCO as a subsidiary
22	2013	Caihong Group Corporation (Caihong) and China Electronics Technology Group Corporation (CETC)	Caihong merged into CETC as a subsidiary

* All mergers are reported and updated on the official website of the SASAC. See 央企变更 [Changes of Central SOEs], available at: www.sasac.gov.cn/n2588035/n2641579/n2641660/index.html.

($112 billion).[92] As regards vertical mergers, one remarkable example is the merger between electricity producer China Guodian Corporation (Guodian) and coal producer Shenhua Group Corporation Limited (Shenhua) in 2017 to create 'the world's largest power company by capacity, with combined assets of 1.8 trillion yuan'.[93] While the restructuring of SOEs has also been carried out at the local level, to date, the reform seems to have prioritised the mergers of central SOEs.[94] Overall, the restructuring and reorganisation of SOEs, at least at the central level, has advanced the efforts of the previous round of reform to create national champions in strategic industries.[95] As the reform continues

---

[92] Lei Zhao, 'World's Largest Shipbuilder Unveiled Following Merger', *China Daily*, 27 November 2019, available at: www.chinadaily.com.cn/a/201911/27/WS5ddd77fea310cf3e3557a2ff.html.

[93] Huang Kaixi, Deng Yucong and Denise Jia, 'China Combines Two State-Owned Nuclear Firms into Powerhouse', *CaiXin News Agency*, 1 February 2018, available at: www.caixinglobal.com/2018-02-01/china-combines-two-state-owned-nuclear-firms-into-powerhouse-101205786.html.

[94] Wendy Leutert, 'State-Owned Enterprise Mergers: Will Less be More?', in 'Big Is Beautiful? State-Owned Enterprise Mergers under Xi Jinping', *European Council on Foreign Relations*, 30 November 2016, available at: www.ecfr.eu/publications/summary/china_state_owned_enterprise_mergers_under_xi_jinping7196.

[95] François Godement, 'Introduction', in 'Big Is Beautiful? State-Owned Enterprise Mergers under Xi Jinping', *European Council on Foreign Relations*, 30 November 2016, available

to proceed in that direction, the tension between the growing concentration and influence of SOEs in pillar industries and the market-oriented reform of SOEs will intensify.

2.3.5 State Asset Management System

The fifth and final element concerns improvement of the state-owned asset management system.[96] This reform aims to transform the functions of state assets regulatory bodies (i.e. SASAC and its local branches) by shifting the focus of the supervision from enterprise to capital, defining the boundaries of the supervision and clarifying their rights and responsibilities. The reform has led to the creation of two types of companies, namely, State Capital Investment Companies (SCICs) and State Capital Operation Companies (SCOCs), or collectively State Capital Investment and Operation Companies (SCIOs). These companies specialise in the management of state assets and operate under the authority granted by the SASAC or its local branches. While the management of state assets will be guided by the market, it is also required to serve national strategies, industrial policies and the capital needs of the most competitive SOEs. Thus, SCIOs are essentially subordinates of central or local SASACs and are expected to support national or provincial industrial policy and the development of strategic and emerging industries.[97] By the end of 2019, there were 21 SCIOs established at the central level and more than 150 at the local level.[98]

The differences between SCICs and SCOCs are not clearly defined in the existing regulatory documents. However, practice suggests that they may serve different functions. For example, China Chengtong Holdings Group Ltd. (Chengtong), an SCOC created in 2016, initiated the China Structural Reform Fund to participate in the reorganisation of SOEs,[99] including the mixed ownership reform of China United Network Communications Limited, as discussed in Section 2.3.3. By contrast, the

---

at: www.ecfr.eu/publications/summary/china_state_owned_enterprise_mergers_under_xi_jinping7196.

[96] See Guiding Opinions, n. 56, section 4.
[97] Naughton, 'The Current Wave of State Enterprise Reform in China', n. 52, 291–2.
[98] Shuping Ma, 'A Comparison between the Two Types of State Capital Investment and Operation Companies', *China Economic Times*, 15 April 2021, available at: www.cet.com.cn/ycpd/sdyd/2825396.shtml.
[99] Chang Lyu, 'Massive Fund to Help Reform Giant SOEs', *China Daily*, 27 September 2016, available at: www.chinadaily.com.cn/business/2016-09/27/content_26904633.htm

China Reform Holdings Corp., an SCIC established around the same time as Chengtong, partnered with two banks and one investment fund to inject RMB 200 billion into innovative technology and industrial upgrading projects.[100] Accordingly, the reform seems to have led to a division of labour between SCOCs and SCICs, with the former focusing on the restructuring of SOEs (such as the mixed ownership reform) and the latter on investment in priority industries.[101] More significant than the possible functional differences between SCOCs and SCICs is the common purpose that SCIOs serve and their far-reaching impacts on the SOE reform. As indicated in Table 2.2, SCIOs are established through mergers of large SOEs to create a massive fund to finance the reorganisation of SOEs or investment in strategic industries. These reforms will considerably strengthen and expand the influence of SOEs or the state in targeted industries and will increase concerns about China's state capitalism.

2.4 A Summary of Current Status and Future Reform

China's four decades of protracted SOE reform has failed to reduce the scale of state capitalism. Having been dedicated to bolstering the state sector and to reinforcing the role of the Party/state in pursuing various policy goals, the current reform is heading in a direction which strengthens state capitalism and is likely to reverse the promised market-oriented transformation. By 2020, the number of Chinese

---

[100] Matthew Miller, 'China to Reform SOEs Using Investment Firms, Asset Managers: Xinhua', *The Tomson Reuters*, 25 February 2016, available at: www.reuters.com/article/us-china-soe-reform/china-to-reform-soes-using-investment-firms-asset-managers-xinhua-idUSKCN0VY15O; Engen Tham and David Stanway, 'China Launches $30 Bln State-Controlled Venture Capital Fund', *The Tomson Reuters*, 18 August 2016, available at: www.reuters.com/article/china-funds/china-launches-30-bln-state-controlled-venture-capital-fund-idUSL3N1AZ1SX.

[101] State-Owned Assets Supervision and Administration Commission Research Bureau, 探索与研究: 国有资产监管和国有企业改革研究报告 *(2014–2015) [Reports on the Supervision of Stated-Owned Assets and The Reform of Stated-Owned Enterprises (2014–2015)]* (Beijing: China Economic Publishing House, 2017) 65; Deloitte, 'Key Points on the Reorganization/Establishment of State-Owned Capital Investment Companies and State-Owned Capital Operating Companies' (2016), available at: www2.deloitte.com/cn/en/pages/operations/articles/soe-transformation-whitepaper-issue5.html; PWC, 'Reform Strategies and Implementation for State Capital Investment and Operation Companies', 2020, available at: www.pwccn.com/zh/blog/state-owned-enterprise-soe/research-state-capital-investment-reform-transformation-strategy-operating-companies-key-points-implementation-2.html.

companies on the Fortune Global 500 list of the world's largest corporations had increased to 124 (compared to 85 in 2013), including 48 central SOEs and 32 local SOEs and, for the first time, surpassed the number of US companies on the list.[102] The restructuring of central SOEs had increased the power of some of the world's largest Chinese companies. For example, after the merger of China Silk Corp. into Poly Group in 2019, Poly Group's ranking rose from 242nd in 2019 to 191st in 2020.[103]

China's Fourteenth Five-Year Plan (2021–2025), released on 12 March 2021, maintains the commitment to deepen market-oriented SOE reform in the five elements discussed in Section 2.3.[104] The reform places more emphasis on the critical role that SOEs should play in strategic sectors, particularly in fostering technological independence and global competitiveness.[105] Thus, despite the rapid growth of the private sector and progressive market opening in China, SOEs will remain one of the principal mechanisms in China's pursuit of strategic goals for the foreseeable future.[106] Consequently, the reform is likely to further strengthen rather than weaken China's state capitalism.

---

[102] Liu Qingshan and Yuan Shimeng, 《独家解读 2020 年《财富》世界五百强上榜国企名单：入围企业结构更加均衡 发展质量持续提升》 [Understanding Chinese SOEs on the Fortune Global 500 in 2020], (2020) No. 8, *State-Owned Assets Report* [国资报告], 10 October 2020, available at: www.sasac.gov.cn/n2588025/n4423279/n4517386/n15645543/c15647699/content.html.

[103] Ibid.

[104] 《中华人民共和国国民经济和社会发展第十四个五年规划和2035年远景目标纲要》 [Outline of the 14th Five-Year Plan for the National Economic and Social Development and the 2035 Long Term Goals], adopted at the Fourth Session of the Thirteenth National People's Congress on 11 March 2021, available at: www.gov.cn/xinwen/2021-03/13/content_5592681.htm. SASAC, '2021 Work Plan of SASAC SOE Reform Department', 23 March 2021, available at: www.sasac.gov.cn/n2588030/n2588924/c17725438/content.html. For a more detailed analysis of the reform agenda under the 14th Five Year Plan, see PWC, 'Understanding SOE Reform in the 14th Five Year Period', March 2021, available at: www.pwccn.com/zh/blog/state-owned-enterprise-soe/interpretation-of-the-key-contents-of-the-reform-of-soe-in-the-14th-five-year-plan-mar2021.html.

[105] Ibid. See also Wang Qianqian, 《开局"十四五"，再启新征程》 [SASAC Report: New Journey under the Fourteenth Five-Year Plan] (2021) No. 1, *State-Owned Assets Report* [国资报告], 12 March 2021, available at: www.sasac.gov.cn/n2588025/n4423279/n4517386/n17140332/c17140607/content.html.

[106] Benjamin Liebman and Curtis Milhaupt, 'Introduction: The Institutional Implications of China's Economic Development', in Benjamin Liebman and Curtis Milhaupt (eds.), *Regulating the Visible Hand? The Institutional Implications of Chinese State Capitalism* (New York: Oxford University Press, 2016), xv.

2.5 Conclusion

Since the start of the economic reform in 1978, China's SOEs have gone a long way. While many SOEs were on the brink of bankruptcy at the beginning of the reform, in the years since, they have become bigger, stronger and more profitable. Many SOEs are now leading players in key sectors and rank high in both domestic and international league tables. In this chapter, we have conducted a thorough examination of the contours of the SOE reform in all of its five phases. We find that, notwithstanding significant progress made in the last two decades of the last century, the reform has been stalled or even retracted since the beginning of the new century. The current round of reform, commenced in 2013, aims to further advance and enhance the position of SOEs in strategic sectors. Domestically, this approach is very likely to lead to the retreat of private firms. As SOEs increase their strength at the international level, the future does not bode well for firms from other parts of the world either. Are the existing WTO rules adequate in dealing with the challenges that Chinese SOEs pose to the world trading system? We will explore this question in Chapters 4 and 5.

3

State Capitalism in China's Accession to the WTO

Concerns and Solutions

3.1 Introduction

Concerns over China's economic system are not new. Rather, when China applied to resume its membership status in the General Agreement on Tariffs and Trade (GATT), it was still in an early stage of reforms of state-owned enterprises (SOEs), as discussed in Chapter 2. Thus, the compatibility between China's economic system and the multilateral trading system became a major issue in the accession process. This chapter recounts the concerns of the GATT/WTO Members, the responses of China and its evolving approach, and how, after numerous rounds of discussions, the Members finally found the solutions to address specific problems with China's state capitalism, as captured in the accession package.

3.2 China and the GATT

As one of the victorious Allied Powers, the Republic of China (ROC) participated in the work of the Preparatory Committee for the UN Conference on Trade and Employment from 1946 to 1947, which tried to establish the International Trade Organization (ITO).[1] When the ITO failed to come into being due to the unfavourable political environment in the United States, China joined twenty-two other countries in signing

---

[1] For an overview of China's participation in the early dates of the GATT, see Henry Gao, 'China's Participation in the WTO: A Lawyer's Perspective', (2007) 11 *Singapore Year Book of International Law* 41; See also Shi Guangsheng,《中国加入世界贸易组织知识读本(4): 中国加入世界贸易组织谈判历程》 *[Reader on China's Accession to the World Trade Organization (Four): Negotiation History of China's Accession to the World Trade Organization]* (人民出版社[People's Press], 1st ed, 2011), 12–14; Xiangping Liu, '《金問泗與關貿總協定》 [Jin Wensi and the General Agreement on Tariffs and Trade]' (2008) 5 二十一世紀(網絡版)*[Ershiyi Shiji (Wanglou Ban)]*, 2–6, available at: www.cuhk.edu.hk/ics/21c/media/online/0204056.pdf.

the Protocol of Provisional Application of the GATT and became one of its founding contracting parties on 21 April 1948.[2]

A year later, however, the Republican government lost the Civil War against the Communist Party of China (CPC or Party) and was forced to retreat to the outlying island of Taiwan. The CPC took control of the bulk of the Chinese mainland and established a rival government – the People's Republic of China (PRC) – on 1 October 1949. While the new government never officially announced its intentions toward the GATT,[3] the establishment of a trade organization of socialist countries – the Council for Mutual Economic Assistance – in 1949[4] made it unlikely that the PRC was keen to participate in the GATT, a 'capitalist club' boycotted by the Union of Soviet Socialist Republics (USSR) since the very beginning.[5]

This resulted in a rather bizarre situation, as the exiled Republican government could not honour its tariff reduction obligations for the goods shipped to the mainland while the CPC could enjoy the preferential tariffs for all goods originating from the mainland.[6] Upon discovering this, the United States threatened the Republican government with termination of most-favoured-nation (MFN) treatment,[7] and the latter

---

[2] Ibid., 7; See also General Agreement on Tariffs and Trade, opened for signature 30 October 1947, 61 Stat. A-11, TIAS 1700, 55 UNTS. 194 (GATT) (listing 'the Republic of China' as one of the founding contracting parties in the preamble).

[3] According to Article 55 of the Common Program of the Chinese People's Political Consultative Conference of 1949, which served as China's interim Constitution until 1954, 'with respect to the treaties and agreements made by the Kuomintang government and foreign governments, the Central People's Government of the People's Republic of China shall conduct examination and may either recognize, repeal, revise or renegotiate them according to their respective contents'. Several treaties were recognised or repealed according to this provision, but the Chinese government never explicitly stated how it would deal with the GATT. See Gao, 'China's Participation in the WTO', n. 1, 42.

[4] While China never joined the CMEA for ideological and historical reasons, it has maintained economic exchange with CMEA countries. See Jude Howell, 'Foreign Trade Reform and Relations with International Economic Institutions', in Christopher Hudson (ed), *The China Handbook* (New York: Routledge, 2013), 173, 17.; Raphael Shen, *China's Economic Reform: An Experiment in Pragmatic Socialism* (Westport: Praeger Publishers, 2000), 97.

[5] See Richard N. Gardner, *Sterling–Dollar Diplomacy: The Origins and the Prospects of Our International Economic Order* (New York: McGraw-Hill Book Company, New Expanded Ed., 1969), xxii.

[6] Liu Xiangping, '《金問泗與關貿總協定》[Jin Wensi and the General Agreement on Tariffs and Trade]', n. 1, 7.

[7] Ibid.; see also Shi,《中国加入世界贸易组织知识读本(4)》[Reader on China's Accession to the World Trade Organization (Four)], n. 1, 14; Gao, 'China's Participation in the WTO', n. 1, 42–3.

responded by formally withdrawing from the GATT, which took effect on 5 May 1950.[8]

The murky state of the law on succession makes the validity of Taiwan's withdrawal an interesting case study, as one could well argue that, because Taiwan, as of 1949, no longer represented China, it also did not have the right to withdraw from the treaty on China's behalf in 1950. However, China did not protest at the time. It had more pressing concerns, including being embroiled in the Korean War. Even when it restored its seat in the United Nations in 1971,[9] China still did not raise the issue.[10] However, on 16 November 1971, the GATT Contracting Parties, being prudent, decided by consensus to terminate the observer status of the Republican government, a position it had occupied since 1965.[11] Upon hearing the news, then-Chinese Premier Zhou Enlai instructed the Chinese Ministry of Foreign Trade and Ministry of Foreign Affairs to examine what position China should adopt on the GATT. On 30 November 1971, the two Ministries submitted a joint report, in which they noted that the GATT was 'a tool for the imperialists, especially American imperialists to expand foreign trade and grab world markets'.[12] While they concluded that participating in the GATT would be beneficial for China in the long term, they advised that the MFN rules under the GATT would prevent China from adopting

---

[8] Contracting Parties, Communication from Secretary-General of United Nations Regarding China, GATT/CP/54, 8 March 1950.

[9] See Restoration of the lawful rights of the People's Republic of China in the United Nations, A/RES/2758(XXVI), 5 October 1971, 2 (deciding 'to restore all its rights to the People's Republic of China and to recognize the representatives of its Government as the only legitimate representatives of China to the United Nations, and to expel forthwith the representatives of Chiang Kai-shek from the place which they unlawfully occupy at the United Nations and in all the organizations related to it').

[10] While the GATT 1947 was not a specialised agency of the United Nations, it generally followed the decisions of the United Nations on political issues. See *GATT Analytical Index: Guide to GATT Law and Practice*, 877 (6th ed. 1995). Thus, even though China did not raise the issue of GATT membership itself at the time, the GATT Contracting Parties still decided to revoke the Taiwan government's observer status, which it had acquired since 1965. See GATT, Contracting Parties Twenty-Seventh Session, Summary Record of the First Meeting, SR.27/1, 19 November 1971, 1–4; see also Gao, 'China's Participation in the WTO', n. 1, 43–4.

[11] See GATT, 'Contracting Parties Twenty-Seventh Session, Summary Record of the First Meeting', n. 10, 1–4.

[12] 《关于'关税及贸易总协定'问题的请示》[Chinese Ministry of Foreign Trade and Ministry of Foreign Affairs, Report on the 'GATT' Issue], 30 November 1971, as quoted in Shi,《中国加入世界贸易组织知识读本(4)》[Reader on China's Accession to the World Trade Organization (Four)], n. 1, 19–21.

different trade policies towards different types of countries.[13] Moreover, joining the GATT would require China to assume various obligations such as opening markets and reducing trade barriers, all of which were impossible for China to implement at that time as it still practised the centrally planned economic system with strict controls on foreign trade.[14] Thus, the Ministries advised that China should hold off from participating.[15]

Upon the launch of the economic reform and opening up in the late 1970s, China started to realise the importance of the GATT. In November 1982, the Ministry of Foreign Economic and Trade (MOFET), Ministry of Foreign Affairs, State Economic Commission, Ministry of Finance, and General Customs Administration submitted a joint report to the State Council requesting participation in the GATT.[16] The report noted that China's foreign trade was rapidly developing with the adoption of the reform and opening up policy, and trade with members of the GATT already constituted 80 per cent of its overall trade.[17] Thus, it was in China's interest to join the GATT and enjoy the MFN tariffs.[18] The report suggested that China file a formal application after the necessary preparatory work had been undertaken.[19]

In January 1983, the State Council adopted the advice.[20] As part of the preparatory work, China sent delegations to Pakistan, Hungary and Yugoslavia to learn from their accession experiences in 1983.[21] In the following year, China invited GATT officials to hold a seminar in Beijing and a Hungarian official to provide advice to China. The Hungarian representative emphasised the importance of economic reforms, especially those on the price differentials between the domestic and international markets.[22] In particular, he emphasised that having a market-determined price is crucial in acceding to the GATT on the basis of tariff concessions, instead of quantitative import commitments as in

---

[13] Ibid., 21.
[14] Ibid.
[15] Ibid.
[16] Ibid., 24–6.
[17] Ibid., 24.
[18] Ibid.
[19] Ibid., 26.
[20] Ibid.
[21] Ibid., 28–9.
[22] Ibid., 29–30.

the case of the Romanian accession, which would require China to import a fixed quantity of products every year.[23]

3.3 Resumption of GATT Contracting Party Status

In late 1984, China joined the GATT as an observer.[24] Between 30 September and 2 October 1985, the GATT Contracting Parties held a Special Session to discuss the new round of trade negotiations (i.e. the Uruguay Round) and China sent a delegation.[25] After the Special Session, China held the first informal consultations with the 'Quad' (the US, the European Communities (EC), Japan and Canada) and stated three principles:[26]

(1) China was to re-join the GATT by resuming its contracting party status rather than a new accession;
(2) China was ready to make tariff concessions and assume obligations commensurate with its development levels and to enter substantive negotiations with the Contracting Parties; and
(3) China would participate in the GATT as a developing country.

The United States expressed reservations on China's bid by noting that China was still a non-market economy (NME).[27] This concern was shared by the EC, which also noted that China still practiced state trading and its price mechanism and import systems were quite different from those of market economies and potentially incompatible with the principles of free trade embedded in the GATT.[28] This was the very first time that such concerns were raised by GATT members on the compatibility

---

[23] Ibid., 30.
[24] China first requested to observe the meetings of individual GATT sessions in 1982. See People's Republic of China: Attendance at Thirty-Eighth Session, L/5344, 24 September 1982. In 1984, China submitted a formal request to have observer status in meetings of the Council of Representatives and its subordinate bodies. See China – Request for Observer Status, L/5712, 16 October 1984. Since then, China has been attending GATT meetings regularly as an observer. See Julia Ya Qin, 'GATT Membership for Taiwan: An Analysis in International Law' (1992) 24 *New York University Journal of International Law and Politics* 1059, 1072.
[25] GATT, Contracting Parties Special Session, Summary Record of the First Meeting, 4SS/SR/1, 14 October 1985.
[26] Shi,《中国加入世界贸易组织知识读本(4)》[Reader on China's Accession to the World Trade Organization (Four)], n. 1, 34.
[27] Ibid.
[28] Ibid., 36.

between China's economic system and the GATT, an issue that would keep resurfacing in China's formal accession process.

On 10 July 1986, China formally submitted the application to resume its status as a GATT contracting party.[29] In March 1987, the GATT established a working party to examine China's status.[30] Reflecting China's insistence on 'resumption, not accession', the working party was aptly named 'Working Party on China's Status as a Contracting Party'[31] (hereinafter Working Party) rather than the usual 'Working Party on Accession'. At the same time, because the GATT does not have rules governing the resumption of contracting party status, for all practical purposes, the Working Party followed the procedure for that of an accession working party.[32] China also accepted this as a practical compromise, and indicated in its resumption request that it 'is prepared to enter into negotiations with GATT contracting parties'.[33] Such negotiations would involve two steps: first, bilateral tariff negotiations with any contracting party that expressed interest; second, multilateral negotiations in the Working Party to work out the accession protocol, annexes and the Working Party report. Pursuant to this procedure, thirty-seven contracting parties requested bilateral negotiations with China.[34]

The first of these bilateral negotiations actually took place even before the formal establishment of the Working Party. This was the bilateral consultation between China and the United States, held in Beijing in November 1986, where the US representative – Assistant United States Trade Representative (USTR) Douglas Newkirk – stated:

> No country is more eager than the US to welcome China into the GATT. The US and China would negotiate hand in hand, rather than by pointing fingers at each other. The US believes that, the participation of China in

---

[29] GATT, China's Status as a Contracting Party: Communication from the People's Republic of China, L/6017, 26 October 1986.
[30] GATT, Minutes of Meeting: Held in the Centre William Rappard on 4 March 1987, C/M/207, 30 March 1987, 9–12.
[31] GATT, Working Party on China's Status as a Contracting Party – Membership and Terms of Reference, L/6191, 19 June 1987.
[32] As stated in its Terms of Reference, the Working Party 'will examine the foreign trade regime of the People's Republic of China, develop a draft Protocol setting out the respective rights and obligations, provide a forum for the negotiation of a schedule, address as appropriate other issues concerning the People's Republic of China and the GATT, including procedures for decision-making by the CONTRACTING PARTIES'.
[33] See GATT, 'China's Status as a Contracting Party', n. 29.
[34] GATT, Working Party on China's Status as a Contracting Party – Membership and Terms of Reference, L/6191/Rev.3, 18 April 1989.

the international trading system will bring positive results to all sides, and help China to achieve economic modernisation.[35]

While Newkirk fully supported China's decision to introduce the market mechanism and adopt price mechanisms reflecting supply and demand, he also expressed some concerns, especially whether China's reform process could create fully market price-based mechanisms to guide traders in commercial decisions.[36] This concern was also reflected as one of the five main demands of the United States until mid-1989, which required China to set out in its accession documents a detailed plan for the establishment of the market-based price mechanism fully reflecting production elements and the supply–demand relationship, and explain the timetable and scope of such reform.[37] In response to the concerns of the United States, China included detailed discussions of its economic reform in the Memorandum on China's Foreign Trade Regime submitted in February 1987, which noted that the 'objective of the reform is to establish a new system of planned commodity economy of Chinese style'.[38]

What, then, is a 'planned commodity economy'? People who are well-versed in Chinese political economy would understand that this is just a euphemism for 'market economy', disguised in such a way as to overcome the ideological oppositions from Party hardliners. Yet, to outsiders, this was too difficult to decipher and can easily be subject to misleading interpretations. This was confirmed by a note by the GATT secretariat in March 1988, which cited the concern by a member (the US)[39] of the Working Party that 'China was a non-market economy country whose ability to extend GATT rights to other contracting parties might be compromised by its centrally-controlled economic and trade system.'[40] Thus, this member noted that 'a key aspect of the examination in the

---

[35] Bicheng Suo, 《中国加入世界贸易组织谈判文件资料选编》 [*Basic Instruments and Selected Documents on the Negotiations for China's Accession to the World Trade Organization*] (中国商务出版社[China Commerce and Trade Press], 2012), 5.

[36] Ibid., 5–6.

[37] Ibid., 7.

[38] GATT, China's Status as a Contracting Party, Memorandum on China's Foreign Trade Regime, L/6125, 18 February 1987, 4.

[39] The GATT secretariat note did not identify the member, but corroborations from Chinese sources confirm that the member is the United States. See Shi,《中国加入世界贸易组织知识读本(4)》 [Reader on China's Accession to the World Trade Organization (Four)], n. 1, 59–60.

[40] GATT, Working Party on China's Status as a Contracting Party, Introduction and General Statements, Note by the Secretariat, Spec(88)13, 29 March 1988, 12.

Working Party had to be the extent to which China's economic reform process had been, or had not been, implemented and what contracting parties could expect in the future'.[41] It is worth noting that the association of the GATT with the concept of market economy is not a view held only by the United States. Instead, it seems to reflect the consensus of GATT members, including even former Communist countries. For example, in a memo submitted in its accession process, Yugoslavia explicitly noted that 'the existence of a market economy, as well as competition between economic entities within a Member state, constitute the basic pre-requisites for the application of GATT regulations'.[42]

To alleviate these concerns, China submitted another memo in April 1988, which further explained that the objective of the reform was to transit 'from an operational mechanism of the economy entirely regulated by planning to a system which integrates market with planning'.[43] In particular, China clarified that '[t]he term "planned commodity economy" means socialist commodity economy. It may be translated into "socialist market economy"'.[44] Notably, this is the very first time that China admitted that the goal of the reform was to establish a 'socialist market economy'. Furthermore, in another statement given in the same month, the head of the Chinese delegation explicitly acknowledged that 'GATT is drawn up on the basis of market economy'[45] and China was not yet 'a full market economy'.[46]

These exchanges on China's economic reform, with China's ultimate confirmation that the goal of the reform was to establish a 'socialist market economy', were testaments to China's eagerness to fully embrace market-oriented reform in the 1980s. At the international level, main players such as the United States also wanted to use China as an example

---

[41] Ibid.
[42] GATT, Status of Yugoslav Economic Organizations (Enterprises), Memorandum submitted by the Yugoslav Government for the information of the Working Party, L/961, 11 March 1959.
[43] GATT, Working Party on China's Status as a Contracting Party: Communication from China, The Progress and Objective of China's Economic Structural Reform, Spec(88)29, 1 June 1988, 2.
[44] Ibid., 8.
[45] GATT, Working Party on China's Status as a Contracting Party: Communication from China, Statement by Mr. Shen Juren, Vice minister of Foreign Economic Relations and Trade, Head of the Chinese delegation at the Third session of the Working Party on China, Spec(88)37, 11 July 1988, 6.
[46] Ibid., 7.

to encourage similar changes in the Communist bloc.[47] The combination of positive domestic and international environments helped to move things quickly so that, by the beginning of 1989, the Working Party was ready to start the drafting of the Accession Protocol.[48] However, this process stalled after China cracked down on student protesters on 4 June 1989 and the West imposed sanctions on the country as a result.[49]

For the next two-and-a-half years, the Working Party went into hibernation.[50] It was not until 1992, when the Fourteenth National Congress of the Communist Party adopted a Resolution to make the 'Socialist Market Economy' the goal of the reform,[51] that the accession negotiation resumed. Nonetheless, this did not solve all the problems, as many observers were sceptical about China's willingness to embrace true capitalism. For example, Douglas Newkirk, the then Assistant USTR, stated bluntly that '[t]he GATT was not written with a Socialist Market Economy in mind'.[52] Moreover, as the Resolution of the Communist Party was not a law passed by the National People's Congress, it was hard for outsiders to understand its significance. It was not until the goal was incorporated into China's Constitution in 1993[53] that others began to

---

[47] Yongzheng Yang, 'China's WTO Accession: The Economics and Politics' (2000) 34 *Journal of World Trade* 77, 88–9.

[48] Shi,《中国加入世界贸易组织知识读本(4)》[Reader on China's Accession to the World Trade Organization (Four)], n. 1, 73–6.

[49] The Working Party meeting originally scheduled in June 1989 was cancelled due to concerns by the participants over 'political and economic upheaval in China'. See Charan Devereaux, Robert Z. Lawrence and Michael Watkins, *Case Studies in US Trade Negotiation Volume 1: Making the Rules* (Washington, DC: Peterson Institute for International Economics, 2006), 252.

[50] Jeffrey Gertler, 'China's WTO Accession: The Final Countdown', in Deborah Z. Cass, Brett Williams and George Barker (eds.), *China and the World Trading System: Entering the New Millennium* (Cambridge: Cambridge University Press, 2003), 56; see also James McGregor, 'China's Entry into GATT is Stalled by Thorny "Socialist Market Economy"', *Wall Street Journal* (New York, 3 March 1993), A11.

[51] Zemin Jiang,《加快改革开放和现代化建设步伐，夺取有中国特色社会主义事业的更大胜利》[Accelerate Steps of Reform and Opening Up and the Development of Modernization, Seize Greater Success in the Endeavor on Socialism with Chinese Characteristics], Report, the Fourteenth National Congress of the China Communist Party, 12 October 1992, available at: www.gov.cn/test/2007-08/29/content_730511.htm.

[52] Raj Bhala, 'Enter the Dragon: An Essay on China's WTO Accession Saga' (2000) 15(6) *American University International Law Review* 1469, 1480.

[53] Article 15 of the Constitution used to state, '[t]he state practices planned economy on the basis of Socialist public ownership' and was amended to '[t]he state practices Socialist market'.《中华人民共和国宪法修正案（1993年）》[Amendment to the Constitution of the People's Republic of China (1993)], adopted by the First Session of

appreciate that China was indeed taking the commitment to market-based reforms seriously.

During the first half of the 1990s, China participated in the Uruguay Round negotiations in the hope that discussions on its status could be concluded in time for it to become a founding member of the WTO.[54] Unfortunately, the world had changed significantly by this point. The Cold War was over, and China had lost its symbolic value as a reformer within the Communist bloc. With the former Soviet countries also eager to join the GATT, the terms of accession for China were increasingly regarded as a template for other transition economies.[55] Thus, Western governments imposed more rigorous terms.[56] At the same time, the Uruguay Round negotiations turned out to be much more difficult than originally imagined, and most countries concentrated their resources on the Uruguay Round rather than on talks with China. Also, for the first time in history, the Uruguay Round included negotiations on trade in services and trade-related intellectual property rights. Rules on non-tariff measures were also strengthened. These issues posed new challenges to China, as it lacked experience in these new areas. For example, China did not have detailed regulations on import relief measures or experience in conducting such investigations until 1997, two years after the establishment of the WTO.[57]

On the other hand, China itself had also changed since the 1980s. First, the 1990s saw China's rise as a major trader, with goods 'Made in China' flooding many parts of the world. Many countries, both developed and developing, felt the threat of China not only in the world market but in their domestic markets too. For them, letting China accede to the GATT to enjoy expanded market access opportunities without demanding a pound of flesh would have been unthinkable. At the same time, with the income level of the Chinese on the rise, more and more Western companies started to recognise the potential of China as the largest untapped market in the world. They demanded better market access opportunities

---

the Eighth National People's Congress, 29 March 1993, available at: www.npc.gov.cn/wxzl/wxzl/2000-12/05/content_4585.htm.
[54] See Bhala, 'Enter the Dragon', n. 52, 1480.
[55] Nicholas Lardy, *Integrating China into the Global Economy* (Washington, DC: Brookings Institution Press, 2002) 63.
[56] Ibid.
[57] Gregory Shaffer and Henry Gao, 'China's Rise: How It Took on the U.S. at the WTO' (2018) 1 *University of Illinois Law Review* 115, 152–3.

in China, which went beyond tariff concessions, and this too required extensive negotiation.

Even though China declared its intention in early 1994 to complete substantive negotiations by the end of that year,[58] when the WTO was established on 1 January 1995, the end of the accession negotiations was still nowhere in sight.[59]

3.4 WTO Accession

Frustrated that China did not become a founding Member of the WTO as it had wished, the head of the Chinese delegation Gu Yongjiang stated at the meeting of the Working Party on 20 December 1994 that 'while China does not wish to close the door for negotiation, China will not take the initiative to request bilateral negotiations or meetings of the Working Party'.[60] All work of the Working Party stopped for the better part of 1995,[61] and it was not until November 1995 that China submitted a new request for accession to the WTO.[62] Subsequently, the GATT Working Party was converted into a WTO Accession Working Party in December 1995.[63] President Jiang Zemin personally set out three principles on WTO accession.[64] First, as an international organisation, the WTO would not be complete without the participation of China. Second, China should join as a developing country. Third, China's accession should be based on a balance of rights and obligations. As we will soon see from the detailed analysis of the terms of the Chinese accession deal, however, China failed to achieve most of these goals.

---

[58] In his letter to the Director General and contracting parties to the GATT on 25 January 1994, then Chinese premier Li Peng stated China's wish to 'conclude the negotiation to resume its GATT membership quickly and become a founding Member of the WTO'. See Shi,《中国加入世界贸易组织知识读本(4)》[Reader on China's Accession to the World Trade Organization (Four)], n. 1, 118.

[59] Shi,《中国加入世界贸易组织知识读本(4)》[Reader on China's Accession to the World Trade Organization (Four)], n. 1, 134-9.

[60] Ibid., 135-9.

[61] Ibid., 436-42.

[62] WTO, Communication from China, WT/ACC/CHN/1, 7 December 1995.

[63] Ibid.

[64] Wen Gong, '《让历史铭记——中国加入世贸组织谈判备忘录》[Let History Remember: Memo on China's Accession to the WTO]', *People's Daily*, 31 October 2005, available at: www.gov.cn/ztzl/content_87675.htm.

China conducted market access negotiations with forty-four WTO Members.[65] Among these negotiations, the most critical was the US–China negotiation, which was concluded in November 1999.[66] The agreement with the United States was the most comprehensive, covering both market access on goods and services, as well as rules issues, especially those on trade remedies.[67] In 2000, China signed a bilateral agreement with the EC, which was less comprehensive, focussing on sectors of specific interest to the EC, such as automobiles, telecommunications, insurance and distribution.[68]

On 10 November 2001, at the Fourth Session of the Ministerial Conference in Doha, Qatar, WTO Members adopted the Protocol on the Accession of China to the WTO[69] (Accession Protocol or AP), which was approved by China's National People's Congress Standing Committee the next day. One month later, the Accession Protocol took effect and China finally became a Member of the WTO.

3.5 Concerns and Solutions on China's State Capitalism Model

With an accession negotiation spanning fifteen years, China's WTO accession process was, until then, the longest in GATT/WTO history. This record was broken by Russia ten years later, but China's accession package remains the most complicated in the history of the WTO. This is not only due to China's large trade volume, which ranked sixth largest at the time of accession. More importantly, the protracted negotiations reflect some major Members' deep concerns about the unique nature of the Chinese economic system, which was in the process of a transition from a centrally planned economy to a 'socialist market economy'.[70] Almost twenty years after China's WTO accession, this transition, as many have criticised, has not yet been completed and has even been reversed by China's current SOE reforms, discussed in Chapter 2. As a consequence, the longstanding concerns about China's economic model, industrial policies and trade practices continue to intensify.

---

[65] See Gertler, 'China's WTO Accession', n. 50, 57.
[66] Ibid., 56–7.
[67] Shi,《中国加入世界贸易组织知识读本(4)》[Reader on China's Accession to the World Trade Organization (Four)], n. 1, 280–7.
[68] Ibid., 387–8.
[69] Protocol on the Accession of the People's Republic of China, WT/L/432, 23 November 2001 (Accession Protocol or AP).
[70] See McGregor, 'China's Entry into GATT is Stalled by Thorny "Socialist Market Economy"', n. 50.

Reflecting these concerns, discussions over China's unique economic model persisted throughout China's accession process. As recounted in the Working Party Report on the Accession of China[71] (Working Party Report or WPR), these concerns mainly focus on four issues: (1) the role of SOEs, (2) pricing policies and distortions, (3) industrial policies and subsidies, and (4) trading rights.

3.5.1 The Role of SOEs

Given the importance of SOEs in the Chinese economy, it is no wonder that they became a major issue in the accession negotiation. However, as shown by the Working Party Report, the existing WTO Members did not waste time debating ideological issues such as how to make China accept abstract concepts of the market economy. Instead, they mainly focused on the more pragmatic and mercantilist issues of making sure that SOEs would not prevent China from fulfilling its market access concessions. More specifically, two issues were raised.

The first concerned the impact of the behaviour and conduct of SOEs on commercial transactions. The Working Party Report noted:

> In light of the role that state-owned and state-invested enterprises played in China's economy, some members of the Working Party expressed concerns about the continuing governmental influence and guidance of the decisions and activities of such enterprises relating to the purchase and sale of goods and services. Such purchases and sales should be based solely on commercial considerations, without any governmental influence or application of discriminatory measures.[72]

This summary has at least two major implications. First, the focus of the Members' concerns was not on the systemic implications of SOEs, but on the effect of government influence on the purchase and sale decisions of SOEs. Second, despite these concerns, the Members did not expect China to eliminate SOEs, either immediately upon accession or gradually over a phase-in period. Instead, the expectation was limited to certain constraints of the behaviour and conduct of SOEs without restricting China's right to maintain a state sector and use SOEs for economic goals and industrial policies as long as China does not breach its accession commitments.

---

[71] Report of the Working Party on the Accession of China, WT/ACC/CHN/49, 1 October 2001 (Working Party Report or WPR).
[72] Ibid., para. 44.

3.5 CONCERNS AND SOLUTIONS ON CHINA'S MODEL 55

In response, China made two commitments. First, paragraph 46 of the Working Party Report provides:

> China would ensure that all state-owned and state-invested enterprises would make purchases and sales based solely on commercial considerations, e.g., price, quality, marketability and availability, and that the enterprises of other WTO Members would have an adequate opportunity to compete for sales to and purchases from these enterprises on non-discriminatory terms and conditions.

This commitment confirms that, like other market participants, Chinese SOEs will play by the same market-based rules, that is, by conducting its transactions on the basis of commercial considerations. Moreover, it also confirms that China will not use SOEs to undercut its WTO commitments but will instead provide firms from other WTO Members non-discriminatory access to do business with SOEs.

Second, in view of the concern over possible government influence on SOE decisions, China further committed, under the same paragraph, that 'the Government of China would not influence, directly or indirectly, commercial decisions on the part of state-owned or state-invested enterprises, including on the quantity, value or country of origin of any goods purchased or sold, except in a manner consistent with the WTO Agreement.' Overall, the two commitments were designed to make sure that all transactions are conducted by the SOEs on the basis of commercial considerations and without the influence of the Chinese government. While these commitments are not further elaborated in the Working Party Report or the Accession Protocol, they can be interpreted in a broad manner so as to address most of today's challenges that Chinese SOEs pose to the world trading system. Such potential of these commitments will be discussed in detail in Chapter 5.

While the above commitments appear to be a major concession from China, such an arrangement was actually to its own advantage too as China was able to avoid making quantitative import commitments like former Socialist countries such as Poland.[73] Traditionally, economic activities in Communist countries were arranged by state planning, which covers not only domestic production and consumption but also

---

[73] Alexander Polouektov, 'Non-Market Economy Issues in the WTO Anti-Dumping Law and Accession Negotiations: Revival of a Two-tier Membership?' (2002) 36(1) *Journal of World Trade* 1, 9–11. See also Kazimierz Grzybowski, 'Socialist Countries in GATT' (1980) 28(4) *American Journal of Comparative Law* 539, 547–8.

foreign trade.[74] The state would decide the amount of exports and imports each year and, as everything was planned by the state, there was no need for tariffs as trade measures. The GATT contracting parties, most of which were capitalist countries, were worried that the Communist countries could simply choose to decide by state planning to not import anything at all, thus nullifying the value of any tariff concessions that they had negotiated with such countries. To avoid this problem, it appeared to make more sense to require the Communist countries to agree to import an increasingly larger amount of goods every year. In appearance, quantitative import commitments seem to be no different from tariff concessions because a country could easily convert tariff concessions into the amount of goods imported every year. In practice, however, because most countries usually have a cushion between bound and applied tariffs, quantitative import commitments may well translate into a much higher tariff concession. Moreover, as a quantitative import commitment requires increases in imports every year, the contracting party so committed would effectively lose the flexibility needed to deal with unexpected changes in the domestic and world markets. By agreeing to commitments on commercial decisions of SOEs, China had avoided such highly restrictive and burdensome quantitative import commitments.

The second SOE-related issue concerned the application of Article III:8(a) of GATT 1994, which creates a carve-out for government procurement measures. In particular, WTO Members sought confirmation from China that 'any measure relating to state-owned and state-invested enterprises importing materials and machinery used in the assembly of goods, which were then exported or otherwise made available for commercial sale or use or for non-governmental purposes, would not be considered to be a measure relating to government procurement.'[75] In essence, the Members were seeking assurance that the purchase and sale activities of Chinese SOEs would not be exempted as government procurement, as China did not accept the Government Procurement Agreement in its accession. In response, China confirmed under paragraph 47 of the Working Party Report that,

> without prejudice to China's rights in future negotiations in the Government Procurement Agreement, all laws, regulations and measures

---

[74] See Gao, 'China's Participation in the WTO', n. 1, 46.
[75] Working Party Report, n. 71, para. 44.

relating to the procurement by state-owned and state-invested enterprises of goods and services for commercial sale, production of goods or supply of services for commercial sale, or for non-governmental purposes would not be considered to be laws, regulations and measures relating to government procurement. Thus, such purchases or sales would be subject to the provisions of Articles II, XVI and XVII of the GATS and Article III of the GATT 1994.

In retrospect, this commitment is a double-edged sword for both China and the other WTO Members. On the one hand, it made sure that the procurement of SOEs is not regarded as part of government procurement and instead is subject to normal WTO rules. On the other hand, by recognising the separation between SOEs and the Chinese government, the other WTO Members inadvertently made it harder to argue that SOEs are essentially an extension of the government when it comes to the 'public body' determination under the Agreement on Subsidies and Countervailing Measures[76] (SCM Agreement), which will be further discussed in Chapter 5.

3.5.2 Pricing Policies and Distortions

Another major concern in China's WTO accession negotiations was on China's pricing policies in general, as WTO Members struggled to understand price controls and state pricing in China. This was a unique problem for China, which was caught in the transition from the old planned economy to the new socialist market economy for the better part of its accession process. Under the old system, the state dictated the prices of all products, be it raw materials or finished products, agricultural or industrial products, and services. As China started its economic reform, the state first granted some firms the autonomy to set prices for surplus products produced above the planned production quota, which was then gradually expanded to other sectors. Yet, as the economy grew too hot with rapid inflation, the Chinese government often resorted to macro-economic adjustment polices to control prices. Concerned with the effects that such price controls can have on the market and trade, WTO Members requested China to 'allow prices for traded goods and services in every sector to be determined by market forces, and multi-tier

---

[76] Agreement on Subsidies and Countervailing Measures, 15 April 1994, Marrakesh Agreement Establishing the World Trade Organization, Annex 1A, 1869 UNTS 14 (SCM Agreement).

pricing practices for such goods and services should be eliminated'.[77] While they recognised that China may maintain price controls on goods and services listed in Annex 4 to the Accession Protocol, they were of the view that price controls should 'be adopted only in extraordinary circumstances and should be removed as soon as the circumstances justifying their adoption were addressed'.[78]

China, in its reply, went to great length to explain its pricing policies, which it summarised as 'a mechanism of market-based pricing under macro-economic adjustment'[79] and expanded with extensive examples from individual sectors in the next eight paragraphs of the Working Party Report. Yet, like the discussion on SOEs in Section 3.5.1, the concerns of WTO Members ultimately boiled down to whether the pricing policies would be used in a way that undermines China's WTO commitments and adversely affects other WTO Members' commercial interests. To address these concerns, China agreed to the following commitments:

First, China will enhance the transparency of its pricing policies by publishing 'in the official journal the list of goods and services subject to state pricing and changes thereto, together with price-setting mechanisms and policies'.[80] Presumably, those which are not on the list shall not be subject to state pricing, and will be determined by the market.

Second, China also confirmed that 'price controls would not be used for purposes of affording protection to domestic industries or services providers'.[81] In other words, this commitment provides the guarantee that the pricing policies would not be used for protectionist purposes.

Third, in response to the concern that China could maintain prices at below market rates to limit imports,[82] China also explicitly confirmed that its price controls 'would not have the effect of limiting or otherwise impairing China's market-access commitments on goods and services'.[83] Instead, it 'would apply its current price controls and any other price controls upon accession in a WTO-consistent fashion, and would take account of the interests of exporting WTO Members as provided for in Article III:9 of the GATT 1994'. According to GATT Article III:9,

---

[77] Working Party Report, n. 71, para. 50.
[78] Ibid., para. 51.
[79] Ibid., para. 52.
[80] Ibid., para. 60.
[81] Ibid., para. 62.
[82] Ibid., para. 63.
[83] Ibid., para. 64.

3.5 CONCERNS AND SOLUTIONS ON CHINA'S MODEL 59

contracting parties applying internal maximum price control measures shall take account of the interests of exporting countries, so as to avoid prejudicial effects on their exports. This apparently reflects the concern over cases where a country establishing a maximum control price for a commodity was 'such an important consumer that its price was likely to become the effective world price'.[84] This would certainly be the case for China, which is the top importer of so many commodities. But the Chinese accession was not the first to incorporate such commitments, as El Salvador also made a similar commitment in its accession in 1990.[85]

Despite China's commitments to bring its pricing policies in line with WTO rules, some WTO Members still had concerns about price distortions in the Chinese market, especially in the context of anti-dumping (AD) and countervailing investigations. This concern led to the creation of special rules to facilitate AD and countervailing investigations by authorities of other WTO Members. We deal with the special AD rule here and then the special countervailing rule in Section 3.5.3. By definition, dumping refers to international price discrimination whereby the export price of goods is lower than the price at which the goods are sold in the domestic market of the exporting country (i.e. normal value). Where such sales cause a material injury to the relevant industries in the importing country, that country may take AD measures typically in the form of import tariffs against the imports so as to remove the injury. During China's accession negotiations, some Members were concerned about the difficulties in using the production costs and prices of final goods in the Chinese market for the calculation of normal values because 'China was continuing the process of transition towards a full market economy'.[86] Accordingly, this concern was essentially about the Chinese government intervention in the market rendering prices of goods not being determined by market forces but being distorted and artificially lowered. Thus, Chinese domestic prices do not represent market prices or normal values of goods and cannot be used for comparison with export prices in determining whether dumping exists. In response to this concern, China agreed to the NME methodology which allows WTO Member authorities that are conducting AD investigations to assume that China is an NME unless China satisfies certain market economy conditions

---

[84] WTO, 'GATT Analytical Index – Article III National Treatment on Internal Taxation and Regulation', at 197, available at: www.wto.org/english/res_e/booksp_e/gatt_ai_e/art3_e.pdf.
[85] Ibid.
[86] Working Party Report, n. 71, para. 150.

contemplated in the domestic laws of these Members or the Chinese producers/exporters under investigation establish that market economy conditions prevail in the industry concerned.[87] Where China fails to rebut this assumption, the authorities are entitled to resort to non-Chinese or surrogate/benchmark prices or costs in a market economy third country to calculate normal values.

While accepting this special rule, China raised its own concerns about the abuse of AD by some WTO Members by treating China as an NME.[88] Notably, from the early stage of the accession negotiations, China had opposed any NME obligations and maintained that the general GATT rules should apply.[89] This special AD rule was one of the thorniest issues in the US–China bilateral negotiation which was key to the success of China's accession negotiations. During the bilateral talks, China regarded the special AD rule as bluntly discriminatory and initially rejected it.[90] Due to the United States' insistence, the two sides reached a compromise that the special AD rule must be subject to an expiration timeframe. This eventually led to the inclusion of a sunset clause under Section 15(d) of the Accession Protocol that the special rule shall be terminated after fifteen years of China's accession.[91] Thus, despite the ongoing debate over whether the special AD rule shall expire due to the operation of the sunset clause,[92] the records of the US–China

---

[87] Accession Protocol, n. 69, Section 15(a).
[88] Working Party Report, n. 71, para. 151.
[89] GATT, Working Party on China's Status as a Contracting Party: Communication from China, Spec(88)37, 11 July 1988, 7.
[90] Weihuan Zhou and Delei Peng, 'EU – Price Comparison Methodologies (DS516): Challenging the Non-Market Economy Methodology in Light of the Negotiating History of Article 15 of China's WTO Accession Protocol' (2018) 52(3) *Journal of World Trade* 505, 524.
[91] Ibid., 524–7.
[92] See e.g. James Nedumpara and Weihuan Zhou, *Non-Market Economies in the Global Trading System: The Special Case of China* (Singapore: Springer, 2018); Jorge Miranda, 'Interpreting Paragraph 15 of China's Protocol of Accession' (2014) 9(3) *Global Trade and Customs Journal* 94; Edwin Vermulst, Juhi Dion Sud and Simon Evenett, 'Normal Value in Anti-Dumping Proceedings against China Post-2016: Are Some Animals Less Equal Than Others?' (2016) 11(5) *Global Trade and Customs Journal* 212; Christian Tietje and Karsten Nowrot, 'Myth or Reality? China's Market Economy Status under WTO Anti-Dumping Law after 2016', Policy Paper, Transnational Economic Law Research Center Policy Papers No. 34, December 2011; 'China: NME at the Gates? Article 15 of China's WTO Accession Protocol: A Multi-Perspective Analysis', Research Paper, European Institute for Asian Studies Research Paper, November 2016; Weihuan Zhou, 'China's Litigation on Non-Market Economy Treatment at the WTO: A Preliminary Assessment' (2017) 5(2) *Chinese Journal of Comparative Law* 345; Mirek

negotiations show convincingly that the compromise reached was that, while China accepted the special rule, the United States agreed that it would remain applicable for fifteen years only.[93] This compromise was not based on or conditional upon whether China transitions into a full-fledged market economy but was merely intended to enable WTO Members to apply a discriminatory method to facilitate AD actions against China for an agreed period of time.

This observation is not affected by paragraph 150 of the Working Party Report which, as noted, documents the concern of some Members about China's NME status creating difficulties in using Chinese prices for determining normal values. Notably, unlike Section 15(b) of the Accession Protocol which sets out a special rule to tackle Chinese subsidies (which is discussed in Section 3.5.3), paragraph 150 is not incorporated into Section 15(a) but is explicitly excluded from the list of commitments undertaken by China.[94] Accordingly, this exclusion arguably reinforces the observation that the inclusion of the special AD rule must not be interpreted or understood as a commitment of China to fundamentally change its economic system or development model.

Again, on pricing policies, the main concern was to make sure that such policies would not be used by China in ways that evade its WTO commitments, rather than banning the use of price controls and forcing China to adopt specific pricing mechanisms.

3.5.3 Industrial Policies and Subsidies

China's use of industrial policies, especially subsidies, which could have trade-distorting effects, was the third major concern of WTO Members. In particular, they sought clarification on whether financial contributions by SOEs (including banks) should be regarded as those by government actors within the scope of Article 1.1(a) of the SCM Agreement.[95] Instead of answering the question directly, the Chinese representative simply noted that 'such financial contributions would not necessarily give rise to a benefit within the meaning of Article 1.1(b) of the SCM

Tobias Hosman, 'China's NME Status at the WTO: Analysis of the Debate' (2021) 20(1) *Journal of International Trade Law and Policy* 1. The disputes over the special anti-dumping rule will be further considered in Chapter 4.
[93] See Zhou and Peng, 'EU – Price Comparison Methodologies (DS516)', n. 90, 527–9.
[94] Working Party Report, n. 71, para. 342.
[95] Ibid., para. 172.

Agreement'.⁹⁶ At the same time, the representative confirmed that 'China's objective was that state-owned enterprises, including banks, should be run on a commercial basis and be responsible for their own profits and losses'.⁹⁷ Of course, such non-committal language could hardly satisfy the other WTO Members. Thus, in line with the pragmatist tradition of the WTO, more concrete commitments were included in China's Accession Protocol.

First, China agreed that subsidies provided to SOEs will be viewed as specific if they are 'the predominant recipients of such subsidies or ... receive disproportionately large amounts of such subsidies'.⁹⁸ Contrary to popular belief, the WTO's SCM Agreement does not prohibit all subsidies. Instead, only those subsidies regarded as 'specific' are actionable.⁹⁹ Only two types of subsidies, that is, export subsidies and import substitution subsidies, are prohibited and are deemed to be 'specific' per se. The specificity of other types of subsidies must be established by showing that they are specific to certain enterprises, industries or regions.¹⁰⁰ Thus, the ownership of an enterprise was not one of the specificity criteria until China's accession, and even then it is limited to China. Does the addition of such an 'ownership-specific' criterion reflect a systemic concern over China's unique economic system? We do not think this is the case for the following reasons. First, if this were indeed regarded as a systemic concern, the WTO Members would probably request China to eliminate all such subsidies, either immediately upon accession as regarding export subsidies and import-substitution subsidies¹⁰¹ or over a transition period. Second, while an explicit reference to ownership as a specificity criterion is unprecedented, the concept can still be regarded as being derived from normal WTO rules on specificity. The SCM Agreement rules on enterprise specificity only refer to 'an enterprise ... or group of enterprises' without detailed rules on how to determine if certain enterprises fall into one group. It could be argued that ownership-type could be used as a classification criterion. The language on factors to be considered in determining whether a subsidy is *de facto* specific is also informative, as it refers to 'predominant use by

---

⁹⁶ Ibid.
⁹⁷ Ibid.
⁹⁸ Accession Protocol, n. 69, Section 10.2.
⁹⁹ SCM Agreement, n. 76, Art. 1.2.
¹⁰⁰ Ibid., Art 2.1–2.
¹⁰¹ Accession Protocol, n. 69, 10.3.

3.5 CONCERNS AND SOLUTIONS ON CHINA'S MODEL

certain enterprises, the granting of disproportionately large amounts of subsidy to certain enterprises',[102] which is the same language used in China's Accession Protocol. Moreover, the same paragraph in the SCM Agreement also noted that, in considering these factors, 'account shall be taken of the extent of diversification of economic activities within the jurisdiction of the granting authority'. It would not be a stretch to argue that the phrase 'extent of diversification of economic activities' could cover issues such as the ownership types of business entities, as is the case in China. Third, a positive finding of specificity based on ownership is not dispositive by itself, as an injury determination is still needed to make such subsidies illegal under WTO law. This affirms again that the underlying concern was not focused on China's economic model as a whole but more on the spill over effect of Chinese subsidies on other WTO Members. If the Members really had a broader systemic concern, they would have banned all subsidies to SOEs categorically, just like they did with agricultural export subsidies, which China was not allowed to maintain or introduce,[103] even though they were allowed for other WTO Members at the time of China's WTO accession.

Second, China also agreed, in Section 15(b) of its Accession Protocol, that, for benefit calculations under Article 14 of the SCM Agreement, the importing WTO Member may 'use methodologies for identifying and measuring the subsidy benefit which take into account the possibility that prevailing terms and conditions in China may not always be available as appropriate benchmarks ... if there are special difficulties' in the application of normal rules under the SCM Agreement. In other words, the investigating Member may resort to alternative benchmarks in its benefits determination, a process similar to the NME methodology contemplated in Section 15(a). As we will discuss in Chapter 5, this language makes it much easier for other WTO Members to determine the existence of benefits in cases involving Chinese firms. Moreover, unlike the NME methodology, which was supposed to expire fifteen years after China's accession, there is no end date for the application of the alternative benchmark mechanism. The inference we could draw here is that the other WTO Members expected that the unique market conditions in China may continue to exist for a very long time after its WTO accession. For them, the existence of such unique market conditions itself is not a problem, as it is already addressed by the 'special difficulties' language. As

---

[102] SCM Agreement, n. 76, Art. 2.1(c).
[103] Accession Protocol, n. 69, 12.1.

confirmation of this reading, we can refer to paragraph 171 of the Working Party Report, which denies China the special treatment normally available for debt forgiveness programs adopted by transition economies in privatisation programmes under Article 27(13) of the SCM Agreement. This means that the direct forgiveness of debts by the Chinese government in privatisation programmes would also be actionable. Had the WTO Members really had systemic concerns with the prevalence of SOEs in China, they would not have included a commitment which creates the perverse effect of discouraging China to privatise its SOEs.

3.5.4 Trading Rights

The fourth major issue arising from China's state-led economic model concerned trading rights, that is, the right to import and export goods. Before the commencement of China's economic reform and opening up, China had a long history of restricting trading rights to a handful of state-owned trading companies.[104] While the reform led to progressive liberalisation of trading rights,[105] China maintained an 'examination and approval' system under which only entities that satisfied certain licensing criteria may become a foreign trade operator and engage in import and export activities.[106]

During China's accession negotiations, WTO Members raised two concerns on trading rights. First, they were concerned that 'the activities of China's state trading enterprises were not sufficiently transparent and were not in accordance with WTO obligations'.[107] Thus, they requested that China 'ensure that the import purchasing practices and procedures of state trading enterprises were fully transparent, and in compliance with the requirements of the WTO Agreement' and 'refrain from taking any measure to influence or direct state trading enterprises as to the quantity, value, or country of origin of goods purchased or sold, except in accordance with the requirements of the WTO Agreement'.[108] In

---

[104] See Lardy, *Integrating China into the Global Economy*, n. 55, 40.
[105] Ibid., 41–2 (noting that prior to China's WTO accession, the Chinese government had authorized 35,000 firms of all types to engage in foreign trade). See also Working Party Report, n. 71, para. 80.
[106] Xin Zhang, *International Trade Regulation in China: Law and Policy* (Portland, OR: Hart Publishing, 2006), 26–32.
[107] Working Party Report, n. 71, para. 208.
[108] Ibid., para. 209.

response, China tried to explain that 'its state trading enterprises had full management autonomy and responsibility for their own profits and losses'.[109] But, for some members of the Working Party, this did not appear sufficient. Instead, they reiterated the request for China to 'undertake a commitment to ensure that all state trading enterprises complied with the requirements of the WTO Agreement'.[110] This resulted in Section 6 of the Accession Protocol, where China agreed to two specific obligations:

First, disciplines on the purchase activities of state trading firms and state intervention on their activities, in relation to which China agreed that it

> shall ensure that import purchasing procedures of state trading enterprises are fully transparent, and in compliance with the WTO Agreement, and shall refrain from taking any measure to influence or direct state trading enterprises as to the quantity, value, or country of origin of goods purchased or sold, except in accordance with the WTO Agreement.

Second, transparency on the pricing mechanisms for state trading firms, where China agreed to 'provide full information on the pricing mechanisms of its state trading enterprises for exported goods'.

While these two commitments provide some assurance that state trading enterprises in China will operate in a WTO-consistent way, the old system that relied predominantly on state trading was still foreign for many WTO Members. More specifically, Members were concerned that trading rights remained limited to 'some Chinese enterprises' and that such a limitation was inconsistent with some fundamental rules of the GATT (i.e. GATT Articles XI and III).[111] There was, therefore, a request for China to create a system whereby the rights to import and export are made generally available and the process and criteria based on which trading rights are granted be transparent.[112] More specifically, the expectation was that, after a transition period, all firms in China, both Chinese and foreign, are entitled to trade in all products, regardless of the scope of business in their business licenses.[113] In response, China agreed to, within three years of accession, grant all enterprises in China 'the right to trade in all goods throughout the customs territory of China, except

---

[109] Ibid., para. 210.
[110] Ibid.
[111] Ibid., para. 80.
[112] Ibid.
[113] Ibid., para. 82.

for those goods listed in Annex 2A which continue to be subject to state trading'.[114] Such a right will be granted to both Chinese firms and all foreign individuals and enterprises, including those 'not invested or registered in China'.[115] China also agreed that its system of examination and approval of trading rights would be eliminated and 'any requirements for obtaining trading rights would be for customs and fiscal purposes only and would not constitute a barrier to trade'.[116] For foreign entities, China also undertook to grant trading rights 'in a non-discriminatory and non-discretionary way'.[117] On 1 July 2004, China implemented the commitment to liberalise trading rights in its newly amended Foreign Trade Law[118] by replacing the licensing system with a registration system. Under the new system, trading rights are granted automatically to any enterprises, institutions or individuals as long as they are registered with the Ministry of Commerce or its local branches or designated bodies.[119]

Again, as we can see from the negotiations on trading rights, the concern WTO Members had with China's economic system was not systemic but practical. These commitments were designed to make sure that the state trading enterprises in China would make their import and export decisions on the basis of commercial considerations and in a transparent manner. Moreover, as shown by China's commitment to

---

[114] Accession Protocol, n. 69, 5.1.
[115] Ibid., 5.2.
[116] Working Party Report, n. 71, para. 84.
[117] Ibid., para. 84(b).
[118] 《中华人民共和国对外贸易法》(1994) [Foreign Trade Law of the People's Republic of China 1994], adopted by the 7th Session of the Standing Committee of the 8th National People's Congress on 12 May 1994, effective on 1 July 1994; revised on 6 April 2004, and on 7 November 2016, effective on the same date.
[119] 《对外贸易经营者备案登记办法》(2004) [Measures for the Filing and Registration of Foreign Trade Operators 2004], Order No 14 of the Ministry of Commerce, promulgated on 25 June 2004, effective on 1 July 2004; revised on 18 August 2016, 30 November 2019 and on 10 May 2021. There was a notable exception to this fundamental overhaul of the trading rights system concerning the remaining restrictions on the right to import certain cultural products. These restrictions were challenged by the United States in the China – Publications and Audiovisual Products dispute in 2007. For a detailed discussion of this dispute and its outcomes, see generally Henry Gao, 'The Mighty Pen, the Almighty Dollar, and the Holy Hammer and Sickle: An Examination of the Conflict between Trade Liberalization and Domestic Cultural Policy with Special Regard to the Recent Dispute between the United States and China on Restrictions on Certain Cultural Products' (2007) 2 *Asian Journal of WTO and International Health Law and Policy* 313; Weihuan Zhou, *China's Implementation of the Rulings of the World Trade Organization* (Oxford: Hart Publishing, 2019) 52–68.

liberalise trading rights, when WTO Members regarded an issue as a problem, they sought to resolve it by creating specific commitments rather than leaving it unaddressed. Conversely, the lack of sweeping disciplines on China's state capitalism itself is telling and demonstrates that WTO Members were not so concerned with China's unique economic model per se. Instead, their concerns were focused on the specific features of the Chinese system that were inconsistent with WTO rules. This is why these issues were explicitly discussed and addressed in the accession documents.

3.6 Conclusion

To summarise the discussions in this chapter, WTO Members never intended to use China's accession to the GATT and WTO to force China to abandon its unique economic system. Instead, the concerns were mainly with specific aspects of the Chinese economic model, that is, the role of SOEs, pricing policies, industrial policies and subsidies and trading rights. More specifically, the main focus was to craft specific rules for China to ensure that these aspects would not be used by China to undermine its WTO commitments. In other words, our review of the accession negotiations shows that the concern with China's state capitalism model was more specific than systemic, which is why the solutions proffered were more surgical than sweeping.

Such China-specific commitments, except those explicitly noted in China's WTO accession package, are not conditional upon the adoption of specific types of reforms within China, or even the progression of the reform according to a specific pace. We understand the frustration some commentators might have had when China's economic reform became stalled or even reversed in recent years, but we do not think that this therefore justifies a revisionist version of China's WTO accession process to support the argument that China did indeed agree to comprehensive reforms of its economic system as the price for its WTO accession. While some people might criticise the members of China's WTO accession Working Party for their alleged lack of imagination and failure to include more rules to counter China's state capitalism, we do not share this view. Instead, we would agree with Robert Howse that 'the basic understanding of the original GATT was that the multilateral trading system is neutral as between state enterprises and private enterprises; provided Members of the WTO do not use state enterprises to circumvent their general obligations under the WTO treaties, there is no special impediment or burden on the choice for state ownership'.[120]

Moreover, we would regard the approach taken in China's WTO accession as a confirmation of the faith among WTO Members in the ability of the WTO to provide an interface of economic relations between countries with different economic systems. In Chapters 4 and 5, we will explore further the potentials and limits of existing WTO rules in tackling (China's) state capitalism.

---

[120] Robert Howse, 'Official Business: International Trade Law and the Resurgence (or Resilience) of the State as an Economic Actor' (Forthcoming) *University of Pennsylvania Journal of International Law*, 5, available at: https://ssrn.com/abstract=3892415.

4

The Limits of General WTO Rules

4.1 Introduction

Chapters 4 and 5 explore the capacity of the WTO to discipline the behaviour and conduct of Chinese state-owned enterprises (SOEs). This chapter discusses the limitations of the major relevant rules under the General Agreement on Tariffs and Trade[1] (GATT) in relation to (1) honouring tariff concessions by import monopolies, (2) the non-discrimination requirement on state trading enterprises (STEs), (3) trade restrictions by STEs, (4) transparency and (5) anti-dumping (AD) measures. We show that the first three rules are limited in terms of the types of policy instruments covered and the scope of obligations. The transparency mechanisms have been ineffective at ensuring the submission of adequate notifications by WTO Members in general and at inducing China to provide sufficient information on SOEs. Finally, the WTO jurisprudence has developed in a way that gradually removes the flexibility of using AD to address market distortions caused by state intervention.

4.2 The Limitations of GATT/WTO Rules in Challenging State Capitalism

Many GATT/WTO rules are designed to control and reduce the degree of governmental interference with commercial transactions to achieve a better allocation of international resources and increase economic welfare worldwide.[2] More specifically, they impose a series of general rules to limit governments' ability to use various policy instruments such

---

[1] General Agreement on Tariffs and Trade, opened for signature 30 October 1947, 61 Stat. A-11, TIAS 1700, 55 UNTS 194 (GATT).
[2] John H. Jackson, *World Trade and the Law of the GATT* (Indianapolis: Bobbs-Merrill Company, 1969) 329.

as tariffs, quantitative restrictions, certain customs rules and formalities, internal taxes and regulations and subsidies. These rules, however, are ill-equipped to deal with SOEs, as noted by Jackson, Davey and Sykes:

> Many GATT rules ... restrict the types of regulations which governments can impose on international traders, but do not purport to regulate the traders themselves. If the government is the trader or controls the trader, the rules may be ineffective since decisions ostensibly made independently by the trader may in fact reflect actions of the government.[3]

Indeed, GATT draftsmen realised that governments may act through firms or enterprises to indirectly influence trade.[4] Thus, several GATT provisions seek to regulate such conduct by prohibiting:

- the imposition of import mark-ups by import monopolies (Article II:4);
- import or export restrictions through state trading operations (the interpretative note to GATT Articles XI, XII, XIII, XIV and XVIII); and
- discriminatory conduct by STEs (Article XVII).

However, as will be discussed in this section, these rules are limited to certain types of policy instruments and a narrow scope of obligations. In addition, GATT Article VI and the WTO Anti-Dumping Agreement[5] (AD Agreement) allow WTO Members to take action against 'dumping', a practice in which companies sell goods in a foreign market at a price (i.e. export price) lower than the price of those goods in the market of exportation (i.e. normal value). AD, typically in the form of import tariffs, has become one of the most popular instruments used by countries to tackle the so-called unfair trade practice which is sometimes made possible by state intervention in the market.[6] However, we believe that the development of WTO jurisprudence has, and rightly so,

---

[3] John H. Jackson, William J. Davey and Alan O. Sykes, *Legal Problems of International Economic Relations – Cases, Materials and Text*, 4th ed. (Saint Paul, MN: West Group, 2002) 402.

[4] Jackson, *World Trade and the Law of the GATT*, n. 2, 331.

[5] Agreement on the Implementation of Article VI of GATT 1994, Marrakesh Agreement Establishing the World Trade Organization, Marrakesh, 15 April 1994, 1868 UNTS 201, Annex 1A.

[6] However, it is interesting to note that the GATT negotiations of the anti-dumping rules were intended to restrict the abuse of anti-dumping measures without treating dumping as unfair practice. See Douglas A. Irwin, Petros C. Mavroidis and Alan O. Sykes, *The Genesis of the GATT* (Cambridge: Cambridge University Press, 2008) 144.

gradually removed the flexibility for governments to use AD to address price distortions generated by state intervention.

4.2.1 Non-discrimination and State Trading Enterprises

The non-discrimination principle, enshrined in the most-favoured-nation (MFN) rule (GATT Article I:1) and the national treatment (NT) rule (GATT Article III), is one of the fundamental pillars of the WTO edifice. The activities of government-related enterprises may undermine the operation of these rules if they discriminate among imports or between imported and domestic goods based on origin. Accordingly, one of the key proposals during the negotiations of the GATT was the imposition of an obligation on governments to ensure that STEs 'operate on a non-discriminatory basis, allowing their sales and purchases to be governed only by commercial considerations'.[7] This obligation was eventually codified in GATT Article XVII:1 which reads in its substantive parts:

(a) Each contracting party undertakes that if it establishes or maintains a State enterprise, wherever located, or grants to any enterprise, formally or in effect, exclusive or special privileges, such enterprise shall, in its purchases or sales involving either imports or exports, act in a manner consistent with the general principles of non-discriminatory treatment prescribed in this Agreement for governmental measures affecting imports or exports by private traders.

(b) The provisions of sub-paragraph (a) of this paragraph shall be understood to require that such enterprises shall, having due regard to the other provisions of this Agreement, make any such purchases or sales solely in accordance with commercial considerations, including price, quality, availability, marketability, transportation and other conditions of purchase or sale, and shall afford the enterprises of the other contracting parties adequate opportunity, in accordance with customary business practice, to compete for participation in such purchases or sales.

Two major elements may affect the scope of Article XVII:1 in dealing with SOEs: the covered enterprises and the scope of obligations.

---

[7] Jackson, *World Trade and the Law of the GATT*, n. 2, 331.

Article XVII:1 deals with STEs which are defined under Article 1 of the Understanding on the Interpretation of Article XVII (STE Understanding) as follows: 'Governmental and non-governmental enterprises, including marketing boards, which have been granted exclusive or special rights or privileges, including statutory or constitutional powers, in the exercise of which they influence through their purchases or sales the level or direction of imports or exports.' This definition leaves two major issues unclarified: (1) the scope of 'exclusive or special rights or privileges' and (2) the degree of influence required to become an STE. These two issues are arguably at the core of determining whether an enterprise is subject to the obligations under Article XVII:1. Since it is impossible to envisage all trade-distorting activities of STEs, Article XVII:1 seeks to tackle the underlying sources of such trade distortions, namely, the use of special rights and privileges by an enterprise to influence trade.[8] Without limiting the scope of 'exclusive or special rights or privileges'[9] or requiring any specific degree of influence, Article XVII:1 is flexible enough to cover a broad range of enterprises including SOEs and private firms that utilise special rights or privileges bestowed by governments to influence trade through 'purchases or sales' activities. Along these lines, the Working Party on STEs, established under Article 5 of the STE Understanding, produced an illustrative list of notifiable STEs.[10] While the list did not define STEs, it considered a wide spectrum of government-enterprise relationships and enterprise activities, showing the willingness of WTO Members to maintain a flexible definition.[11] Accordingly, in the context of China's SOE reform, Public Welfare SOEs and Special Commercial SOEs would fall within the definition of

---

[8] See Ernst-Ulrich Petersmann, 'GATT Law on State Trading Enterprises: Critical Evaluation of Article XVII and Proposals for Reform', in Thomas Cottier and Petros Mavroidis (eds.), *State Trading in the Twenty-First Century* (Ann Arbor: The University of Michigan Press, 1998) 71, 72.

[9] The only limits on the scope of 'exclusive or special rights or privileges' are set out in the interpretative note to Article XVII:1(a) which excludes governmental measures 'imposed to insure standards of quality and efficiency in the operation of external trade, or privileges granted for the exploitation of national natural resources but which do not empower the government to exercise control over the trading activities of the enterprise in question'. These limits were compromises reached in the original negotiations of the GATT. See Jackson, *World Trade and the Law of the GATT*, n. 2, 341–2.

[10] WTO, Working Party on State Trading Enterprises, Illustrative List of Relationships between Governments and State Trading Enterprises and the Kinds of Activities Engaged in by These Enterprises, G/STR/4, 30 July 1999.

[11] Andrea Mastromatteo, 'WTO and SOEs: Article XVII and Related Provisions of the GATT 1994' (2017) 16(4) *World Trade Review* 601, 607.

STEs because they undertake governmental functions or carry out government-mandated policies. Article XVII:1 can also be applied to General Commercial SOEs or private enterprises insofar as special rights or privileges are conferred upon these entities, enabling them to influence trade through 'purchases or sales' or associated activities. As regards the activities of enterprises, it is worth noting that there is no requirement that the enterprises undertake import or export activities. Rather, it would suffice if their purchases or sales affect trade.[12]

In contrast to the potentially broad coverage of STEs, the substantive obligations imposed by Article XVII:1(a) and (b) are limited. According to Jackson, these provisions were intended to impose an MFN obligation only.[13] However, the question of whether Article XVII:1(a) also covers an NT obligation remains unsettled to date.[14] In *Canada – FIRA*, the GATT panel, in *obiter dictum*,[15] concurred with Canada's submission that only the MFN obligation falls within the scope of Article XVII:1(a).[16] Canada's submission relied on two major arguments: (1) the reason why the word 'principle' is used in the plural is that the GATT contains a number of MFN-type obligations; and (2) by referring to 'imports or exports', Article XVII:1(a) does not concern 'the treatment by the state-trading enterprise of imported or domestic products in its domestic market'.[17] In contrast, the WTO panel subsequently in *Korea – Beef* observed that the general principle of non-discrimination under Article XVII:1(a) 'includes at least the provisions of Articles I and III of GATT'.[18] Consequently, the panel found that the Korean measure at

---

[12] GATT, Panel on Subsidies and State Trading, Final Report on State Trading, L/1146, 11 March 1960, 5. The Working Party on STEs provided a non-exhaustive list of activities ranging from direct involvement in importation or exportation (e.g. imports control, quota administration, licensing) to those relating to domestic sales or purchases (e.g. production, distribution, credit guarantees, storage, promotion, packaging, transportation). This also suggests that the covered activities are not limited to 'purchases or sales' *per se* but include activities associated with purchases or sales.

[13] Jackson, *World Trade and the Law of the GATT*, n. 2, 345–7.

[14] For a review of the relevant GATT/WTO panels' decisions, see Petersmann, 'GATT Law on State Trading Enterprises', n. 8, 80–4; Mastromatteo, 'WTO and SOEs', n. 11, 608–9.

[15] For a discussion of whether the WTO dispute settlement system is modelled on the Common Law doctrine of precedent, see Henry Gao, 'Dictum on Dicta: Obiter Dicta in WTO Disputes', (2018) 17(3) *World Trade Review* 509.

[16] Panel Report, *Canada – Administration of the Foreign Investment Review Act*, L/5504–30s/140, adopted 7 February 1984, para. 5.16 (*Canada – FIRA*).

[17] Ibid., para. 3.16.

[18] WTO Panel Report, *Korea – Measures Affecting Imports of Fresh, Chilled and Frozen Beef*, WT/DS161/R, WT/DS169/R, adopted 10 January 2001, para. 753 (*Korea – Beef*). This

issue constituted an NT-type violation.[19] The panel's findings were not appealed. In *Canada – Wheat*, the Canadian Wheat Board (CWB) Export Regime granted a range of 'exclusive and special privileges' to the CWB relating to the purchase and sale of certain Canadian wheat.[20] The Appellate Body (AB) was asked to consider the relationship between paragraphs (a) and (b) of Article XVII:1 and hence did not provide further clarification on the exact scope of the non-discrimination principles.[21] The AB merely stated that Article XVII:1(a) is an 'anti-circumvention' provision which

> seeks to ensure that a Member cannot, through the creation or maintenance of a State enterprise or the grant of exclusive or special privileges to any enterprise, engage in or facilitate conduct that would be condemned as discriminatory under the GATT 1994 if such conduct were undertaken directly by the Member itself.[22]

One may argue that for Article XVII:1(a) to fully perform the 'anti-circumvention' function, it is necessary for it to cover both the MFN rule and the NT rule. However, in the same case, the AB also observed that the interpretation of Article XVII:1 must take into account the other GATT rules that apply to the behaviour of STEs.[23] Thus, the argument that Article XVII:1(a) extends to the NT rule may be qualified if GATT Article III itself is sufficiently broad to capture NT-type discriminatory conduct by STEs. In *Canada – Provincial Liquor Boards (EEC)*, the GATT panel observed in *dictum* that Article III:4 is applicable to STEs 'at least when the monopoly of the importation and monopoly of the distribution in the domestic markets were combined, as was the case of

---

dispute concerned the consistencies of Korea's regulatory regime for beef with a number of GATT rules. Under Article XVII:1, the issue related to the practices of the Livestock Products Marketing Organisation (LPMO), the Korean state trading agency for beef.

[19] Ibid., para. 769. The panel found that the LPMO's practice of delaying 'its sales of imported beef into the Korean market while having important stocks' violated the non-discrimination principles contemplated in Article XVII:1(a). This finding suggests a NT-type violation whereby imported beef was treated less favourably than domestic beef in terms of distribution in the Korean market.

[20] Appellate Body Report, *Canada – Measures Relating to Exports of Wheat and Treatment of Imported Grain*, WT/DS276/AB/R, adopted 27 September 2004, para. 11 (*Canada – Wheat*).

[21] Ibid., para. 88.

[22] Ibid., para. 85. In Paragraph 87 of the Report, the AB's interpretation of the non-discrimination principles merely shows that such principles cover both *de jure* and *de facto* discrimination.

[23] Ibid., para. 150.

the provincial liquor boards in Canada'.[24] In *Canada – Provincial Liquor Boards (US)*, the GATT panel ruled that the different systems for the delivery of domestic and imported beer, maintained by a number of provincial liquor agencies, treated imported beer less favourably and hence violated Article III:4.[25] Specifically, the panel held:

> Article III:4 did not differentiate between measures affecting the internal transportation of imported products that were imposed by governmental monopolies and those that were imposed in the form of regulations governing private trade ... Canada's right under the General Agreement to establish an import and sales monopoly for beer did not entail the right to discriminate against imported beer inconsistently with Article III:4 through regulations affecting its internal transportation.[26]

While the issue of whether discriminatory conduct of STEs should be adjudicated under Article III or Article XVII:1 remains controversial, the GATT panels' recourse to the former in the above cases suggests that they were reluctant to determine whether Article XVII:1(a) imposes an NT obligation. In future cases, it is reasonable to believe that WTO tribunals will seek to condemn both MFN-type and NT-type discriminatory conduct by STEs through the application of the relevant WTO rules.

Another important issue is whether Article XVII:1(b) establishes a stand-alone obligation beyond non-discrimination, that is, requiring STEs to 'make ... purchases or sales solely in accordance with commercial considerations' (Commercial Considerations Requirement) and 'afford the enterprises of the other contracting parties adequate opportunity ... to compete for participation in such purchases or sales' (Adequate Opportunity Requirement). In *Canada – Wheat*, the United States argued that the Commercial Considerations Requirement constitutes a separate obligation whereby STEs must 'make sales solely in accordance with commercial considerations'.[27] The AB disagreed, holding that the opening phrase of Article XVII:1(b) makes it 'abundantly clear' that the remainder of that provision merely defines and clarifies the

---

[24] GATT Panel Report, *Import, Distribution and Sale of Alcoholic Drinks by Canadian Provincial Marketing Agencies*, L/6304-35S/37, adopted 22 March 1988, para. 4.26 (*Canada – Provincial Liquor Boards (EEC)*).

[25] GATT Panel Report, Canada – *Import, Distribution and Sale of Certain Alcoholic Drinks by Provincial Marketing Agencies*, DS17/R-39S/27, adopted 18 February 1992, paras. 5.10–5.16 (*Canada – Provincial Liquor Boards (US)*).

[26] Ibid., para. 5.15.

[27] Appellate Body Report, *Canada – Wheat*, n. 20, paras. 82–3.

requirement in Article XVII:1(a) and does not create obligations separate or independent from non-discrimination.[28] The AB concluded that 'Article XVII:1 was intended to impose disciplines on one particular type of STE behaviour, namely discriminatory behaviour, rather than to constitute a comprehensive code of conduct for STEs' or impose 'comprehensive competition-law-type obligations on STEs'.[29]

Regarding the Adequate Opportunity Requirement, the AB rejected the US's allegation that 'the CWB must offer the requisite opportunity to any enterprise that is ... selling wheat in the same market as the CWB'. Instead, the AB ruled that this requirement 'refer[s] to the opportunity to become the STE's counterpart in the transaction, *not* to an opportunity to replace the STE as a participant in the transaction'.[30]

In light of the discussions above, while Article XVII:1 is sufficiently broad to capture SOEs, it is limited to anti-discrimination and does not address other trade-distorting behaviour of SOEs. Other than discrimination, Article XVII:1 does not prohibit anti-competitive behaviour by SOEs and does not require SOEs to act as private entities, thereby giving WTO Members the flexibility to use SOEs for various regulatory purposes.[31] Finally, the application of Article XVII:1 may be qualified by the availability of other WTO rules applicable to the trade-distorting conduct of SOEs. As the AB observed in *Canada – Wheat*, 'Article XVII:1 was never intended to be the sole source of the disciplines imposed on STEs' and 'a number of additional obligations, under different covered agreements, operate to further constrain the behaviour of STEs'.[32] These obligations include, *inter alia*, GATT Article II:4, the *Ad* Note to Articles XI, XII, XIII, XIV and XVIII and GATT Article VI as implemented by the Agreement on Subsidies and Countervailing Measures (SCM Agreement) and the AD Agreement.[33] In practice, GATT/WTO tribunals have relied on the other disciplines, in preference to Article XVII:1, to condemn the conduct of STEs.[34]

---

[28] Ibid., paras. 89–91.
[29] Ibid., paras. 97–8, 145.
[30] Ibid., paras. 152, 157 (original emphasis).
[31] See Bernard Hoekman and Joel Trachtman, 'Canada–Wheat: Discrimination, Non-Commercial Considerations, and the Right to Regulate through State Trading Enterprises' (2008) 7(1) *World Trade Review* 45, 58, 62, 64.
[32] Appellate Body Report, *Canada – Wheat*, n. 20, para. 98.
[33] Ibid., para. 98 and FN 102–5.
[34] Mastromatteo, 'WTO and SOEs', n. 11, 609.

4.2.2 Tariffs and Import Monopoly

Another fundamental GATT/WTO rule, as codified in GATT Article II:1, serves to protect the value of tariff concessions by preventing a WTO Member from increasing import tariffs beyond the 'bound' levels recorded in its WTO 'Schedule of Concessions on Goods' (Goods Schedule). This rule limits the permissible conduct of governments but is not directly applicable to the activities of companies. Thus, if a trading company acquires a monopoly position in the importation of certain goods, it may simply make a business decision to increase the resale price of those goods in the domestic market, which would effectively offset the benefits of tariff concessions. To address this situation, GATT Article II:4 stipulates:

> If any contracting party establishes, maintains or authorizes, formally or in effect, a monopoly of the importation of any product described in the appropriate Schedule annexed to this Agreement, such monopoly shall not, except as provided for in that Schedule or as otherwise agreed between the parties which initially negotiated the concession, operate so as to afford protection on the average in excess of the amount of protection provided for in that Schedule...

The scope of Article II:4 in dealing with SOEs is limited in at least two aspects. First, it concerns whether an entity maintains a monopoly position in the importation of goods. SOEs that do not have such a monopoly position would fall outside the ambit of Article II:4. Second, it applies to 'bound' goods only and does not apply to goods that are 'unbound' (i.e. not included in Goods Schedules), although the current coverage of bound tariff lines is broad.[35]

With respect to the scope of obligations, Article II:4 requires that the maximum permissible monopoly protection must not, on average, exceed the amount of protection specified in the Goods Schedule.[36] The *Ad* Note to Article II:4 suggests that the relevant provisions of Article 31 of the Havana Charter would assist in the interpretation of this obligation. Article 31(4) of the Havana Charter relevantly provides that a 'bound' import duty

> shall represent the maximum margin by which the price charged by the import monopoly for the imported product (exclusive of internal taxes

---

[35] WTO, *World Trade Report: Six Decades of Multilateral Trade Cooperation: What Have We Learnt?* (Geneva: WTO, 2007) 221.
[36] Jackson, *World Trade and the Law of the GATT*, n. 2, 356–7.

conforming to the provisions of Article 18 [i.e. GATT Article III], transportation, distribution and other expenses incident to the purchase, sale or further processing, and a reasonable margin of profit) may exceed the landed cost . . .[37]

Accordingly, several GATT panels interpreted Article II:4 as only allowing for protection that has been included in Goods Schedules. In *Canada – Provincial Liquor Boards (EEC)*, since all imported alcoholic beverages are bound under Canada's Goods Schedule, the panel ruled that applying a profit margin on imported alcoholic beverages higher than that on 'like' domestic ones ran afoul of Article II:4.[38] The panel held:

> 4.16 . . . the phrase "a reasonable margin of profit" should be interpreted in accordance with the normal meaning of these words in their context of Article II and Article 31 of the Havana Charter, and that *"a reasonable margin of profit" was a margin of profit that would be obtained under normal conditions of competition (in the absence of the monopoly)*. The margin of profit would have on the average to be the same on both domestic and the like imported products so as not to undermine the value of tariff concessions under Article II.
>
> 4.19 . . . the mark-ups which were higher on imported than on like domestic alcoholic beverages (differential mark-ups) could *only* be justified under Article II:4, to the extent that they represented *additional costs necessarily associated with marketing of the imported products*, and that calculations could be made on the basis of average costs over recent periods. (emphasis added)

Thus, an import monopoly may charge, beyond an import duty, the costs associated with importation and a 'reasonable amount of profit'. However, a profit margin obtained from a monopoly position – that is, not under normal conditions of competition – is not 'reasonable' and would constitute a 'mark-up' prohibited by Article II:4. This finding was confirmed by the GATT panel in *Korea – Beef (Australia)*.[39]

Regarding the costs associated with importation, the panel in *Canada – Provincial Liquor Boards (US)* clarified that they must reflect the variable costs directly associated with the importation of the goods or

---

[37] GATT Analytical Index, Article II Schedules of Concessions, 91–2, available at: www.wto.org/english/res_e/booksp_e/gatt_ai_e/art6_e.pdf.

[38] GATT Panel Report, *Canada – Provincial Liquor Boards (EEC)*, n. 24, paras. 4.3–4.19.

[39] GATT Panel Report, *Republic of Korea – Restrictions on Imports of Beef – Complaint by Australia*, L/6504–36S/202, adopted 7 November 1989, para. 106.

the 'charges for fixed assets employed that were calculated in proportion to the use of these assets by the imported product'.[40] Accordingly, the panel found that the cost-of-service differential between imported and domestic products, which was equivalent to the differential profit margin applied previously in *Canada – Provincial Liquor Boards (EEC)*, did not represent 'additional costs necessarily associated with the marketing of imported products'.[41] To date, Article II:4 has not been considered by WTO tribunals, suggesting that import monopolies 'are less of an issue nowadays' than they were during the GATT era.[42]

4.2.3 Quantitative Restrictions and State Trading Enterprises

Import or export quantitative restrictions (i.e. quotas), which are generally prohibited under GATT Article XI:1, may also be applied via STEs. Thus, the *Ad* Note to Articles XI, XII, XIII, XIV and XVIII stipulates: 'Throughout Articles XI, XII, XIII, XIV and XVIII, the terms "import restrictions" or "export restrictions" include restrictions made effective through state-trading operations.'[43] This *Ad* Note has been applied in a number of disputes to successfully challenge the conduct of STEs. For example, in *Canada – Provincial Liquor Boards (EEC)*, the GATT panel found that 'the practices concerning listing/delisting requirements and the availability of points of sale [as maintained by the Canadian import and distribution monopoly of alcoholic beverages] which discriminate against imported alcoholic beverages were restrictions made effective through state-trading operations contrary to Article XI:1'.[44] In *Korea – Beef*, the WTO panel clarified that in cases where an STE exercises effective controls over both the importation and the distribution channels, 'the imposition of any restrictive measure, including internal measures, will have an adverse effect on the importation of the products

---

[40] GATT Panel Report, *Canada – Provincial Liquor Boards (US)*, n. 25, para. 5.19.
[41] Ibid., paras. 5.18, 5.21.
[42] Petros Mavroidis, *The Regulation of International Trade: GATT*, 1 vol (Cambridge, MA: MIT Press, 2016) 172.
[43] While Articles XII, XIV and XVIII provide for certain exceptions to the general principle for balance of payments and economic development reasons, Article XIII requires that any permitted import or export quotas are allocated on a non-discriminatory basis. The latter means that administration of quotas through STEs in a discriminatory manner is also prohibited.
[44] GATT Panel Report, *Canada – Provincial Liquor Boards (EEC)*, n. 24, para. 4.25.

concerned', which will trigger the application of the *Ad* Note.[45] Consequently, the panel found that because the Livestock Products Marketing Organisation (Korea's state trading agency for beef) had an exclusive import right to over 30 per cent of imported beef, its refusal to distribute imported beef in the domestic market constituted import restrictions on foreign beef contrary to Article XI:1 through the application of the *Ad* Note.[46]

Given the definition of STEs, the scope of the *Ad* Note is not confined to import or export monopolies or STEs with exclusive rights over importation or exportation. However, like Articles XVII:1 and II:4, the *Ad* Note merely deals with one type of trade-restrictive policy instrument. The combined scope of these provisions is therefore limited, as they leave other forms of trade-distorting measures unregulated. Finally, it should be noted that the *Ad* Note does not prohibit Members from using STEs for importation or exportation *per se*. As ruled by the WTO panel in *India – Quantitative Restrictions*, 'the mere fact that imports are effected through state trading enterprises would not in itself constitute a restriction. Rather, for a restriction to be found to exist, it should be shown that the operation of this state trading entity is such as to result in a restriction.'[47] This suggests that, to establish a violation of the *Ad* Note, the facts that 'trading rights' (i.e. the right to import and export) are granted to an entity with exclusive or special privileges (i.e. an STE) and that there are no imports of the subject goods during certain periods are not, in themselves, sufficient.[48] One must further prove that the absence of imports is caused by the STE.

4.2.4 Transparency

Transparency has long been one of the most fundamental principles of the multilateral trading system.[49] In general, the GATT/WTO rules on transparency comprise three key elements including (1) publication and

---

[45] WTO Panel Report, *Korea – Beef*, n. 18, para. 751. The panel also observed that 'when dealing with measures relating to agricultural products' (i.e. beef in this case), a violation of the Ad Note 'would necessarily constitute a violation of Article 4.2 of the WTO Agreement on Agriculture and Footnote 1 to that provision which essentially prevent Members from maintaining quantitative import restrictions through STEs' (paras. 759–62).

[46] Ibid., paras. 767–8.

[47] WTO Panel Report, *India – Quantitative Restrictions on Imports of Agricultural Textile and Industrial Products*, WT/DS90/R, adopted on 22 September 1999, para. 5.134.

[48] Ibid., para. 5.135.

[49] For a comprehensive analysis on China's implementation of the transparency obligations, see Henry Gao, 'The WTO Transparency Obligations and China' (2018) 12(2) *Journal of Comparative Law* 329.

4.2 LIMITATIONS OF GATT/WTO RULES

administration of trade-related laws, regulations and other governmental measures, (2) notification of such regulatory measures under various WTO agreements through the relevant WTO committees and (3) periodic review of trade policies and regulations pursuant to the Trade Policy Review Mechanism (TPRM).

Article X of the GATT sets out the basic transparency obligation which requires WTO Members to publish trade-related laws, regulations and other governmental measures and to administer these measures 'in a uniform, impartial and reasonable manner'. Steve Charnovitz pointed out that the origin of the provision can be traced back to the 1923 International Convention Relating to the Simplification of Customs Formalities,[50] but Padideh Ala'i argued that, as the United States proposed the language, this provision was heavily influenced by the US Administrative Procedure Act (APA), which was passed in June 1946.[51] According to Ala'i, as the APA had made the US administrative processes more transparent for foreign traders to conduct business in the United States, the United States proposed Article X in the GATT to level the playing field for US traders who often faced opaque and informal administrative structures in foreign markets.[52]

The US draft, initially entitled 'Publication and Administration of Trade Regulations–Advance Notice of Restrictive Regulations', was first incorporated as Article 38 in the Havana Charter for the International Trade Organization (ITO).[53] When the ITO failed to come into being, it was inherited by the GATT as Article X under a slightly different title – 'Publication and Administration of Trade Regulations'.[54] Notwithstanding the minor change in title, the substantive content of the article remained the same.[55] However, this provision was rarely used in the GATT era. As noted by Charnovitz, in the history of the GATT, this provision was invoked only once, that is, in the *EEC – Apples* case.[56] Moreover, even in that case,

---

[50] Steve Charnovitz, 'Transparency and Participation in the World Trade Organization' (2014) 56(4) *Rutgers Law Review* 927, 929.
[51] Padideh Ala'i and Mathew D'Orsi, 'Transparency in International Economic Relations and the Role of the WTO', in Robert G. Vaughn (eds.), *Research Handbook on Transparency* (Cheltenham: Edward Elgar, 2014) 370.
[52] Ibid.
[53] Sylvia Ostry, 'China and the WTO: Transparency' (1998) 3 *UCLA Journal of International Law and Foreign Affairs* 1, 3.
[54] Ibid.
[55] Ibid., 3–4.
[56] Charnovitz, 'Transparency and Participation in the World Trade Organization', n. 50, 929. GATT Panel Report, *European Economic Community – Restrictions on Imports of Apples – Complaint by the United States*, L/6513 – 36S/135, adopted 22 June 1989.

transparency was not the main claim and was instead only incidental to the main claims on quantitative restrictions under Articles XI and XIII. According to Ala'i, the reason for the low usage is because the focus of trade negotiations in GATT, at least for its first two decades, was mainly on reduction of tariffs.[57] As tariff is the most transparent trade measure, there was not much need to invoke the transparency obligation. Interestingly, this also explains why Article X was invoked in the *EEC – Apples* case, as it is mainly concerned with import quota, which by its nature is among the most opaque and non-transparent trade measures.

Under the WTO, trade negotiations have expanded significantly beyond tariff reductions[58] to cover a wide spectrum of non-tariff measures such as trade remedies measures, technical barriers, sanitary and phytosanitary measures, services regulations and intellectual property rights measures. Because most of these measures concern behind-the-border regulatory measures that are difficult to police, transparency has become 'an indispensable element of the multilateral trading system', as noted by the WTO in its official publication commemorating the Twenty Year Anniversary of the WTO.[59]

As an underlying WTO principle, transparency serves to reduce 'information asymmetries among governments, and between the state, economic actors, and citizens' and is essential for the systemic stability of the trading system.[60] The general obligations contemplated in GATT Article X, as mentioned, cover all trade measures affecting trade in goods. This provision is incorporated into other agreements such as Article III of the General Agreement on Trade in Services (GATS) and Article 63 of the Agreement on Trade-Related Aspects of Intellectual Property Rights (TRIPs). As these two provisions are modelled after Article X, we will concentrate on Article X in our discussions. Article X includes three paragraphs, two of which are relevant to the transparency obligation.

---

[57] See Ala'i and D'Orsi, 'Transparency in International Economic Relations and the Role of the WTO', n. 51, 368.
[58] The trade negotiations conducted under the auspices of the GATT were so successful that, by 1994, the average tariff for industrial countries had been drastically reduced from 20–30 per cent in 1947 to less than 4 per cent. See World Trade Report 2007, n. 35, 207–9.
[59] WTO, *The WTO at Twenty: Challenges and Achievements* (Geneva: WTO, 2015), 51.
[60] See generally Petros Mavroidis and Robert Wolfe, 'From Sunshine to a Common Agent: The Evolving Understanding of Transparency in the WTO' (2015) 21(2) *Brown Journal of World Affairs* 118; Robert Wolfe, 'Letting the Sunshine in at the WTO: How Transparency Brings the Trading System to Life', WTO Staff Working Paper ERSD-2013-03, 1–44.

4.2 LIMITATIONS OF GATT/WTO RULES

Under the first paragraph, WTO Members are required to publish promptly all trade-related 'laws, regulations, judicial decisions and administrative rulings of general application' and international trade agreements. Under the second paragraph, WTO Members may not enforce measures 'effecting an advance in a rate of duty or other charge on imports under an established and uniform practice, or imposing a new or more burdensome requirement, restriction or prohibition on imports, or on the transfer of payments therefor ... before such measure has been officially published'.

In addition, there are agreement-specific obligations that set out transparency requirements in various sector or measure-specific agreements. They mainly focus on due process and notification requirements. For example, under Article 6 of the AD Agreement and Article 12 of the SCM Agreement, authorities shall not only provide public notices on the key stages in the investigation process but also give interested parties the opportunity to supply information and participate in the process. As noted by the WTO, these requirements are 'intended to increase the transparency of determinations, with the hope that this will increase the extent to which determinations are based on fact and solid reasoning'.[61] Moreover, notification requirements can be found in almost every agreement ranging from the Technical Barriers to Trade (TBT)[62] and Sanitary and Phytosanitary (SPS) measures[63] agreements to the Agreement on Trade-Related Investment Measures (TRIMS).[64]

As these transparency obligations differ in nature and effect, we can also divide them into the following two categories:

- Passive or paper transparency, which is mainly about the obligation to provide the information so as to help traders to understand the various government regulations affecting trade. This includes the publication and notification obligations.

---

[61] WTO, 'Technical Information on Anti-dumping', available at: www.wto.org/english/tratop_e/adp_e/adp_info_e.htm.

[62] Agreement on Technical Barriers to Trade (TBT), 15 April 1994, Marrakesh Agreement Establishing the World Trade Organization, Annex 1A, 1868 U.N.T.S. 120, Art. 10.

[63] Agreement on the Application of Sanitary and Phytosanitary Measures (SPS), 15 April 1994, Marrakesh Agreement Establishing the World Trade Organization, Annex 1A, 1867 U.N.T.S. 493, Art. 7.

[64] Agreement on Trade-Related Investment Measures (TRIMs), 15 April 1994, Marrakesh Agreement Establishing the World Trade Organization, Annex 1A, 1868 U.N.T.S. 186, Art. 6.

- Positive or participatory transparency, which requires the relevant authorities to provide the information to various stakeholders to enable these actors to assess the implications of and even influence policy-making. Such provisions go beyond the narrow one-way publication and notification requirements under the previous category and instead prescribe a two-way process whereby the authorities would provide the information to the stakeholders first, then the stakeholders are given an opportunity to comment on the information and the authorities will then make decisions based on these comments. Such requirements apply not only to the drafting of trade-related laws and regulations,[65] but also to the decision-making process in administrative proceedings such as anti-dumping and subsidy investigations.

Transparency is even more crucial to the operation of the trading system when dealing with non-market economies (NMEs) or SOEs, whose impact on trade is often difficult to observe.[66] During the 1954–1955 Review Session, GATT Article XVII:4 was added to ensure adequate disclosure of the activities of STEs and to bring them under closer international scrutiny.[67] Sub-paragraphs (a)–(c) of Article XVII:4, respectively, require Members to notify the products traded by STEs, the import mark-up applied by import monopolies and any STE operations that have adversely impacted the interests of other Members. Sub-paragraph (d) excludes confidential information from the disclosure obligations. Subsequently, the GATT Contracting Parties adopted standard questionnaires and procedures for STE notifications in 1960 and 1962, which however did not facilitate adequate notifications.[68] The STE Understanding was then designed to improve the notifications by (1) requiring Members to review their policies regarding the submission of STE notifications to the Council for Trade in Goods, (2) encouraging Members to maximise transparency on the notification of STE operations and the effect on trade and (3) allowing other Members to make counter-notifications against inadequate notifications. The Working

---

[65] See e.g. SPS Agreement, Annex B, para. 5; TBT Agreement, Art. 2.9.2 and Annex 3, para. L.
[66] See Eliza Patterson, 'Improving GATT Rules for Nonmarket Economies' (1986) 20(2) *Journal of World Trade* 185, 199–200.
[67] See Jackson, *World Trade and the Law of the GATT*, n. 2, 349–50.
[68] GATT Analytical Index, Article VI Anti-Dumping and Countervailing Duties, 481–2, available at: www.wto.org/english/res_e/booksp_e/gatt_ai_e/art6_e.pdf. Jackson, *World Trade and the Law of the GATT*, n. 2, 350–4.

Party on STEs was tasked with reviewing notifications and counter-notifications. In 2003, the Working Party produced a revised questionnaire requesting a wide range of information on STEs, their activities and impact on trade.[69] Despite these efforts, notifications have remained strikingly inadequate, with a decreasing number of notifications over the notification periods despite the expansion of WTO membership.[70] In the latest notification period in 2020, only 30 new and full notifications were submitted, while a majority of WTO Members including China did not submit a notification.[71]

In China's accession process, transparency was regarded as one of the most problematic areas. As summarised in the Working Party Report on the Accession of China,

> some members noted the difficulty in finding and obtaining copies of regulations and other measures undertaken by various ministries as well as those taken by provincial and other local authorities. Transparency of regulations and other measures, particularly of sub-national authorities, was essential since these authorities often provided the details on how the more general laws, regulations and other measures of the central government would be implemented and often differed among various jurisdictions. Those members emphasized the need to receive such information in a timely fashion so that governments and traders could be prepared to comply with such provisions and could exercise their rights in respect of implementation and enforcement of such measures. The same members emphasized the importance of such pre-publication to enhancing secure, predictable trading relations.[72]

To address these concerns, China agreed to a series of obligations in addition to the general transparency obligations just discussed. These wide-ranging China-specific obligations include, *inter alia*, publication of relevant rules and other relative normative documents, provision of official journals and opportunities for comment prior to implementation of such rules, establishment of enquiry points to provide access to

---

[69] WTO, Working Party on State Trading Enterprises, Questionnaire on State Trading, G/STR/3/Rev.1, 14 November 2013.

[70] WTO, Report (2020) of the Working Party on State Trading Enterprises, adopted 2 November 2020, G/L/1370, G/STR/26, 9 November 2020; WTO, Working Party on State Trading Enterprises, Status of Notifications Submitted by WTO Members under Article XVII:4(A) of the GATT 1994 and Paragraph 1 of the Understanding on the Interpretation of Article XVII of the GATT 1994, G/STR/25/Rev.1, 9 November 2020.

[71] Ibid.

[72] Report of the Working Party on the Accession of China, WT/ACC/CHN/49, 1 October 2001, para. 324 (WPR).

relevant information on the rules and related measures prior to their introduction, to make available to WTO Members translations into one or more of the official languages of the WTO all relevant rules in good time prior to their introduction, and to allow a transitional review conducted by the General Council and subsidiary bodies of the WTO mandated to oversee China's commitments. While China has taken a range of actions to implement its WTO-plus transparency obligations, there are notable deficiencies such as the lack of publication of sub-central governmental measures, insufficient responses by certain enquiry points and a general lack of implementation by local governments.[73]

As far as the notification of SOEs is concerned, China's Trade Policy Review (TPR) documents in 2016 did contain information on SOEs. However, the information provided was too sparse to satisfy the purpose of STE notifications.[74] This sparseness contrasted with the WTO Secretariat's Report on China's TPR which contained much more detailed information on the operation of Chinese SOEs and identified certain areas where more information was required.[75] Many WTO Members raised questions about Chinese SOEs and requested concrete details of the SOE reform, reflecting a significant lack of transparency in China's submissions and a lack of knowledge on the (potential) impact of SOEs on trade and competition.[76] In its following two rounds of TPR in July 2018 and October 2021, China provided almost no further information on issues relating to SOEs including the SOE reform,[77] even though these issues remained a major matter of concern.[78] The WTO Secretariat Report on the latest Trade Policy Review of China also noted that the information on China's industrial subsidies remains strikingly

---

[73] See Gao, 'WTO's Transparency Obligations and China', n. 49, 340–55.
[74] WTO Trade Policy Review Body, Trade Policy Review Report by China, WT/TRP/G/342, 15 June 2016, 12–13.
[75] Trade Policy Review Body, Trade Policy Review Report by the Secretariat, WT/TRP/S/342, 15 June 2016.
[76] WTO Trade Policy Review Body, Trade Policy Review – China, Minutes of the Meeting, WT/TRP/M/342, 26 September 2016, paras. 3.19, 4.211, 4.348. See also Robert Wolfe, 'Sunshine over Shanghai: Can the WTO Illuminate the Murky World of Chinese SOEs?' (2017) 16(4) *World Trade Review* 713, 721–4.
[77] WTO Trade Policy Review Body, Trade Policy Review Report by China, WT/TRP/G/375, 6 June 2018. WTO Trade Policy Review Body, Trade Policy Review – Report by China, WT/TPR/G/415, 15 September 2021.
[78] WTO Trade Policy Review Body, Trade Policy Review Report by the Secretariat, WT/TRP/S/375, 6 June 2018. WTO Trade Policy Review Body, Trade Policy Review – Report by the Secretariat, WT/TPR/S/415, 15 September 2021.

inadequate, particularly due to the involvement of SOEs, even though China claimed to have made a full notification of subsidies in 2019.[79]

In general, the records of notification of subsidies granted to or through SOEs have been poor.[80] The inadequacy of notifications under the different WTO transparency mechanisms reveals the limitations or ineffectiveness of the relevant WTO rules in ensuring transparency. The underlying causes of this ineffectiveness stem from, amongst others, the ambiguities in the definition and coverage of STEs, the exclusion of confidential information from notifications, and Members' lack of capacity or incentives to collect and provide the required information.[81] These causes apply to WTO Members in general and do not make China a unique case. Nevertheless, given the role of SOEs in the Chinese economy and the complexities of China's SOE reform, the lack of transparency in the operation, activities, and impact of Chinese SOEs creates particularly acute challenges for the WTO.

4.2.5 Anti-dumping

AD has been one of the most frequently invoked policy instruments in dealing with NMEs. When an NME is involved, investigating authorities (IAs) may decide to replace the price of the subject goods sold in its market with a surrogate price of 'like goods' in a market economy third country in order to determine the dumping margins. The justification for using surrogate prices typically relates to alleged state intervention and resultant distortions in the NME market. As the NME price is regarded as having been artificially lowered by the government, the surrogate price selected is generally higher than that price, thereby leading to higher dumping margins and AD duties. In this way, AD duties are used to counteract the injurious effect of state intervention in an NME exporting country on the relevant domestic industry of the importing country.

China has been treated as an NME in many jurisdictions and suffers hefty and often inflated AD duties.[82] The extent to which the WTO AD rules allow the use of surrogate prices has been vigorously debated and

---

[79] See WTO Trade Policy Review Body, 'Trade Policy Review – Report by the Secretariat', n. 78, at 76–7.
[80] See Wolfe, 'Sunshine over Shanghai', n. 76, 720.
[81] Ibid., 720, 724.
[82] For a comprehensive volume on the evolution of the NME anti-dumping methodology under the WTO rules and the laws and practices in various major jurisdictions using China as a case study, see James Nedumpara and Weihuan Zhou (eds.), *Non-Market*

remains contentious.[83] Instead of fully engaging in that debate, our analysis here focuses on the major constraints on the use of AD to tackle NME-related issues under the WTO AD rules.

Like the other WTO rules, GATT Article VI and the AD Agreement are not designed to deal specifically with NMEs. Arguably, the only AD rule that does so is the second Supplementary Provision to paragraph 1 of GATT Article VI which reads:

> It is recognized that, in the case of imports from a country which has a complete or substantially complete monopoly of its trade and where all domestic prices are fixed by the State, special difficulties may exist in determining price comparability for the purposes of paragraph 1, and in such cases importing contracting parties may find it necessary to take into account the possibility that a strict comparison with domestic prices in such a country may not always be appropriate.[84]

In *EC – Fasteners*, the AB confirmed that this *Ad* Note 'allows investigating authorities to disregard domestic prices and costs of ... an NME in the determination of normal value and to resort to prices and costs in a market economy third country'.[85] However, the AB also ruled that surrogate prices and costs may be invoked only when both of the prescribed conditions are found to exist in an economy, that is, 'the

---

Economies in the Global Trading System: The Special Case of China (Singapore: Springer, 2018).

[83] See e.g. Weihuan Zhou, 'Appellate Body Report on EU – Biodiesel: The Future of China's State Capitalism under the WTO Anti-Dumping Agreement' (2018) 17(4) *World Trade Review* 609; Jochem de Kok, 'The Future of EU Trade Defence Investigations against Imports from China' (2016) 19(2) *Journal of International Economic Law* 515; Ilaria Espa and Philip Levy, 'The Analogue Method Comes Unfastened – The Awkward Space between Market and Non-Market Economies in EC-Fasteners (Article 21.5)' (2018) 17(2) *World Trade Review* 313; Sherzod Shadikhodjaev, 'Input Cost Adjustments and WTO Anti-Dumping Law: A Closer Look at the EU Practice' (2018) 18(1) *World Trade Review* 81.

[84] This rule was added to the GATT during the Review Session of 1954–5 to deal with certain NMEs. Article 2.7 of the AD Agreement provides that Article 2 of the agreement is 'without prejudice to' this Ad Note. The wording 'without prejudice to' suggests that the interpretation of the other provisions of Article 2 must not 'detrimentally affect, encroach upon, or impair' the right of WTO Members under the Ad Note. See Appellate Body Report, *China – Measures Affecting Trading Rights and Distribution Services for Certain Publications and Audiovisual Entertainment Products*, WT/DS363/AB/R, adopted 19 January 2010, para. 219.

[85] Appellate Body Report, *European Communities – Definitive Anti-Dumping Measures on Certain Iron or Steel Fasteners from China*, WT/DS397/AB/R, adopted 28 July 2011, para. 285 (*EC – Fasteners*). For a legal and economic analysis of this case, see Chad Bown and Petros Mavroidis, 'One (Firm) Is Not Enough: A Legal-Economic Analysis of EC – Fasteners', (2013) 12(2) *World Trade Review* 243.

complete or substantially complete monopoly of trade and the fixing of all prices by the State'.[86] Thus, the *Ad* Note applies to an extreme type of NME only and does not apply to other types where state intervention exists to a lesser degree. Given the level of liberalisation and competition in the Chinese market, any claim that China remains such an extreme type of NME must be rejected.[87] Commentators have repeatedly and correctly pointed out that the current Chinese economy is at least comparable to many other WTO Members, such that the application of the *Ad* Note to China can hardly be justified.[88]

The concern that the *Ad* Note may no longer apply to China led to the inclusion of a China-specific rule in Section 15 of China's Accession Protocol.[89] In essence, Section 15 allows WTO Members to treat China as an NME in AD investigations and to use benchmark prices (as opposed to Chinese prices) to determine normal values. Paragraph (d) of Section 15 stipulates that a certain part of this section shall remain in force for fifteen years until 11 December 2016. China believed that the expiration of the relevant part has removed the basis for other countries to treat it as an NME in AD actions, whereas others (particularly the US and the EU) maintained a different position.[90] China brought a dispute against the EU on this issue on 12 December 2016 but requested a suspension of the panel proceedings on 14 June 2019 before the panel report was to be released.[91] Since China did not ask the panel to resume

---

[86] Appellate Body Report, *EC – Fasteners*, n. 85, FN 460.

[87] See e.g. David Palmeter, 'The WTO Antidumping Agreement and the Economies in Transition', in Thomas Cottier and Petros Mavroidis (eds.), *State Trading in the Twenty-First Century* (Ann Arbor: The University of Michigan Press, 1998) 115, 117.

[88] See e.g. William Watson, 'Will Nonmarket Economy Methodology Go Quietly into the Night?', Cato Institute Policy Analysis No. 763, 28 October 2014, 1, 8; Matthew R. Nicely, 'Time to Eliminate Outdated Non-Market Economy Methodologies' (2014) 9(4) *Global Trade and Customs Journal* 160–1; Lisa Toohey and Jonathan Crowe, 'The Illusory Reference of the Transitional State and Non-Market Economy Status' (2014) 2(2) *Chinese Journal of Comparative Law* 314, 333–4 (arguing that the distinction between market economy and NME is fundamentally flawed given 'the diversity of regulatory regimes and market mechanisms around the world').

[89] Protocol on the Accession of the People's Republic of China, WT/L/432, 23 November 2001 (AP).

[90] Scholars and policymakers have also debated about this issue intensively. See generally Weihuan Zhou and Delei Peng, 'EU – Price Comparison Methodologies (DS516): Challenging the Non-Market Economy Methodology in Light of the Negotiating History of Article 15 of China's WTO Accession Protocol', (2018) 52(3) *Journal of World Trade* 505.

[91] For a summary of this dispute, see WTO, *European Union – Measures Related to Price Comparison Methodologies* (DS516) – Current Status, available at: www.wto.org/english/

its work within the one-year timeframe envisaged in Article 12.12 of WTO's Dispute Settlement Understanding,[92] this dispute was effectively terminated on 15 June 2020.[93] As a result, the issue of whether Section 15 continues to provide a basis for WTO Members to treat China as an NME remains unsettled. Nevertheless, some WTO Members have started to change laws or practices to gradually shift away from relying on Section 15 to the general rules under the AD Agreement.[94]

The remaining and increasingly more important question, therefore, is 'to what extent the AD Agreement allows the use of surrogate prices and costs in dealing with exports from NMEs?' Article 2.2 of the AD Agreement states:

> When there are no sales of the like product *in the ordinary course of trade in the domestic market of the exporting country or when, because of the particular market situation or the low volume of the sales in the domestic market of the exporting country, such sales do not permit a proper comparison*, the margin of dumping shall be determined by comparison with a comparable price of the like product when exported to an appropriate third country, provided that this price is representative, or with *the cost of production in the country of origin plus a reasonable amount for administrative, selling and general costs and for profits.* (emphasis added)

Thus, a normal value is generally established by reference to the price of the subject goods in the market of the exporting country. However, a surrogate price based on sales in a third country or a constructed normal value (CNV) may be employed where (1) there are 'no domestic sales of like products in the ordinary course of trade'; (2) a 'particular market situation' (PMS) exists in the domestic market; or (3) there is a 'low volume of sales in the country of exportation'. The third circumstance concerns the technical issue of whether there are sufficient sales in the

---

tratop_e/dispu_e/cases_e/ds516_e.htm; WTO, *European Union – Measures Related to Price Comparison Methodologies*, Communication from the Panel, WT/DS516/13, 17 June 2019. For a discussion of China's request for suspension, see Henry Gao and Weihuan Zhou, 'The End of the WTO and the Last Case', *East Asia Forum*, 10 July 2019, available at: www.eastasiaforum.org/2019/07/10/the-end-of-the-wto-and-the-last-case/.

[92] Understanding on Rules and Procedures Governing the Settlement of Disputes, Marrakesh Agreement Establishing the World Trade Organization, Annex 2, 1869 UNTS 401, 33 ILM 1226 (1994).

[93] WTO, *European Union – Measures Related to Price Comparison Methodologies*, Lapse of Authority for the Establishment of the Panel, WT/DS516/14, 15 June 2020.

[94] See e.g. Weihuan Zhou and Andrew Percival, 'Debunking the Myth of "Particular Market Situation" in WTO Antidumping Law', (2016) 19(4) *Journal of International Economic Law* 863.

domestic market for the determination of normal values and is not concerned about state interventions in an NME. The first two circumstances may be relevant to the consideration of NME-related issues in AD actions.

With respect to the 'ordinary course of trade' (OCT) test, the AB, in *US – Hot-Rolled Steel*, observed that the test affords IAs 'discretion to determine how to ensure that normal value is not distorted through the inclusion of sales that are not "in the ordinary course of trade"'.[95] The AB clarified that transactions concluded on terms and conditions that are incompatible with 'normal' commercial practice 'for sales of the like product' would not satisfy the test.[96] The AB contemplated a number of circumstances where sales may be treated as not being made in the OCT, such as internal transfers within a single economic entity and sales between affiliated entities.[97] It emphasised that, in conducting the OCT test, price is merely one of the relevant factors and must be 'assessed in light of the other terms and conditions of the transaction', such as sales volume, transport and insurance.[98] The AB held that both lower-priced sales and higher-priced sales not in the OCT must be excluded from the determination of normal values to avoid distortions.[99] While the AB's rulings did not exhaust the circumstances in which sales are not made in the OCT, they suggested strongly that the test concerns the terms and conditions of transactions between *enterprises* and does not concern market distortions caused by state intervention. In other words, the test focuses on distortions arising from commercial activities rather than those caused by governmental or regulatory activities. For example, the OCT test would apply to the sale of goods by a Chinese SOE to a related entity at a price lower than their market value or on terms and conditions more favourable than the sale of the goods to unrelated entities. However, whether the sale of the SOE has benefited from subsidies for the production of the goods or has been influenced by other government policies may not be relevant to the OCT test. As long as the sale is concluded on normal terms and conditions, the existence of state interventions in the market would not prevent the sale from satisfying the

---

[95] Appellate Body Report, *United States – Anti-Dumping Measures on Certain Hot-Rolled Steel Products from Japan*, WT/DS184/AB/R, adopted 23 August 2001, para. 148.
[96] Ibid., para. 140.
[97] Ibid., paras. 141, 143.
[98] Ibid., para. 142.
[99] Ibid., paras. 145, 148.

OCT test. In this sense, the OCT test would be of limited use in dealing with market distortions caused by government interventions, although the scope of the test is to be further elucidated by the WTO adjudicators.

Compared with the OCT test, the PMS test tends to provide more flexibility to capture state-caused market distortions in AD actions. As of this writing, the meaning and scope of the term PMS has been considered only by one WTO panel in a recent dispute brought by Indonesia against Australia's AD measures on A4 Copy Paper (*Australia – A4 Copy Paper*).[100] The panel rejected Indonesia's argument that government action is, in principle, excluded from the coverage of AD remedies and should be addressed under the SCM Agreement.[101] Instead, it ruled that 'a situation arising from government action in whole or in part' may constitute a PMS.[102] The panel, however, found that Australia failed to consider whether the PMS concerned had precluded a 'proper comparison' between domestic and export prices pursuant to Article 2.2 of the AD Agreement. For the panel, a finding that the PMS existed and distorted the cost of pulp in the Indonesian market did not necessarily mean that distortion made any comparison between domestic paper price and export price misleading.[103] Therefore, although this decision created room for the term PMS to capture state-led market distortions, it imposed a significant constraint on the use of this approach for the application of a CNV. The panel's interpretation of the 'proper comparison' test suggests a test of even-handedness. That is, if the situation concerned has lowered the domestic and export prices to the same degree, then the comparability of the domestic price would not be affected, which therefore must be used for the determination of dumping margins. However, if the situation has had a larger or exclusive impact on the domestic price, then a 'proper comparison' between the two prices would be precluded, and the use of a CNV would be justified. This

---

[100] Australia has been the most frequent user of the PMS method in anti-dumping actions. See Weihuan Zhou, 'Australia's Anti-Dumping and Countervailing Law and Practice: An Analysis of Current Issues Incompatible with Free Trade with China' (2015) 49(6) *Journal of World Trade* 975.

[101] Panel Report, *Australia – Anti-Dumping Measures on A4 Copy Paper*, WT/DS/529/R, adopted 27 January 2020, para. 7.53 (*Australia – A4 Copy Paper*). For a detailed discussion of the panel report, see Weihuan Zhou and Delei Peng, 'Australia – Anti-Dumping Measures on A4 Copy Paper' (2021) 115(1) *American Journal of International Law* 94.

[102] Panel Report, *Australia – A4 Copy Paper*, n. 101, para. 7.55.

[103] Ibid., paras. 7.86–7.89.

even-handedness approach should be welcomed. It would be unnecessary to resort to CNVs if a market situation causes the same level of distortions in domestic and export prices such that the two prices remain comparable. The panel did not clarify how the even-handedness test should be applied. Nevertheless, the fact that a PMS in an upstream market typically affects the cost of production for domestic and export sales in the same way would make it difficult for IAs to substantiate that the comparability of the domestic sales is affected.

A finding that a PMS has precluded a 'proper comparison' between domestic and export prices merely justifies the *adoption* of a CNV. However, it is the *calculation* of the CNV that determines the magnitude of dumping margins. The level of a CNV typically hinges on the cost of production used for the calculation. In this regard, Article 2.2.1.1 of the AD Agreement provides:

> ... costs shall *normally* be calculated on the basis of records kept by the exporter or producer under investigation, provided that such records are *in accordance with the generally accepted accounting principles of the exporting country and reasonably reflect the costs associated with the production and sale of the product under consideration.* (emphasis added)

Thus, there are two conditions for the determination of whether costs recorded by producers and exporters should be used for the calculation of a CNV. The first condition merely requires that costs be recorded in accordance with generally accepted accounting principles and hence provides no flexibility for consideration of whether recorded costs are distorted by state intervention. The second condition, according to the AB in *EU – Biodiesel*, requires that the cost records suitably and sufficiently reflect the actual costs incurred and does not allow for consideration of the reasonableness of the costs themselves.[104] Therefore, the 'reasonably reflecting test' also provides no flexibility for considering whether state intervention distorts recorded costs. In *Australia – A4 Copy Paper*, however, the panel distinguished the *EU – Biodiesel* decision, finding that Australia's application of surrogate production costs was not based on the reasonably reflecting test, but was rather based on an

---

[104] Appellate Body Report, *European Union – Anti-Dumping Measures on Biodiesel from Argentina*, WT/DS473/AB/R, adopted 26 October 2016 (*EU – Biodiesel*). For a detailed analysis of the Appellate Body Report, see Meredith Crowley and Jennifer Hillman, 'Slamming the Door on Trade Policy Discretion? The WTO Appellate Body's Ruling on Market Distortions and Production Costs in EU – Biodiesel (Argentina)' (2018) 17(2) *World Trade Review* 195; Zhou, 'Appellate Body Report on EU – Biodiesel', n. 83.

assessment of the *reasonableness* of the recorded costs, that is, whether the costs were '*competitive* market costs associated with the production'[105] (emphasis added). In other words, as the reasonably reflecting test does not provide room for consideration of the reasonableness of recorded costs, the panel believed that Australia was not applying that test so that the *EU – Biodiesel* decision does not apply.[106] Instead, the panel held that the term 'normally' may provide some flexibility for IAs to consider the reasonableness of costs and to replace distorted production costs with a competitive benchmark. It ruled that there may be circumstances in which benchmark costs may be employed even though the two conditions of Article 2.2.1.1 are fulfilled.[107] The panel's interpretation of 'normally' created the flexibility for the use of surrogate costs in the presence of government-induced price distortions. While the panel did not clarify exactly what circumstances may fall within the scope of 'normally',[108] it does not impose any substantive limitation either. In this sense, the panel has extended the scope of the AD Agreement in a way that the AB sought to restrain in *EU – Biodiesel*.

Where a surrogate cost is applied, adjustments of the cost must be made for the purpose of the construction of normal values. In *EU – Biodiesel*, while the AB agreed that out-of-country cost information may be considered when in-country cost information cannot be obtained, it ruled that such information must be adjusted to reflect the cost of production in the country of origin as required under Article 2.2.[109] The AB found that the EU authorities had failed to make such adjustments in that dispute because they '... specifically selected the surrogate price for soybeans to remove the perceived distortion in the cost of soybeans in Argentina. As the Panel stated, the EU authorities selected and used this particular information precisely because it did not represent the cost of soybeans in Argentina.'[110] By requiring adjustments to be made to the surrogate cost to ensure it reflects the alleged market situations in Argentina, the AB's ruling imposed an additional restraint on the use of AD to deal with state intervention in NMEs.[111] Here too, the *Australia – A4 Copy Paper* panel deviated from the AB's approach. It

---

[105] Panel Report, *Australia – A4 Copy Paper*, n. 101, para. 7.102.
[106] Ibid., paras. 7.103–7.107.
[107] Ibid., paras. 7.110–7.115.
[108] Ibid., para. 7.117.
[109] Appellate Body Report, *EU – Biodiesel*, n. 104, para. 6.73.
[110] Ibid., para. 6.81.
[111] See Zhou, 'Appellate Body Report on EU – Biodiesel', n. 83, 620–4.

held that Article 2.2 'requires the investigating authority to consider available alternatives for replacing recorded costs *so as to use the costs that are unaffected by the distortion to the extent possible*'[112] (emphasis added). This suggests that the required adjustments to benchmarks are limited to the components of producers' costs unaffected by government-caused distortions,[113] whereas the *EU – Biodiesel* decision has arguably required such adjustments to include all conditions in the relevant market including distortions caused by state intervention.

In short, WTO AD jurisprudence has evolved in a way that gradually removes flexibility in the use of AD to address state intervention and market distortions in NMEs. To the extent that the panel decision in *Australia – A4 Copy Paper* reintroduces such flexibility, it can hardly be reconciled with the AB's approach in *EU – Biodiesel*. Given the paralysis of the AB, it would be interesting to see whether future panels will adopt the more restrictive approach in *EU – Biodiesel* or the more flexible approach adopted in *Australia – A4 Copy Paper*.

4.3 Conclusion

This chapter has offered a detailed analysis of the major GATT/WTO rules that may be applied to constrain the market-distortive behaviour of SOEs with an aim to revealing the limitations of these rules. Specifically, the rules that prohibit the discriminatory conduct of STEs, the erosion of tariff concessions through import monopolies, and import and export restrictions through STEs have a limited coverage of policy instruments and substantive obligations. The major challenge for WTO's transparency mechanisms lies in enforcement, and the efficacy of the transparency rules requires an effective mechanism to induce implementation. While having been widely used to address market distortions caused by state intervention, the development of the WTO's AD law has gradually removed the flexibility for governments to use AD for that purpose. Overall, the WTO does not impose a comprehensive code of conduct on the anti-competitive behaviour of *enterprises* including SOEs.[114]

---

[112] Panel Report, *Australia – A4 Copy Paper*, n. 101, para. 7.162.
[113] Ibid., para. 7.164.
[114] Aaditya Mattoo, 'Dealing with Monopolies and State Enterprises: WTO Rules for Goods and Services', WTO Staff Working Paper TISD9801, 17 January 1997, 1.

Instead, it merely prohibits Member *governments* from using certain policy instruments to undermine the expected conditions of competition. The remaining question is whether China's WTO-plus obligations have provided additional tools to tackle China's state capitalism. We explore this issue in Chapter 5.

5

The Potential of WTO Rules on Industrial Subsidies and China-Specific Obligations

5.1 Introduction

Recognising the limitations of general WTO rules (as discussed in Chapter 4), WTO Members negotiated China-specific rules to address various challenges that were perceived as being unique to China. This chapter offers a critical analysis of China's WTO-plus obligations on subsidies, pricing, and the commercial behaviour of SOEs as well as the major rules on industrial subsidies set out in the Agreement on Subsidies and Countervailing Measures[1] (SCM Agreement). We argue that these rules have provided sufficient tools to challenge Chinese industrial subsidies and the conduct of SOEs that cause market distortions. Therefore, at the same time that WTO Members are contemplating the need for new rules, they should make more active use of these existing rules.

5.2 China's WTO-Plus Obligations on State-Owned Enterprises

China's accession instruments – that is, the Protocol on the Accession of China[2] (Accession Protocol or AP) and the Report of the Working Party on the Accession of China[3] (Working Party Report or WPR) – set out some broad commitments that can be applied to address China's state capitalism. These rules, however, have been strikingly under-utilised to date.

---

[1] Agreement on Subsidies and Countervailing Measures, Marrakesh Agreement Establishing the World Trade Organization, Marrakesh, 15 April 1994, in force 1 January 1995, 1869 UNTS 14, Annex 1A.
[2] Protocol on the Accession of the People's Republic of China, WT/L/432, 23 November 2001 (Accession Protocol or AP).
[3] Report of the Working Party on the Accession of China, WT/ACC/CHN/49, 1 October 2001 (Working Party Report or WPR).

The first is Section 6.1 of the AP, which reads:

> China shall ensure that import purchasing procedures of state trading enterprises are fully transparent, and in compliance with the WTO Agreement, and shall refrain from taking any measure to influence or direct state trading enterprises as to the quantity, value, or country of origin of goods purchased or sold, except in accordance with the WTO Agreement.

This commitment is elaborated and expanded in paragraph 46 of the WPR, which states:

> *The representative of China further confirmed that China would ensure that all state-owned and state-invested enterprises would make purchases and sales based solely on commercial considerations, e.g. price, quality, marketability and availability*, and that the enterprises of other WTO Members would have an adequate opportunity to compete for sales to and purchases from these enterprises on non-discriminatory terms and conditions. In addition, the Government of China would not influence, directly or indirectly, commercial decisions on the part of state-owned or state-invested enterprises, including on the quantity, value or country of origin of any goods purchased or sold, except in a manner consistent with the WTO Agreement. (emphasis added)

Unlike GATT Article XVII:1,[4] paragraph 46 does not seem to be limited to a non-discrimination obligation but provides a more comprehensive restriction on the conduct of SOEs and state-invested enterprises (SIEs). Specifically, the emphasised section of the first sentence makes no reference to non-discrimination and requires that the 'purchases and sales' activities of these entities be based solely on commercial considerations. While paragraph 46 does not define the term 'commercial considerations' and merely provides several examples of the factors that may be considered, this rule can be further developed by case law. Here, the WTO tribunals in *Canada – Wheat* have offered some guidance for its application. The panel opined that central to the application of the 'commercial considerations' rule are the factors to be considered.[5] In this respect, the panel observed that the rule requires STEs to make purchase or sale decisions based on 'terms which are economically advantageous for themselves and/or their owners, members, beneficiaries, etc.' as opposed to 'such considerations as the nationality of potential

---

[4] For a detailed discussion of Article XVII:1, see Chapter 4.
[5] Panel Report, *Canada – Measures Relating to Exports of Wheat and Treatment of Imported Grain*, WT/DS276/R, adopted 27 September 2004, paras. 6.92–6.95.

buyers or sellers, the policies pursued by their governments, or the national (economic or political) interest'.[6] On appeal, the Appellate Body (AB) endorsed the panel's interpretation that the rule encompasses 'a range of different considerations that are defined in any given case by the type of "business" involved (purchases or sales), and by the economic considerations that motivate actors engaged in business in the relevant market(s)' such that whether a decision is 'commercial' requires a case-by-case analysis.[7] Thus, paragraph 46 can be interpreted as imposing a general requirement for commercial behaviour from the enterprises concerned in a wide range of activities as broad as those covered under GATT Article XVII:1 (which has been discussed in detail in Chapter 4). The second sentence of paragraph 46, which elaborates Article 6.1 of the AP, contains a similarly broad obligation, although the activities covered seem to be limited to purchases and sales relating to the quantity, value or country of origin of goods.

Moreover, an important distinction exists between the obligations set out in the first sentence and the second sentence of paragraph 46: the latter refers to the WTO Agreement while the former does not. The lack of reference to the WTO Agreement may well mean that the exceptions under the GATT cannot be invoked to justify deviations from the stated obligation. In *China – Publications and Audiovisual Products* and *China – Raw Materials*, the AB ruled that the use of GATT exceptions to justify a breach of China's commitments under its accession instruments must be based on certain textual support. In the former dispute, the textual support was found in the opening language of Section 5.1 of the AP, that is, '[w]ithout prejudice to China's right to regulate trade in a manner consistent with the WTO Agreement'.[8] In the latter, however, the AB found no such textual support and hence that China has no recourse to GATT Article XX to justify its violations of Section 11.3 of the AP.[9] Similar to Section 11.3, the first sentence of paragraph 46 does

---

[6] Ibid., paras. 6.87–6.88.
[7] Appellate Body Report, *Canada – Measures Relating to Exports of Wheat and Treatment of Imported Grain*, WT/DS276/AB/R, adopted 27 September 2004, paras. 140–4.
[8] Appellate Body Report, *China – Measures Affecting Trading Rights and Distribution Services for Certain Publications and Audiovisual Entertainment Products*, WT/DS363/AB/R, adopted 19 January 2010, paras. 216–33.
[9] Appellate Body Report, *China – Measures Related to the Exportation of Various Raw Materials*, WT/DS394/AB/R, WT/DS395/AB/R, WT/DS398/AB/R, adopted 22 February 2012, paras. 279–307. Section 11.3 states 'China shall eliminate all taxes and charges applied to exports unless specifically provided for in Annex 6 of this Protocol or applied in conformity with the provisions of Article VIII of the GATT 1994.'

not provide any textual support for China to use GATT exceptions to justify breaches of the 'commercial considerations' and non-discrimination rules.

Whether such an ambitious obligation was intended by China during the accession negotiations is questionable because it would overly restrict China's capacity to pursue regulatory or policy goals via SOEs. It is also potentially unfair that other WTO Members are not subject to such onerous obligations and enjoy 'a great deal of regulatory freedom [in] ... using STEs as instruments of economic policy'.[10] These concerns may necessitate that paragraph 46 be interpreted in a cautious and restrictive manner that pays due deference to China's regulatory freedom. However, based on its text, paragraph 46 seems to provide abundant flexibility for WTO Members to challenge the non-commercial activities of Chinese SOEs.

Another important commitment made by China is set out in Section 9.1 of the AP, which reads:

> China shall, subject to paragraph 2 below, allow prices for traded goods and services in every sector to be determined by market forces, and multi-tier pricing practices for such goods and services shall be eliminated.

This commitment reflects WTO Members' concerns about China's extensive use of price controls in various sectors at the time of the accession negotiations.[11] Like paragraph 46 of the WPR, this commitment expands far beyond an obligation of non-discrimination and applies to *all* governmental measures on *all* prices in *all* sectors other than a few exempted ones. The exemptions from this broad obligation are confined to a short list of goods and services that may be subject to government pricing or government guidance pricing as envisaged in Annex 4.[12] Notably, there is no exemption for many of the strategic

---

[10] Bernard Hoekman and Joel Trachtman, 'Canada-Wheat: Discrimination, Non-Commercial Considerations, and the Right to Regulate through State Trading Enterprises' (2008) 7(1) *World Trade Review* 45, 64.

[11] See WPR, n. 3, paras. 50–64.

[12] These exemptions include four categories of goods (i.e. tobacco, edible salt, natural gas, and certain pharmaceuticals) and four types of services (i.e. public utilities, and postal and telecommunication services, entrance fee for tour sites, and education services) subject to government price; and six categories of goods (i.e. grain, vegetable oil, processed oil, fertiliser, silkworm cocoons, cotton) and six types of services (i.e. transport services, professional services, commission agents' services, certain banking services, certain prices of residential apartments, and health-related services) subject to government guidance pricing.

5.2 CHINA'S WTO-PLUS OBLIGATIONS ON SOES

and priority sectors considered in China's policy documents (as shown in Chapter 2) and currently controversial sectors such as the steel and aluminium industries. Thus, it can be argued that China must let the market determine prices in all of the covered sectors, including goods and services, and must not affect prices directly or indirectly through any measures or interventions. China is not allowed to expand the list of exempted sectors '[e]xcept in exceptional circumstances and subject to notification to the WTO'.[13] This serves to strictly confine the application of this exception to an extraordinary circumstance that justifies the adoption of price controls.[14] In addition, since Section 9.1 makes no reference to the WTO Agreement, the GATT exceptions may not apply.

The obligations imposed under Section 9.1 and paragraph 46 are strongly interrelated. While the former prevents the Chinese government from intervening in the market, the latter requires the government to ensure that no such interventions are implemented through SOEs or SIEs. Given their broad scope, the two obligations may well operate together to provide sufficient restraints on state intervention (including via SOEs) and thereby address the associated market distortions.

That said, the broad wording of these provisions means that significant gap-filling exercises are required in their interpretation and application. For example, what factors should a WTO panel consider when determining whether Chinese prices are market prices? Similarly, the factors to be considered under the 'commercial considerations' rule also need to be further clarified and developed. Moreover, how could a complaining Member collect sufficient evidence on these issues since the determination of price and other business decisions of enterprises are often confidential? Paragraph 46 and Section 9.1 provide little guidance on these matters and, hence, their exact scope of application would be subject to the development of WTO jurisprudence. A narrow interpretation of key terms such as 'determined by market forces' and 'commercial considerations' would limit the capacity of these rules to address SOE-related issues. Comparably, the SCM Agreement currently offers a more workable mechanism for WTO Members to challenge Chinese industrial subsidies that are essential to its state capitalism, although the utility of paragraph 46 and Section 9.1 should also be further explored.

---

[13] See AP, n. 2, Section 9.2.
[14] See WPR, n. 3, para. 51.

5.3 WTO Subsidy Rules and China-Specific Obligations

Subsidies provided to or by SOEs are key to China's success in and continuous pursuit of a wide range of ambitious industrial policies and economic development goals.[15] There have been growing concerns about the effectiveness of WTO rules in dealing with Chinese subsidies. One of the latest criticisms comes from Bown and Hillman, who identified many shortcomings in the SCM Agreement to address Chinese subsidies, including the definition of subsidies, the difficulties of satisfying the relevant evidentiary burden and lack of notification and retrospective remedies.[16] These concerns are flawed in two major aspects. First, they do not distinguish between deficiencies specific to China and those generally applicable to all WTO Members. For example, it is hard to see why the lack of notification and retrospective remedies applies to China only. Second, they are not based on a detailed assessment of specific types of Chinese subsidies and the potential issues in applying the existing rules to these subsidies. Significantly, they pay little attention to China's WTO-plus obligations.

Through an analysis of the major legal elements under the SCM Agreement and China's relevant WTO-plus obligations in this section, we argue that these rules have provided sufficient flexibility to address Chinese subsidies provided to or through SOEs. Most of the potential challenges in the application of these rules are not China-specific, but applicable to all WTO Members. Therefore, linking these challenges exclusively to China's subsidies or characterising them as 'China-specific problems' is highly questionable and would not help resolve these problems in future negotiations.

5.3.1 Covered Types of Subsidies: Financial Contributions and Income/Price Support

The SCM Agreement does not cover all government actions or measures that may have the effect of distorting trade. Rather, it only applies to certain types of subsidies as defined in Article 1. For a measure to be a

---

[15] For discussions of China's SOE reform and industrial policies, see Chapter 2. Also see generally Weihuan Zhou and Meng Fang, 'Subsidizing Technology Competition: China's Evolving Practices and International Trade Regulation' (2021) 30(3) *Washington International Law Journal* 470.

[16] See Chad Bown and Jennifer Hillman, 'WTO'ing a Resolution to the China Subsidy Problem' (2019) 22(4) *Journal of International Economic Law* 557, 567–72.

covered subsidy, it must constitute a 'financial contribution' or 'any form of income or price support' that is provided by a government, a 'public body' or a 'private body entrusted or directed' to exercise relevant government functions, and confers a 'benefit' to the recipient concerned.

Article 1.1(a)(1) of the SCM Agreement encompasses three types of 'financial contributions': (i) direct transfer of funds; (ii) foregoing or non-collection of government revenue otherwise due (Revenue Foregone); and (iii) provision of goods or services (other than general infrastructure) or purchase of goods. Although the coverage of 'financial contributions' was intended to be exhaustive and arguably to avoid 'a purely effect-based concept of subsidies',[17] it has been interpreted and applied in a flexible and broad manner.[18]

'Direct transfer of funds' covers not only measures such as grants, loans and equity infusion but also 'potential direct transfers of funds or liabilities' such as loan guarantees. These measures and their variations have been found to constitute a 'financial contribution' in a series of cases. They include, *inter alia*, grant payments,[19] non-commercial loans,[20] debt-for-equity swaps and debt rescheduling by way of interest/debt reductions, deferrals and forgiveness,[21] equity infusion,[22]

---

[17] Appellate Body Report, *United States - Measures Affecting Trade in Large Civil Aircraft (Second Complaint)*, WT/DS353/AB/R, adopted 23 March 2012, para. 613 (holding that 'Subparagraphs (i)–(iv) exhaust the types of government conduct deemed to constitute a financial contribution') (*US - Aircraft (2nd complaint)*). See also Wolfgang Muller, *WTO Agreement on Subsidies and Countervailing Measures: A Commentary* (Cambridge: Cambridge University Press, 2017) 62, 7.; Petros C. Mavroidis, *The Regulation of International Trade: The WTO Agreements on Trade in Goods*, 3 vols (Massachusetts: MIT Press, 2016) vol. II, 202–3, 215–16.

[18] Appellate Body Report, *United States - Final Countervailing Duty Determination with Respect to Certain Softwood Lumber from Canada*, WT/DS257/AB/R, adopted 17 February 2004, para. 52 (*US - Softwood Lumber IV*).

[19] Panel Report, *Australia - Subsidies Provided to Producers and Exporters of Automotive Leather*, WT/DS126/R, adopted 16 June 1999, paras. 2.1–2.5, 9.43–9.45. (*Australia - Automotive Leather II*).

[20] Ibid.

[21] Panel Report, *Korea - Measures Affecting Trade in Commercial Vessels*, WT/DS273/R, adopted 11 Apr. 2005, paras. 7.336–7.339, 7.411–7.413 (*Korea - Commercial Vessels*). In the panel's view, while 'interest reductions and deferrals are similar to new loans' and 'interest/debt forgiveness is comparable to a cash grant', debt-for-equity swaps are 'a combination of equity infusion and debt forgiveness'. See also Appellate Body Report, *US - Aircraft (2nd complaint)*, n. 17, para. 615.

[22] See Appellate Body Report, *US - Aircraft (2nd complaint)*, n. 17, paras. 622–4 (involving joint venture arrangements whereby funds were provided (by NASA/USDOD) in exchange for some kind of return such as scientific and technical information (from

transfers of equity interests or shares,[23] and any other forms leading to 'an accrual of financial resources' and other financial claims that improve the financial position of the recipient.[24] The sub-category of *'potential direct transfers of funds or liabilities'* typically involves 'a legally binding promise' or 'an obligation to make a direct transfer of funds which, *in and of itself*, is claimed and capable of conferring a benefit on the recipient that is separate and independent from the benefit that might be conferred from any future transfer of funds' (original emphasis).[25]

Revenue Foregone involves a situation in which a government foregoes or does not collect 'revenue that is otherwise due', typically tax revenues. The current legal test entails a comparison between 'the tax treatment that applies to the alleged subsidy recipients and the tax treatment of comparable income of comparably situated taxpayers' in the jurisdiction concerned.[26] For example, in *US - Aircraft (2nd complaint)*, the AB upheld the panel's affirmative finding of Revenue Foregone on the ground that the Washington State Business and Occupation Tax regime applied a lower tax rate to commercial aircraft and component manufacturers compared to the rates applicable to general manufacturing, wholesaling and retailing activities in the state.[27] If a government does not collect the tax revenue in full at the time that it normally would under the comparable benchmark, that would also amount to Revenue Foregone, as the government effectively gives up the entitlement to 'enjoy the cash available to it and earn interest on it'.[28]

The third category of 'financial contributions' involves two types of in-kind contributions: (1) the provision of goods or services to and (2) the purchase of goods from an enterprise by governments. Goods or services may be provided through the grant of relevant rights leading to the use or

---

Boeing). NASA and USDOD, respectively, stand for United States National Aeronautics and Space Administration and United States Department of Defense).

[23] Panel Report, *European Communities and Certain Member States - Measures Affecting Trade in Large Civil Aircraft*, WT/DS316/R, adopted 1 June 2011, para. 7.1291 (*EC - Aircraft*).

[24] Appellate Body Report, *Japan - Countervailing Duties on Dynamic Random Access Memories from Korea*, WT/DS336/AB/R, adopted 17 December 2007, paras. 247, 250-2 (*Japan - DRAMs (Korea)*).

[25] See Panel Report, *EC - Aircraft*, n. 23, paras. 7.302, 7.304, 7.733, 7.1495.

[26] See Appellate Body Report, *US - Aircraft (2nd complaint)*, n. 17, paras. 812-13.

[27] Ibid., paras. 816-31.

[28] Appellate Body Report, *Brazil - Certain Measures Concerning Taxation and Charges*, WT/DS472/AB/R, WT/DS497/AB/R, adopted 11 January 2019, paras. 5.220-5.221. (*Brazil - Taxation*).

enjoyment of the goods or services. For example, in *US – Softwood Lumber IV*, the AB found that Canada's provincial stumpage arrangements amounted to a provision of goods by giving the eligible enterprises the right to cut standing timber and enjoy exclusive rights over the timber harvested.[29]

The provision of goods or services in the form of 'general infrastructure' is explicitly excluded. In *EC – Aircraft*, the panel observed that 'general infrastructure' refers to 'infrastructure that is not provided to or for the advantage of only a single entity or limited group of entities, but rather is available to all or nearly all entities'.[30] Therefore, even the provision of railroads or electrical distribution systems, for example, may fall within the ambit of subparagraph (iii) if they are made available only to a limited group of entities.[31] Such limitations on access to or use of the infrastructure may arise in law (e.g. where the infrastructure is created for the particular needs of certain entities) or in effect (e.g. where in the absence of an explicit limitation, only certain entities actually have access to the infrastructure).[32] The other sub-category – governments' purchase of goods – may involve a government acquiring things for its own use or for others to use (such as resale to end users of electricity).[33] Whether this category also includes purchases of 'services' remains unsettled.[34]

Contrary to widespread concerns about the potential difficulties of identifying Chinese subsidies due to a lack of transparency, most Chinese subsidies may fall squarely within the ambit of 'financial contributions'. China's high-tech sector, which is central to China's current industrial policies and economic development goals, offers a perfect illustration. The main types of China's high-tech subsidies have taken one of the typical forms of 'financial contributions'. These include, *inter alia*, the various government-initiated investment funds in support of selected

---

[29] Appellate Body Report, *US – Softwood Lumber IV*, n. 18, paras. 68–76.
[30] See Panel Report, *EC – Aircraft*, n. 23, para. 7.1036.
[31] Ibid., para. 7.1039.
[32] Ibid., para. 7.1043.
[33] Panel Report, *Canada – Certain Measures Affecting the Renewable Energy Generation Sector/Measures Relating to the Feed-in Tariff Program*, WT/DS412/R, WT/DS426/R, adopted 24 May 2013, paras. 7.225–7.227; Appellate Body Report, *Canada – Certain Measures Affecting the Renewable Energy Generation Sector/Measures Relating to the Feed-in Tariff Program*, WT/DS412/AB/R, WT/DS426/AB/R, adopted 24 May 2013, para. 5.124 (*Canada – Renewable Energy/Feed-in Tariff Program*).
[34] See Appellate Body Report, *US – Aircraft (2nd complaint)*, n. 17, para. 620.

sectors by way of equity injection, loans and loan guarantees,[35] tax exemptions and reductions for eligible enterprises in priority sectors,[36] the provision of production inputs (such as land and electricity) at preferential rates[37] and input materials (such as steel and aluminium) at less than adequate remuneration,[38] and preferential government

---

[35] Some major examples include the National Integrated Circuit Investment Fund (2014), the Advanced Manufacturing Industry Investment Fund (2016) and more recently the National Manufacturing Industry Transformation and Upgrading Fund (2019). All of these funds were created under the leadership of the competent central authorities, particularly the Ministry of Finance and Ministry of Industry and Information Technology, supported by state banks and followed by the creation of similar funds by local governments. See 'The Establishment of the National Integrated Circuit Investment Fund', Ministry of Industry and Information Technology, 14 October 2014, available at: www.miit.gov.cn/n1146290/n1146402/n7039597/c7053700/content.html; 'The Establishment of the Advanced Manufacturing Industry Investment Fund', State-Owned Assets Supervision and Administration Commission of the State Council, 12 June 2016, available at: www.sasac.gov.cn/n2588025/n2588124/c3822803/content.html; 'Ministry of Finance, China Railway Rolling Stock Corporation and Others Initiated the Establishment of the National Manufacturing Industry Transformation and Upgrading Fund Limited Liability Company with Registered Capital Worth RMB 147.2 Billion', YICAI, 18 November 2019, available at: www.yicai.com/news/100407324.html.

[36] These tax preferences are applied at both central and local levels. See 《中华人民共和国企业所得税法》 [Corporate Income Tax Law of People's Republic of China], adopted by the National People's Congress on 16 March 2007, effective on 1 January 2008; 《国务院关于经济特区和上海浦东新区新设立高新技术企业实行过渡性税收优惠的通知》 [Notice on the Application of Transitional Tax Incentives for Newly-Established High-New Technology Enterprises in Special Economic Zones and Shanghai Pudong New Zone], issued by the State Council on 26 February 2007, available at: www.gov.cn/gongbao/content/2008/content_871687.htm.

[37] See e.g. 《临沂高新技术产业开发区招商引资的有关规定》 [Several Regulations on the Business and Investment Invitation in Linyi High-tech Industrial Development Zone], available at: www.lytoday.com/kfly/yhzc/2013-12/17/content_1600.htm; 'Provincial Pricing Bureau Actively Uses Pricing Policies to Support High-Tech Industry Development in Hubei', Hubei Government, 20 May 2014, available at: www.hubei.gov.cn/xxbs/bmbs/swjj/201405/t20140520_1204265.shtml.

[38] See generally OECD, 'A First Look at the Steel Industry in the Context of Global Value Chains', DSTI/SC(2017)4, 16 March 2017, available at: https://one.oecd.org/document/DSTI/SC(2017)4/en/pdf; OECD, 'Measuring Distortions in International Markets: the Aluminum Value Chain', OECD Trade Policy Papers No. 218, 7 January 2019, available at: www.oecd-ilibrary.org/trade/measuring-distortions-in-international-markets-the-aluminium-value-chain_c82911ab-en (OECD Aluminum Report); Wayne M. Morrison and Rachel Tang, 'China's Rare Earth Industry and Export Regime: Economic and Trade Implications for the United States', Congressional Research Service, 30 April 2012, 1–4, available at: https://fas.org/sgp/crs/row/R42510.pdf.

procurement in favour of domestic goods and services.[39] While the other legal elements must also be examined to determine whether these subsidies are actionable or countervailable, it is not difficult to treat them as 'financial contributions'.

That said, certain forms of financial support are excluded from the coverage of the SCM Agreement. One such measure is contemplated under Footnote 1 of the SCM Agreement which excludes 'duty and tax exemptions or remissions for *exported* products' from being treated as Revenue Foregone. As a result, value-added tax (VAT) rebates are generally permitted (as long as the level of rebates does not go beyond the corresponding VAT rates) and have been widely used by WTO Members.[40] This exception does not apply to *import* duty exemptions.[41] However, a duty drawback scheme, that is, an import duty remission for inputs imported for the production of goods destined for export, falls within the exception provided that the remission does not exceed the import duty actually levied.[42]

VAT rebates and duty drawbacks have been a major component of China's export promotion policies.[43] For instance, China recently made some adjustments to its VAT rebate scheme by increasing the rebate

---

[39] See e.g. 《关于印发政府机关及公共机构购买新能源汽车实施方案的通知》 [Notice on Issuing the Implementation Plan of Government Agencies and Public Institutions' Purchases of New Energy Vehicles], issued by the Government Offices Administration of the State Council, the Ministry of Finance, the Ministry of Science and Technology, the Ministry of Industry and Information Technology and the National Development and Reform Commission on 14 July 2014, available at: www.caam.org.cn/chn/9/cate_99/con_5124489.html; 《关于促进国家高新技术产业开发区高质量发展的若干意见》 [Several Opinions on Enhancing the High Quality Development of National High-Tech Industrial Zones], issued by the State Council on 17 July 2020, available at: www.gov.cn/zhengce/content/2020-07/17/content_5527765.htm.

[40] See generally Youssef Benzarti and Alisa Tazhitdinova, 'Do Value-Added Taxes Affect International Trade Flows? Evidence from 30 Years of Tax Reforms', NBER Working Paper No. 26195, August 2019, available at: www.nber.org/system/files/working_papers/w26195/w26195.pdf.

[41] See Appellate Body Report, *Canada – Certain Measures Affecting the Automotive Industry*, WT/DS139/AB/R, WT/DS142/AB/R, adopted 19 June 2000, paras. 91–2. (*Canada – Autos*).

[42] Panel Report, *European Union – Countervailing Measures on Certain Polyethylene Terephthalate from Pakistan*, WT/DS486/R, adopted 25 May 2018, paras. 7.29–7.30; Appellate Body Report, *European Union – Countervailing Measures on Certain Polyethylene Terephthalate from Pakistan*, WT/DS486/AB/R, adopted 25 May 2018, paras. 5.68, 5.97–5.134. (*EU – PET (Pakistan)*).

[43] See generally Chi-Chur Chao, Eden S. H. Yu and Wusheng Yu, 'China's Import Duty Drawback and VAT Rebate Policies: A General Equilibrium Analysis' (2006) 17(4) *China Economic Review* 432.

rates for eligible exports in general[44] and allowing high-tech firms to use excess input VAT credits.[45] Since the rebate rates are not in excess of the current VAT rate (i.e. 13 per cent), the Chinese VAT scheme remains immune from the subsidy rules, just like similar policies applied by other WTO Members. Nonetheless, it should be noted that such policies are subject to the WTO non-discrimination rules (e.g. GATT Articles I and III). In *China – Value-Added Tax on Integrated Circuits*, for example, China had to cease its discriminatory application of VAT rebates for domestic enterprises in the software and IC industry, allegedly affecting around $2 billion worth of US exports to China.[46] Thus, while the SCM Agreement largely leaves out VAT rebate policies from its coverage, there are other rules that may be applied to restrain the use of such policies. In this regard, the WTO dispute settlement mechanism has proved effective in restraining China's use of trade-distortive subsidies[47] and therefore should continue to be used for that purpose. To the extent that VAT rebates may distort trade and hurt trading partners, it is for WTO Members to decide whether more discipline would be desirable via negotiations. The current lack of discipline on VAT rebates under the SCM Agreement was agreed to by WTO Members and does not cause a deficiency problem specific to China.

Moreover, the issue of whether government purchases of services may be treated as 'financial contributions' remains unresolved. Again, this issue does not create a problem that is specific to China, and any further development of the WTO rulebook or case law will apply to all WTO Members. In this respect, it should be noted that China is actively negotiating to join the WTO Agreement on Government Procurement

---

[44] Ministry of Finance and State Taxation Administration,《关于提高部分产品出口退税率的公告》[Notice on Increasing Tax Rebate Rates for Certain Exports], issued on 17 March 2020, available at: www.chinatax.gov.cn/chinatax/n810341/n810755/c5146338/content.html.

[45] Ministry of Finance and State Taxation Administration,《关于2018年退还部分行业增值税留抵税额有关税收政策的通知》[Notice on Refunds to Excess VAT Credits in Certain Industries in 2018], issued on 27 June 2018, available at: www.chinatax.gov.cn/n810341/n810755/c3556358/content.html. The Notice provided that the ten strategic sectors identified in the MIC 2025 should be prioritised for the refund of excess VAT credits.

[46] For an official summary of this dispute, see WTO, China – Value-Added Tax on Integrated Circuits, WT/DS309, available at: www.wto.org/english/tratop_e/dispu_e/cases_e/ds309_e.htm.

[47] For a comprehensive and detailed discussion of China's implementation of adverse WTO rulings, see Weihuan Zhou, *China's Implementation of the Rulings of the World Trade Organization* (Oxford: Hart Publishing, 2019).

which sets forth rules (e.g. non-discrimination) on government procurement activities that are not available under the existing WTO agreements.[48] Recently, China has proposed to enhance its market access commitments by broadening the scope of covered procurement such as procuring entities and goods and services sectors including some of the strategic sectors.[49] These rules and commitments would provide additional, more specific discipline on China's government procurement activities, thereby reducing the need to resort to the SCM Agreement.

In addition, China's broad obligations under Section 6.1 of the AP and paragraph 46 of the WPR, as discussed in Section 5.2, provide a more comprehensive restriction on the anti-competitive conduct of SOEs and SIEs including government purchases and sales of goods and services. Thus, the SCM Agreement is not, nor is it intended to be, the sole source of discipline on government procurement and sales activities that may cause market distortions and adversely affect other WTO Members.

Finally, the extent to which the SCM Agreement, particularly the residual category on 'any form of income or price support' contemplated under Article 1.1(a)(2), covers indirect subsidies remains debatable. In *China – GOES*, the panel rejected an effect-based approach to the determination of 'price support'. For the panel, 'price support' is concerned with '*direct government intervention in the market with the design to fix the price of a good at a particular level*, for example, through purchase of surplus production when price is set above equilibrium' (emphasis added) as opposed to 'a random change in price merely being a side-effect of any form of government measure'.[50] To date, this ruling remains the only detailed consideration of the meaning of 'income or price support'. Nevertheless, the effect-based approach to the determination of subsidies has been consistently rejected in other disputes. For example, in *US – Export Restraints*, the panel refused to treat export restraints as a

---

[48] The Agreement on Government Procurement is a plurilateral agreement that applies to signatories only. For an official introduction of the agreement, see 'WTO and Government Procurement', WTO, available at: www.wto.org/english/tratop_e/gproc_e/gproc_e.htm. For a discussion of the application of the relevant WTO rules on government procurement in China's high-tech sector, see Daniel C. K. Chow, 'China's Indigenous Innovation Policies and the World Trade Organization' (2013) 34(1) *Northwestern Journal of International Law and Business* 81, 98–104.

[49] WTO, 'China Submits Revised Offer for Joining Government Procurement Pact', 23 October 2019, available at: www.wto.org/english/news_e/news19_e/gpro_23oct19_e.htm.

[50] Panel Report, *China – Countervailing and Anti-Dumping Duties on Grain Oriented Flat-rolled Electrical Steel from the United States*, WT/DS414/R, adopted 16 November 2012, para. 7.86.

'financial contribution' (despite their potential trade-distorting effect).[51] The current jurisprudence, therefore, suggests that measures that may cause price distortions *indirectly* may not be captured by this residual category. One such measure that has been hotly debated in recent years concerns China's export restraints, mainly in the form of export quotas and taxes, on raw materials and rare earths.[52] While these measures are apparently adopted to protect the security of exhaustible natural resources and the environment,[53] they may cause domestic input prices to fall, thereby conferring a cost advantage on downstream entities (such as semiconductors, electric cars).[54] Despite the potential price effects, export restraints do not amount to a government's direct control of price in light of the panel decision in *US – Export Restraints*.[55]

Again, the SCM Agreement is not the sole source of discipline that may be employed to tackle trade-distortive export measures and resultant price distortions. Under the general WTO rules, all export restrictions other than duties, taxes or other charges are prohibited under GATT Article XI:1. Anti-dumping (AD) duties have been routinely applied to address price distortions derived from the raw materials market affecting the price of final goods.[56]

In addition, China has undertaken two relevant WTO-plus obligations. Under Section 11.3 of the AP, China is required to 'eliminate all taxes and charges applied to exports' except for a list of eighty-four tariff items subject to a bound export duty from 20 per cent to 50 per cent. Many raw materials, such as bauxite, coke, fluorspar, magnesium, silicon

---

[51] See Panel Report, *United States – Measures Treating Exports Restraints as Subsidies*, WT/DS194/R, adopted 23 August 2001, paras. 8.62–8.75 (*US – Export Restraints*).

[52] See Bown and Hillman, 'WTO'ing A Resolution', n. 16, 568–9, 574.

[53] 《中国的稀土状况与政策》[Situations and Policies of China's Rare Earth Industry], Information Office of the State Council, 20 June 2012, available at: www.gov.cn/zhengce/2012-06/20/content_2618561.htm.

[54] See Marco Bronckers and Keith Maskus, 'China – Raw Materials: A Controversial Step Towards Evenhanded Exploitation of Natural Resources' (2014) 13(2) *World Trade Review* 393, 402–4.

[55] But see John H. Jackson, *World Trade and the Law of the GATT* (Indianapolis: Bobbs-Merrill Co., Inc, 1969), 383–4 (arguing that the negotiating history of GATT Article XVI:1 has suggested that the definition of subsidy may be broadly interpreted to cover indirect subsidies that increase the export of any products).

[56] For an illustration, see Appellate Body Report, *European Union – Anti-Dumping Measures on Biodiesel from Argentina*, WT/DS473/AB/R, adopted 26 October 2016. For a detailed discussion of this report, see Weihuan Zhou, 'Appellate Body Report on EU–Biodiesel: The Future of China's State Capitalism under the WTO Anti-Dumping Agreement' (2018) 17(4) *World Trade Review* 603.

metal, zinc and a wide spectrum of rare earths, are not included in the list and, hence, must not be subject to export taxes. This WTO-plus obligation has been applied to successfully challenge China's export taxes on raw materials and rare earths in two consecutive disputes.[57] This obligation has significantly limited China's policy space in using export taxes for legitimate regulatory goals while other WTO Members are free to and do apply such taxes for similar goals.[58] Even more broadly and as discussed in Section 5.2, China undertakes to 'allow prices for traded goods and services in every sector to be determined by market forces' under Section 9.1 of the AP. This obligation has the potential to extend beyond 'price or income control' to capture Chinese government intervention in all sectors (other than the few exemptions) where it affects prices directly or indirectly.

5.3.2 Public Body

Anti-subsidy measures may be applied only when the subsidy is provided by a government, a public body or an entrusted private body under Article 1.1 of the SCM Agreement. In his influential article exploring China's unique economic structure and the efficacy of the existing WTO rules in tackling China's state capitalism, Mark Wu treated the determination of 'which Chinese enterprises, banks, and entities' are 'public bodies' as a primary challenge to the application of the SCM Agreement.[59] For Wu and many others, this challenge became particularly acute after the *US – Anti-Dumping and Countervailing Duties (China)* dispute[60] in which the AB ruled that a public body 'must be an

---

[57] See Panel Report, *China – Measures Related to the Exportation of Various Raw Materials*, WT/DS394/R, WT/DS395/R, WT/DS398/R, adopted 22 February 2012; Appellate Body Report, *China – Measures Related to the Exportation of Various Raw Materials*, WT/DS394/AB/R, WT/DS395/AB/R, WT/DS398/AB/R, adopted 22 February 2012; Panel Report, *China – Measures Related to the Exportation of Rare Earths, Tungsten and Molybdenum*, WT/DS431/R, WT/DS432/R, WT/DS433/R, adopted 29 August 2014; Appellate Body Report, *China – Measures Related to the Exportation of Rare Earths, Tungsten and Molybdenum*, WT/DS431/AB/R, WT/DS432/AB/R, WT/DS433/AB/R, adopted 29 August 2014.

[58] Jeonghoi Kim, 'Recent Trends in Export Restrictions on Raw Materials' in OECD, *The Economic Impact of Export Restrictions on Raw Materials* (Paris: OECD Publishing, 2010) 15–20.

[59] See Mark Wu, 'The "China, Inc." Challenge to Global Trade Governance' (2016) 57(2) *Harvard International Law Journal* 261, 301–5.

[60] Ibid. See also e.g. Ru Ding, '"Public Body" or Not: Chinese State-Owned Enterprise' (2014) 48(1) *Journal of World Trade* 167; Michel Cartland, Gerard Depayre and Jan

entity that possesses, exercises or is vested with governmental authority' and 'the mere fact that a government is the majority shareholder of an entity does not demonstrate that the government exercises meaningful control over the conduct of that entity'.[61] This ruling downplays the value of state ownership or interest in an entity as a criterion in a 'public body' determination and emphasises the question of whether the entity has the authority to function as an extension of the government. Critics of the AB's ruling were concerned that the 'authority-based' approach erected a substantial barrier to the determination of 'public bodies', thereby creating loopholes for subsidies granted through SOEs to circumvent the WTO disciplines.[62]

However, we believe that the 'authority-based' approach leaves sufficient room for investigating authorities (IAs) to find a Chinese SOE or SIE to be a 'public body', especially under China's current SOE reform. In *US – Anti-Dumping and Countervailing Duties (China)*, the AB observed that 'the absence of an express statutory delegation of authority [does not] necessarily preclude a determination that a particular entity is a public body'.[63] The AB directed IAs, in applying the 'authority-based' approach, to evaluate 'core features of the entity' and 'its relationship with government'.[64] The AB elaborated as follows:

> In some instances, ... where the evidence shows that the formal indicia of government control are manifold, and there is also evidence that such control has been exercised in a meaningful way, then such evidence may permit an inference that the entity concerned is exercising governmental authority.[65]

Woznowski, 'Is Something Going Wrong in the WTO Dispute Settlement?' (2012) 46(5) *Journal of World Trade* 979, 1001–14.

[61] Appellate Body Report, *United States – Definitive Anti-Dumping and Countervailing Duties on Certain Products from China*, WT/DS379/AB/R, adopted 25 March 2011, paras. 317–18 (*US – Anti-Dumping and Countervailing Duties (China)*).

[62] See Cartland et al., 'Is Something Going Wrong', n. 60, 1008, 1010–12; Wu, 'The "Chine, Inc."', n. 59, 303–5. In our view, the AB's approach is reasonable as it attempts to avoid the over-reaching of 'public body' to cover all SOEs or SIEs. If one accepts that SOEs or SIEs may operate as private entities, then the 'ownership-based' approach is too broad to distinguish SOEs or SIEs acting on behalf of governments from those operating solely in their own interest.

[63] See Appellate Body Report, *US – Anti-Dumping and Countervailing Duties (China)*, n. 61, para. 318.

[64] Ibid., paras. 317, 345.

[65] Ibid., para. 318.

In applying its rulings, the AB accepted the US's finding of China's state-owned commercial banks as 'public bodies' mainly based on evidence relating to (1) state ownership, (2) laws that mandate implementation or consideration of government policies and (3) the influence of the government or the Party on the management and decision-making.[66]

Most recently, the AB revisited the 'function/authority-based' approach in detail in *US – Countervailing Measures (China) (Article 21.5)*. This dispute arose out of the United States' continued application of the 'ownership-based' approach in finding that Chinese SOEs and SIEs providing inputs for the production of certain goods (i.e. certain pipes, steel and aluminium products, wind power and solar panels) were 'public bodies' in a range of countervailing investigations.[67] The United States was found to be in breach of Article 1.1(a)(1) in the original proceedings. In the compliance proceedings, China's core contention was that the US authorities failed to apply the correct legal test. Specifically, China submitted that the 'authority-based' test 'require[s] a particular degree or nature of connection in all cases between an identified government function and the particular financial contribution at issue', and hence cannot be satisfied by 'an abstract review of China's system of governance and state functions'.[68] The AB rejected China's claim and clarified that the focus of the test is on the *entity* concerned and its relationship with government as opposed to the *conduct* alleged to give rise to a 'financial contribution'.[69] Therefore, it is unnecessary to show that the entity is 'meaningfully controlled' by the government in the *specific* conduct.[70] Once an entity is found to be a 'public body', all its conduct 'is *directly* attributable to' the government of the Member concerned (original emphasis).[71]

In our view, the WTO tribunals' application of the 'authority-based' approach has been reasonably balanced by requiring some evidence beyond ownership without imposing excessively high evidentiary

---

[66] Ibid., para. 350.
[67] Panel Report, *United States – Countervailing Duty Measures on Certain Products from China*, WT/DS437/R, adopted 16 January 2015, para. 7.1.
[68] See Appellate Body Report, *United States – Countervailing Duty Measures on Certain Products from China – Resources to Article 21.5 of the DSU by China*, WT/DS437/AB/RW, adopted 15 August 2019, paras. 5.65, 5.77–5.78 (*US – Countervailing Measures (Article 21.5 – China)*).
[69] Ibid., paras. 5.100–5.101.
[70] Ibid., para. 5.103.
[71] Ibid., para. 5.103.

standards. The AB's latest ruling that the 'public body' determination does not require one to show that specific conduct of the entity concerned is 'meaningfully controlled' by the Chinese government has further reduced the evidentiary burden on IAs. In practice, China's industrial policies, directives and other regulatory instruments as well as information on the involvement of the state/Party in corporate management and governance, as the major evidence required under the 'authority-based' test, have been widely documented and are readily accessible nowadays. IAs in major jurisdictions have already collected abundant evidence and have often resorted to such evidence collected by each other in countervailing investigations. The totality of the evidence here would be sufficient to establish a *prime facie* case which would be difficult for the Chinese government to rebut. Thus, in both of the discussed disputes in which the 'authority-based' approach was developed and applied, the tribunals did not disagree with the US authorities on the findings that the evidence on the record was sufficient to show China's state banks and SOEs/SIEs providing inputs to manufacture were meaningfully controlled by the Chinese government to exercise governmental functions.

In addition, China's ongoing SOE reform has added substantial evidence necessary for an affirmative finding of 'public bodies' based on the 'authority-based' test. As discussed in Chapter 2, the SOE classifications constitute an explicit designation of authority for Public Welfare SOEs to undertake government functions in the provision of public goods and services and for Special Commercial SOEs to play a significant role in strategic industries. The government's *meaningful* influence on these entities may be readily inferred according to the limitations on private equity, the mandates on activities, the criteria for performance evaluation, the involvement of the state/Party in management and decision-making, etc. While General Commercial SOEs are intended to operate as private entities, in specific cases they may also undertake government functions, particularly when investing in strategic sectors as State Capital Investment and Operation Companies.

In short, while one may continue to debate the legitimacy and efficacy of the 'authority-based' test, the case law seems to have evolved in a direction that makes 'public bodies' easier to prove than to defend.

5.3.3 *Benefits Conferred*

A government action that constitutes a 'financial contribution' (or 'price or income support') would not be regarded as a 'subsidy' unless it confers a benefit to the recipient under Article 1.1(b) of the SCM Agreement. In developing the legal test of 'benefit conferred', WTO tribunals have relied on Article 14 as an immediate context. In essence, Article 14 states that the calculation of benefit shall be based on the extent to which a financial contribution is made 'on terms more favourable than those available to the recipient in the market'.[72] Therefore, for example, if the financial contribution is in the form of a government loan, then it would constitute a subsidy only if it has been granted on terms more favourable than those of a comparable commercial loan in the market at the time the loan is provided.[73]

One of the most controversial issues in the benefit analysis concerns the application of external benchmarks, especially when a market is dominated or heavily influenced by governments.[74] This analysis involves two major steps: (1) determining an appropriate benchmark and if an external benchmark is employed[75] and (2) making adjustments to that benchmark to ensure it reflects the prevailing conditions in the market of the subsidising country. These two steps may pose challenges for the establishment of 'benefit conferred'.

The first step requires evidence to show that the primary benchmark, such as prices of final goods or inputs or commercial loan rates in the market of the subsidising country, is distorted and hence needs to be replaced with an external benchmark. The AB has taken a cautious approach in determining whether an external benchmark may be applied. It ruled that government predominance in the market does not necessarily mean all prices are distorted; hence, whether that predominance has induced private suppliers to align their prices to the government

---

[72] Appellate Body Report, *Canada – Measures Affecting the Export of Civilian Aircraft*, WT/DS70/AB/R, adopted 20 August 1999, paras. 155, 158 (*Canada – Aircraft*).

[73] See Appellate Body Report, *European Communities and Certain Member States – Measures Affecting Trade in Large Civil Aircraft*, WT/DS316/AB/R, adopted 1 June 2011, paras. 834–5 (*EC – Aircraft*).

[74] See generally Wentong Zheng, 'The Pitfalls of the (Perfect) Market Benchmark: The Case of Countervailing Duty Law' (2010) 19 *Minnesota Journal of International Law* 350; Julia Qin, 'Market Benchmarks and Government Monopoly: The Case of Land and Natural Resources under Global Subsidies Regulation' (2019) 40(3) *University of Pennsylvania Journal of International Law* 575. For a more general critique of the benchmark analysis, see Andrew Lang, 'Governing "As If": Global Subsidies Regulation and the Benchmark Problem' (2014) 67(1) *Current Legal Problems* 135.

[75] Note that a constructed benchmark may involve the use of out-of-country cost information if the in-country production cost is found to be distorted due to government intervention in the relevant upstream market.

price must be assessed on a case-by-case basis.[76] The AB emphasised that it is price distortion that would allow the use of alternative benchmarks, not the role of the government *per se*.[77] It also clarified that the evidence required to prove such distortion may vary depending on the degree of government intervention and such intervention 'does not refer exclusively to market shares, but may also refer to market power'.[78]

These rulings suggest that in sectors in which private actors are more significant than state actors, more compelling evidence on market distortion would be needed. In China's high-tech sector, such as semiconductors, new energy vehicles (NEVs), 5G, big data, etc., for example, private firms have been increasing both market shares and market power through myriads of investments.[79] This market situation, compared with the situation in the industries dominated by state actors (such as steel, energy and resources), would entail a higher burden in substantiating that the provision of goods or services or equity infusion by the private entities, for example, is based on distorted terms and conditions due to government influence so that recourse to alternative benchmarks is warranted. The potential difficulties in proving in-country price distortion may only increase if one considers the AB's general position that the circumstances that would permit the replacement of in-country private prices are 'very limited' under the SCM Agreement.[80] Consequently, there were cases in which the use of an external benchmark was difficult to justify even when a government held a monopolistic position in the relevant market.[81]

---

[76] See Appellate Body Report, *US – Softwood Lumber IV*, n. 18, paras. 90, 100–2.

[77] See Appellate Body Report, *US – Anti-Dumping and Countervailing Duties (China)*, n. 61, para. 446.

[78] Ibid., paras. 443–4.

[79] A recent report of the China Semiconductor Industry Association on 'The Ten Most Competitive Chinese Companies in the Semi-Conductor Industry in 2019' shows that private companies have made up a significant portion in the sector, including design of integrated circuit, semi-conductor manufacturing, semi-conductor testing and packaging, semi-conductor materials, etc. The list is available at: 'The Ten Most Competitive Chinese Companies in the Semi-Conductor Industry in 2019', China Semiconductor Industry Association, 26 August 2020, available at: www.csia.net.cn/Article/ShowInfo.asp?InfoID=95565. In the NEV sector, private companies such as BYD and Geely are becoming the leaders in the market. See 'China's Top 10 Selling New Energy Cars', *China Daily*, 12 October 2018, available at: www.chinadaily.com.cn/a/201810/12/WS5bbfd4c5a310eff303281e78_4.html.

[80] See e.g. Appellate Body Report, *US – Countervailing Measures (Article 21.5 – China)*, n. 68, para. 5.137.

[81] See Qin, 'Market Benchmarks and Government Monopoly', n. 74, 587–606.

The second step requires adjustments to be made to a selected external benchmark to reflect the prevailing market conditions in the subsidising country. This requirement is explicitly set out in Article 14(d), which contemplates certain factors for adjustments including price, quality, availability, marketability, transportation and other conditions of purchase or sale of goods or services in the country of provision or purchase. Such adjustments are also required under the other sub-paragraphs of Article 14. For example, in *US – Anti-dumping and Countervailing Duties (China)*, the AB held that for the purpose of Article 14(b) a benchmark may be employed if 'loans in a given market and in a given currency are distorted by government intervention'; however, such a benchmark must be adjusted to approximate 'a comparable commercial loan which the firm could actually obtain on the market', taking into account factors 'such as date of origination, size, maturity, currency, structure, or borrower's credit risk'.[82]

The difficulties in making these adjustments concern how to ensure they reflect the prevailing conditions of a market so distorted by government intervention as to render the terms and conditions of private transactions in that market unreliable. In other words, if the use of an out-of-country benchmark is intended to remove the in-country market distortions, then making an adjustment to reflect the in-country market conditions may reintroduce such distortions into the benchmark, at least to some extent. In this regard, the AB has explained that 'prevailing market conditions' refer to the terms and conditions determined by market forces, which may include commercial activities of both private and government-related entities.[83] This ruling confirms that the adjustments would need to distinguish between market-based terms and conditions and those distorted by government intervention or even to establish a counterfactual market in the absence of such distortions. This would be a formidable task for which the case law has not provided sufficient guidance. To make it even more complicated, the AB opined, in *US – Softwood Lumber IV*, that the adjustments must reflect and maintain the comparative advantage of the subsidising Member so that countervailing measures are not imposed to 'offset differences in comparative

---

[82] See Appellate Body Report, *US – Anti-Dumping and Countervailing Duties (China)*, n. 61, paras. 484–6.
[83] Appellate Body Report, *United States – Countervailing Measures on Certain Hot-Rolled Carbon Steel Flat Products from India*, WT/DS436/AB/R, adopted 19 December 2014, paras. 4.150–4.151. (*US – Carbon Steel (India)*).

advantages between countries'.[84] While this is an enlightening remark, it tends to make the legal requirements on the adjustments of benchmarks even more obscure and difficult to apply, and may drag WTO Members into endless debate about what constitutes a comparative advantage, to what extent such an advantage may be created by governments, etc.[85]

These challenges associated with the application of the benefit/benchmark test are, again, not specific to China but have arisen in disputes between other WTO Members. As far as China is concerned, these challenges may be addressed through China's WTO-plus commitment under Section 15(b) of the AP. That provision states:

> In proceedings under Parts II, III and V of the SCM Agreement, when addressing subsidies described in Articles 14(a), 14(b), 14(c) and 14(d), relevant provisions of the SCM Agreement shall apply; however, *if there are special difficulties in that application, the importing WTO Member may then use methodologies for identifying and measuring the subsidy benefit which take into account the possibility that prevailing terms and conditions in China may not always be available as appropriate benchmarks. In applying such methodologies, where practicable, the importing WTO Member should adjust such prevailing terms and conditions before considering the use of terms and conditions prevailing outside China.*
> (emphasis added)

This provision was introduced to address the lack of relevant rules on non-market economies under the SCM Agreement for the situation where no marketplace benchmarks are available or readily accessible in China.[86] Unlike the special AD rule under Section 15(a), this special rule on subsidies is not subject to an expiration date. This suggests that anti-subsidy actions were intended to be the preferred solution to address system-wide distortions in China.

Although Section 15(b) has never been applied before, it arguably has the potential to considerably soften the legal requirements for the benchmark analysis, precisely in the two major steps discussed in this section. In the first step, there is almost no obstacle to the invocation of the right to use external benchmarks, as the only condition seems to be that 'special difficulties' exist when using Chinese prices. The scope of 'special difficulties' is not defined or circumscribed in any way, thus providing

---

[84] See Appellate Body Report, *US – Softwood Lumber IV*, n. 18, para. 109.
[85] See Qin, 'Market Benchmarks and Government Monopoly', n. 74, 613–15.
[86] See Julia Ya Qin, 'WTO Regulation of Subsidies to State-Owned Enterprises (SOEs) – A Critical Appraisal of the China Accession Protocol' (2004) 7(4) *Journal of International Economic Law* 863, 870–1, 903.

considerable latitude for IAs to decide that such difficulties exist. These may involve either systemic difficulties resulting from distortions created by government interventions in the whole market or practical difficulties in obtaining or verifying the information on subsidies. For example, such difficulties may exist in cases where IAs find it hard to collect evidence on whether an SOE has received a benefit from subsidies or on the magnitude of such a benefit. Thus, anti-subsidy measures may be justified in cases of insufficient disclosure or lack of notification by China. This could solve a major problem in countervailing investigations, which have been plagued by the failure of the governments of the exporting countries to provide information or reliable information. In any event, the evidentiary requirements under the test of 'special difficulties' would be much less onerous than those under Article 14 of the SCM Agreement.

In the second step, the obligation to make adjustments to a selected benchmark is reduced to a non-obligatory best-endeavours requirement which merely encourages authorities to do so 'where practicable'. Like in the first step, no matter how the term 'practicable' is interpreted, it would be less onerous to leave room for investigators to exercise discretion. If a 'special difficulty' exists due to state intervention in a particular market, the same difficulty may be used to show that adjustments are not 'practicable' as it is practically difficult to identify undistorted terms and conditions. Even in cases where China adduces sufficient evidence to show that such adjustments are practically doable, one would have to decide whether the best-endeavours language should otherwise be mandatory. Overall, it is submitted that Section 15(b) has significantly relaxed the high standards developed by WTO tribunals in determining 'benefits conferred', making it much easier for WTO Members to tackle Chinese subsidies through countervailing actions.

5.3.4 Specificity

A subsidy that is not 'prohibited'[87] is not actionable or countervailable unless it is 'specific' within the meaning of Article 2. This specificity requirement is intended to exclude subsidies that are 'broadly available and widely used throughout an economy' from the SCM Agreement.[88] In

---

[87] Export subsidies and local content subsidies are deemed 'specific' under Article 2.3 of the SCM Agreement.
[88] Panel Report, *United States – Subsidies on Upland Cotton*, WT/DS267/R, adopted 21 March 2005, para. 7.1143. (*US – Upland Cotton*).

essence, it is concerned about whether a subsidy is made available only to 'certain enterprises' or 'geographical regions' in law or, in fact, with a focus on 'limitations on eligibility'.[89] Thus, a subsidy is *de jure* specific if the access to or eligibility for it is *explicitly* limited to certain enterprises (Article 2.1(a)). In contrast, if the eligibility is automatic based on objective criteria or conditions, then the subsidy is ostensibly non-specific (Article 2.1(b)). However, an ostensibly non-specific subsidy may be found to be, in fact, specific in a particular case.[90] *De jure* specificity would usually rely on a written instrument, whereas unwritten subsidies would typically trigger an inquiry into *de facto* specificity.[91] To establish *de facto* specificity, one would need to demonstrate 'a systematic series of actions pursuant to which financial contributions that confer a benefit have been provided to certain enterprises'.[92] All evidence/factors relating to 'specificity' and 'non-specificity' must be considered.[93]

Under the chapeau of Article 2.1, the term 'certain enterprises' encompasses 'an enterprise or industry or group of enterprises or industries'. While an enterprise refers to a firm or business, an industry generally 'relates to producers of certain products'.[94] A subsidy is specific if eligible beneficiaries are limited to 'certain enterprises', regardless of whether similar subsidies are also granted to certain other enterprises.[95] Therefore, it would not be difficult to establish that many Chinese subsidies are *de jure* specific. The relevant national policy documents, such as the Five-Year plans and Made in China 2025, and their implementing regulatory instruments at both national and local levels, explicitly set out the priority sectors and projects and the development goals, and direct the provision of a variety of financial contributions to these sectors. As shown in Chapter 2, for instance, these policies have led to the creation and continuous expansion of the government investment funds to which only enterprises in the selected sectors (e.g. semiconductors,

---

[89] See Appellate Body Report, *US – Anti-Dumping and Countervailing Duties (China)*, n. 61, para. 368.
[90] Ibid., para. 367.
[91] Appellate Body Report, *United States – Countervailing Duty Measures on Certain Products from China*, WT/DS437/AB/R, adopted 16 January 2015, para. 4.129 (*US – Countervailing Measures (China)*).
[92] Ibid., para. 4.141.
[93] See Appellate Body Report, *US – Anti-Dumping and Countervailing Duties (China)*, n. 61, paras. 370–1.
[94] Ibid., para. 373.
[95] See Appellate Body Report, *EC – Aircraft*, n. 73, para. 949.

NEVs) are eligible. Likewise, the preferential tax treatment for eligible enterprises in selected high-tech industries is also specific.

Regional specificity concerns the eligibility for a subsidy being limited to 'certain enterprises' in a designated geographical region. This type of specificity merely requires that a subsidy is limited to a designated region without the need to establish further that it is also limited to a subset of enterprises within the region.[96] Thus, a national subsidy provided to a region is specific even though it is made available to all enterprises in the region. In contrast, a subsidy granted by a local government to enterprises throughout its jurisdiction, that is, not limited to a specific segment of the local jurisdiction, would not be regionally specific.[97] Thus, to the extent that Chinese subsidies are provided by a local government to enterprises in the selected sectors in its entire jurisdiction, such subsidies would be enterprise/industry-specific, not regionally specific.

Complexities may arise where the designated area is a segment of a local jurisdiction. In *US – Anti-dumping and Countervailing Duties (China)*, the panel considered the provision of land-use rights to certain enterprises in an Industrial Park within the jurisdiction of a local government in China (i.e. the Huantai County). It ruled that a designated geographical region may encompass 'any identified tract of land within the jurisdiction of a granting authority' and hence the Industrial Park.[98] However, the panel observed that the subsidy is not specific just because the land was physically located in the designated area. Further evidence was required to show that the land-use rights in the area constituted a 'distinct regime' for the provision of that financial contribution compared with the general provision of land-use rights by the local government in its jurisdiction. In this regard, the panel suggested that the subsidy may not be regionally specific if 'all purchasers of land-use rights throughout the jurisdiction of the granting authority paid exactly the same below-market price for land'.[99] Applying this case law to China's

---

[96] See e.g. Panel Report, 'EC – Aircraft', n. 23, para. 7.1223; Panel Report, *United States – Definitive Anti-Dumping and Countervailing Duties on Certain Products from China*, WT/DS379/R, adopted 25 March 2011, para. 9.135 (*US – Anti-Dumping and Countervailing Duties (China)*).
[97] See Appellate Body Report, *US – Countervailing Measures (China)*, n. 91, para. 4.165.
[98] See Panel Report, *US – Anti-Dumping and Countervailing Duties (China)*, n. 96, paras. 9.140–9.144, 9.156.
[99] Ibid., paras. 9.158–9.160.

high-tech subsidies, for example, we note that industrial parks, high-tech zones and the like are widespread in local jurisdictions in China.[100] However, the facts that they constitute designated areas, and that subsidies are provided to these areas, are insufficient to prove regional specificity. A further step must be taken to show that a subsidy programme provided to such a segment of a jurisdiction is distinct. In practical terms, this programme would be distinct if it is only available to the designated area or offers preferential terms and conditions compared to those provided to enterprises outside the area. This further step would not be a hurdle to establishing that China's high-tech subsidies are regionally specific. For example, the provision of land-use rights and energy inputs to designated areas such as high-tech zones by local governments has been generally based on preferential rates compared to the standard rates applicable in the relevant jurisdictions.[101] This has to do with the fact that these areas are created to fulfil the policy objectives and mandates envisaged by the central government and more specifically to promote the growth of priority sectors within the jurisdictions according to local strengths and advantages. Thus, these subsidies constitute a distinct regime and are regionally specific.

Where there is no written instrument, difficulties may arise in establishing *de facto* specificity. The case law requires the demonstration of 'a systematic series of actions' pointing to 'the existence of an unwritten "subsidy programme"'.[102] In *US - Countervailing Measures (China)*, the AB rejected the panel's ruling that the consistent provision of the relevant input by SOEs was sufficient to show the existence of 'a systematic series of actions'.[103] In the compliance proceedings, the AB, in upholding the findings of the compliance panel, elaborated that *de facto* specificity cannot be established merely based on 'repeated transactions' but requires an assessment of how such transactions constitute 'a systematic subsidy programme'.[104] In its findings of *de facto* specificity, the US authority merely requested information on the industry providing the

---

[100] The catalogue of the High-tech Zones listed in the Ministry of Science and Technology website can be found at: www.most.gov.cn/gxjscykfq/.
[101] See Zhou and Fang, 'Subsidizing Technology Competition', n. 15, 502–3.
[102] See Appellate Body Report, *US - Countervailing Measures (China)*, n. 91, para. 4.141; Appellate Body Report, *US - Countervailing Measures (Article 21.5 - China)*, n. 68, para. 5.233.
[103] See Appellate Body Report, *US - Countervailing Measures (China)*, n. 91, paras. 4.148–4.151.
[104] See Appellate Body Report, *US - Countervailing Measures (Article 21.5 - China)*, n. 68, paras. 5.231–5.233.

relevant input and the number of recipients in the past few years, without explaining how such information substantiated the existence of an unwritten subsidy programme.[105] Only during the compliance proceedings did the United States adduce additional evidence relating to various Chinese policy mandates leading to the provision of the relevant input for nearly 50 years. Both the compliance panel and the AB regarded the additional evidence as 'an *ex post* rationale' and refused to accept it. In any event, the AB stressed that the existence of such policy mandates, in itself, would not suffice and 'a reasoned and adequate explanation' must be provided to show the existence of 'a systematic subsidy programme'.[106]

Thus, compared with *de jure* specificity, demonstrating *de facto* specificity requires a higher evidentiary standard and level of analysis. This would make it more difficult for IAs to tackle hidden or unwritten subsidies through countervailing measures. Although this difficulty applies to all WTO Members, China's longstanding practice of using SOEs to supply input at low costs to certain sectors[107] have generated considerable concerns. However, one may argue that at the end of *US – Countervailing Measures (China)*, the AB was no longer concerned about the sufficiency of evidence after the US provided the additional information in the compliance proceedings. Such information was not accepted by the WTO tribunals simply because it did not form the basis of US findings of *de facto* specificity in its countervailing investigations. In contrast, the remaining concern of the AB seems to be the lack of 'a reasoned and adequate *explanation*' that links the various policy documents to the existence of an unwritten subsidy programme. Admittedly, more guidance would be needed to fully understand the degree of explanation required. However, it would not be unreasonably difficult to offer such an explanation given the existence of the wide range of policy documents that explicitly direct all governments to support selected

---

[105] Ibid., para. 5.237.
[106] Ibid., paras. 5.219, 5.240.
[107] For instance, Chinese SOEs have provided a stable supply of alumina, a key input to electronics products, at below-market or even below-cost prices to local companies: see OECD Aluminum Report, n. 38, 93. Chinese steel SOEs have also received government subsidies over the years, which have enabled them to supply low-priced steel products to downstream industries, such as high-end equipment manufacturing: see Yibo Zhao, 'Profits-Losing BaoSteel Received RMB 1.7 Billion Government Subsidies and Analysis Points Out the Lack of Chance in Stop Losing on Its Own', Sina Finance, 30 December 2015, available at: http://finance.sina.com.cn/chanjing/gsnews/2015-12-30/doc-ifxmxxst0778361.shtml.

sectors through all means, the dominant role of SOEs in the critical upstream industries (such as steel, aluminium, energy, raw materials and rare earths) and the fact that these SOEs have long benefited from government subsidies and other preferential regulatory treatment to be financially capable of supplying lower-priced input for production.[108] In reality, authorities may well utilise the ambiguities and flexibilities left by the *US – Countervailing Measures (China)* decision to treat the provision of production input by Chinese SOEs for less than adequate remuneration as being specific. Such practice has been widely adopted in numerous countervailing investigations against China.

In addition, one may argue that the source of the distortions lies in the subsidies and preferential treatment provided to SOEs, enabling them to supply production input for less than adequate remuneration. Therefore, one way to deal with the subsidies to downstream industries would be to address the source of the problem, that is, to push China to reduce or remove the subsidies to SOEs. In this regard, Section 10.2 of the AP allows WTO Members to deem Chinese subsidies to SOEs as being 'specific' if the SOEs 'are the predominant recipients of such subsidies or ... receive disproportionately large amounts of such subsidies'. This commitment expands the list of specific subsidies beyond the categories enumerated under Article 2 of the SCM Agreement and adds 'ownership' as the key criterion for determining specificity. Given the dominant role of SOEs in certain upstream industries in China and the large amount of subsidies they receive, this WTO-plus commitment would mean that any subsidies provided to SOEs in these sectors would be 'specific'.[109]

More broadly, as discussed in Section 5.2, paragraph 46 of the WPR requires Chinese SOEs and SIEs to make purchases and sales solely based on commercial considerations. It may be argued that the longstanding and consistent practice of Chinese SOEs and SIEs selling input to selected downstream industries for less than adequate remuneration has precluded them from making reasonable returns that would generally be expected in commercial transactions. This obligation, therefore, provides an extra tool to address the problem concerned without the need to resort to the SCM Agreement, thereby avoiding the potential difficulties in establishing *de facto* specificity.

---

[108] See e.g. OECD Aluminum Report, n. 38; Morrison and Tang, 'China's Rare Earth Industry', n. 38, 13–14; Qin, 'WTO Regulation of Subsidies', n. 86, 875–82.

[109] For further discussion of this commitment, see Qin, 'WTO Regulation of Subsidies', n. 86, 890–1.

5.3.5 Concluding Remarks

In summary, while the SCM Agreement does not cover all kinds of government actions, it is broad enough to capture the major subsidies provided under China's ambitious industrial policies, including those granted via SOEs. Where difficulties may arise in establishing some of the major legal conditions contemplated under the SCM Agreement, these difficulties generally apply to all WTO Members. China's WTO-plus obligations have provided additional tools to address most such difficulties and hence to facilitate a finding of actionable or countervailable subsidies. More broadly, these obligations can be applied to tackle market-distortive behaviour and conduct of SOEs and price distortions caused by the Chinese government. Government measures, such as export restraints, VAT rebates, regulatory preferences or incentives, that seem to fall outside the reach of the SCM Agreement can and should be tackled through the application of other WTO rules. Where new and better rules are needed, they can only be created by WTO Members through negotiations.

5.4 Conclusion

Through a critical analysis of the SCM Agreement and the relevant China-specific obligations, this chapter has challenged the mainstream view that the existing WTO rules are inadequate to deal with Chinese SOEs and industrial subsidies. We have argued that the rules on industrial subsidies, coupled with China's WTO-plus obligations, provide sufficient defence against the encroachment of Chinese SOEs beyond its own shores. Since these extra rules have been strikingly under-utilised to date, the claim that the current rules are inadequate is unpersuasive and misleading. Thus, the real problem is not the lack of rules to tackle China's state capitalism, but the lack of utilisation of existing rules. If WTO Members, especially the major players, can start bringing well-coordinated countervailing investigations domestically and 'big, bold' cases[110] challenging China's subsidies and SOEs at the WTO, they will not only help to level the playing field for firms from other countries, but also help China to steer its SOE reform back on the right course.

---

[110] Testimony of Jennifer Hillman, United States–China Economic and Security Review Commission Hearing on U.S. Tools to Address Chinese Market Distortions, 8 June 2018, available at: www.uscc.gov/sites/default/files/Hillman%20Testimony%20US%20China%20Comm%20w%20Appendix%20A.pdf.

Compared to litigation, major WTO Members, particularly the United States and the EU, seem to be more keen to strengthen the existing rules on SOEs via WTO reform or negotiations at sub-multilateral levels. The question then is what approach should be taken in such reform or negotiations. Chapter 6 will review the development of the international regulation of SOEs in the Comprehensive and Progressive Agreement for Trans-Pacific Partnership (CPTPP) and the major post-CPTPP free trade agreements of the United States and the EU and discuss whether they provide a suitable model for future negotiations of SOE rules.

6

Emerging Approaches to Regulating State-Owned Enterprises

The Comprehensive and Progressive Agreement for Trans-Pacific Partnership (CPTPP) and Post-CPTPP Free Trade Agreements

6.1 Introduction

This chapter explores the development of international regulation of state-owned enterprises (SOEs) in major free trade agreements (FTAs). We briefly review the development of SOE rules in select FTAs of the United States and the EU, the two leaders in promoting global rules on SOEs. We then focus on analysing the SOE chapter (i.e. chapter 17) of the Comprehensive and Progressive Agreement for Trans-Pacific Partnership (CPTPP),[1] which is widely regarded as a landmark achievement in the development of SOE rules, notwithstanding some outstanding issues.[2] This is followed by a review of major post-CPTPP FTAs of

---

[1] Comprehensive and Progressive Agreement for Trans-Pacific Partnership, effective on 30 December 2018 (CPTPP). For the full legal text of the CPTPP, see Australian Government, Department of Foreign Affairs and Trade, 'CPTPP Text and Associated Documents', available at: www.dfat.gov.au/trade/agreements/in-force/cptpp/official-documents/Pages/official-documents.

[2] See generally, e.g. Gary Clyde Hufbauer and Cathleen Cimino-Isaacs, 'How Will TPP and TTIP Change the WTO System?' (2015) 18(3) *Journal of International Economic Law* 679; Julien Sylvestre Fleury and Jean-Michel Marcoux, 'The US Shaping of State-Owned Enterprise Disciplines in the Trans-Pacific Partnership' (2016) 19(2) *Journal of International Economic Law* 445; Sean Miner, 'Commitments on State-Owned Enterprises', in Jeffrey Schott and Cathleen Cimino-Isaacs (eds.) *Assessing the Trans-Pacific Partnership: Innovations in Trading Rules*, 2 vols. (Washington, DC: Peterson Institute for International Economics, 2016), vol. II, 91–100; Ines Willemyns, 'Disciplines on State-Owned Enterprises in International Economic Law: Are We Moving in the Right Direction?' (2016) 19(3) *Journal of International Economic Law* 657; Minwoo Kim, 'Regulating the Visible Hands: Development of Rules on State-Owned Enterprises in Trade Agreements' (2017) 58(1) *Harvard International Law*

the United States and the EU to show the extent to which they have further advanced the CPTPP SOE rules. We argue that, compared to existing WTO rules, particularly the China-specific ones, neither the CPTPP SOE chapter nor its further development in subsequent FTAs have provided more rigid or workable rules to tackle Chinese SOEs. Rather, these emerging approaches to strengthening the regulation of SOEs have maintained a narrower coverage of SOEs and extensive exceptions, among other deficiencies. This argument is advanced and illustrated in the context of China's current SOE reform.

6.2 An Overview of SOE Rules in Free Trade Agreements

As the major promoters and norm-setters of global rules on SOEs, the United States and the EU have shared goals and approaches which have been reiterated in a series of their joint statements since 2018. To tackle 'non market-oriented policies and practices ... that create unfair competitive conditions ... and undermine the proper functioning of international trade', they call for more rigorous rules on SOEs and industrial subsidies (amongst other objectives and proposals).[3] More recently, in a joint announcement on 24 March 2021, the United States and the EU decided to further cooperation in dealing with 'the full range of [China-]related challenges and opportunities'.[4] A fundamental challenge, as

---

Journal 225; Jaemin Lee, 'Trade Agreements' New Frontier – Regulation of State-Owned Enterprises and Outstanding Systemic Challenges' (2019) 14(1) *Asian Journal of WTO and International Health Law and Policy* 33; Mitsuo Matsushita and C. L. Lim, 'Taming Leviathan as Merchant: Lingering Questions about the Practical Application of Trans-Pacific Partnership's State-Owned Enterprises Rules' (2020) 19(3) *World Trade Review* 402.

[3] See Office of the United States Trade Representative, 'Joint Statement on Trilateral Meeting of the Trade Ministers of the United States, Japan, and the European Union', 31 May 2018, available at: https://ustr.gov/about-us/policy-offices/press-office/press-releases/2018/may/joint-statement-trilateral-meeting; Office of the United States Trade Representative, 'Joint Statement of the Trilateral Meeting of the Trade Ministers of the United States, European Union, and Japan', 23 May 2019, available at: https://ustr.gov/about-us/policy-offices/press-office/press-releases/2019/may/joint-statement-trilateral-meeting; European Commission, 'Joint Statement of the Trilateral Meeting of the Trade Ministers of Japan, the United States and the European Union', 14 January 2020, available at: https://trade.ec.europa.eu/doclib/docs/2020/january/tradoc_158567.pdf.

[4] See US Department of State, 'Joint Statement by the Secretary of State of the United States of America and the EU High Representative for Foreign Affairs and Security Policy/Vice President of the European Commission', 24 March 2021, available at: www.state.gov/joint-statement-by-the-secretary-of-state-of-the-united-states-of-america-and-the-eu-high-rep

unequivocally contemplated in their respective trade policy agenda, arises from China's 'state-capitalist model' and 'unfair trade practices' that undermine a level playing field for US and EU counterparts.[5] To address this challenge, they both see the need to resort to unilateral, bilateral and multilateral approaches.[6]

While the United States and the EU are keen to develop and strengthen WTO rules on SOEs and industrial subsidies, this is hardly achievable in the foreseeable future given the widely-known difficulties in multilateral negotiations[7] and the high probability that China will resist any rules that are biased against it.[8] As an alternative, both the United States and the EU have taken the bilateral route and have incorporated SOE rules in a range of their own FTAs either as part of a chapter on Competition/Competition Policy or as a stand-alone chapter. Through this approach, they seek to shape international rules and standards on SOEs.[9]

Prior to the CPTPP, most US and EU FTAs focused on addressing anti-competitive conduct and did not develop detailed rules to regulate the behaviour and conduct of SOEs. For example, chapter 16 of the US–Chile FTA (2004),[10] titled 'Competition Policy, Designated Monopolies,

---

resentative-for-foreign-affairs-and-security-policy-vice-president-of-the-european-com mission/.

[5] See Office of the United States Trade Representative, '2021 Trade Policy Agenda and 2020 Annual Report', 1 March 2021, 4, available at: https://ustr.gov/about-us/policy-offices/press-office/press-releases/2021/march/biden-administration-releases-2021-presi dents-trade-agenda-and-2020-annual-report; European Commission, 'Trade Policy Review – An Open, Sustainable and Assertive Trade Policy', COM(2021)66 Final, 18 February 2021, 2, 9–14, available at: https://ec.europa.eu/transparency/regdoc/rep/1/ 2021/EN/COM-2021-66-F1-EN-MAIN-PART-1.PDF.

[6] Ibid.

[7] See e.g. Christoph Moser and Andrew Rose, 'Why Do Trade Negotiations Take So Long?' (2012) 27(2) *Journal of Economic Integration* 280; Manfred Elsig and Thomas Cottier, 'Reforming the WTO: The Decision-Making Triangle Revisited', in Thomas Cottier and Manfred Elsig (eds.), *Governing the World Trade Organization: Past, Present and Beyond Doha* (Cambridge: Cambridge University Press, 2011), 289–312.

[8] For a review of China's reactions towards the US and EU proposals on SOEs, see Henry Gao, 'Rethinking China Trade Policy: Lessons Learned and Options Ahead', National Foundation for American Policy Brief, January 2021, available at: https://nfap.com/wp-content/uploads/2021/01/Rethinking-China-Trade-Policy.NFAP-Policy-Brief.January-2021-2.pdf.

[9] Ibid. See also Fleury and Marcoux, 'US Shaping of State-Owned Enterprise Disciplines', n. 2, 448–9.

[10] United States–Chile Free Trade Agreement, effective on 1 January 2004 (US–Chile FTA), available at: https://ustr.gov/trade-agreements/free-trade-agreements/chile-fta/final-text/

and State Enterprises', targets anti-competitive conduct of designated monopolies and state enterprises and merely prevents these enterprises from engaging in such conduct in exercising designated government functions (Article 16.4). The only specific obligation on state enterprises is non-discrimination in the sale of goods or services (Article 16.4.3). These rules were largely reproduced in some later FTAs, such as chapter 14 of the US–Australia FTA (2005),[11] chapter 13 of the US–Peru FTA (2009),[12] chapter 13 of the US–Colombia FTA (2012)[13] and chapter 16 of the US–Korea FTA (2012 and amended in 2019).[14] Only the US–Australia FTA contains a definition of 'state enterprises' which covers 'an enterprise owned, or controlled through ownership interests, by any level of government' (Article 14.12.9).

EU FTAs prior to the CPTPP took similar approaches. For example, the EU–Chile FTA[15] (2003) has a whole section aimed at avoiding 'the benefits of the liberalization process in goods and services being diminished or cancelled out by anti-competitive business conduct' (Article 172 (1)). Although it also has a separate section on public enterprises and enterprises entrusted with special or exclusive rights, that section largely subjects these enterprises to the rules on competition policy (Article 179). The EU–South Korea FTA (2012)[16] and the EU–Colombia–Peru FTA

---

[11] United States–Australia Free Trade Agreement, effective on 1 January 2005 (US–Australia FTA), available at: https://ustr.gov/trade-agreements/free-trade-agreements/australian-fta/final-text.

[12] United States–Peru Free Trade Agreement, effective on 1 February 2009 (US–Peru FTA), available at: https://ustr.gov/trade-agreements/free-trade-agreements/peru-tpa/final-text.

[13] United States–Colombia Free Trade Agreement, effective on 15 May 2012 (US–Colombia FTA), available at: https://ustr.gov/trade-agreements/free-trade-agreements/colombia-tpa/final-text.

[14] United States–Korea Free Trade Agreement, effective on 15 March 2012, amended on 1 January 2019 (US–Korea FTA), available at: https://ustr.gov/trade-agreements/free-trade-agreements/korus-fta/final-text.

[15] Agreement Establishing an Association between the European Community and Its Member States, of the One Part, and the Republic of Chile, of the Other Part, effective February 2003 (EU–Chile FTA). The two sides commenced negotiations to amend the agreement in 2017. More information of the amendment negotiations and the full legal text of the current agreement are available at: https://ec.europa.eu/trade/policy/countries-and-regions/countries/chile/.

[16] Free Trade Agreement between the European Union and its Member States, of the One Part, and the Republic of Korea, of the Other Part, provisionally applied 1 July 2011, effective on 13 December 2015 (EU–South Korea FTA). More information and the agreement available at: https://ec.europa.eu/trade/policy/countries-and-regions/countries/south-korea/.

6.2 OVERVIEW OF SOE RULES IN FTAS

(2013)[17] deal with state/public enterprises under the Competition chapter based on similar rules as those in the EU–Chile FTA.[18] Both FTAs incorporate GATT Article XVII on state trading enterprises (STEs)[19] without developing more rules on SOEs. Accordingly, these EU FTAs merely regulate discriminatory conduct of SOEs, similar to the approach adopted in the US FTAs.[20]

Among these earlier FTAs, the US–Singapore FTA (2004)[21] stands out as an exception by providing the most detailed rules on SOEs prior to the CPTPP. Chapter 12, titled 'Anticompetitive Business Conduct, Designated Monopolies, and Government Enterprises', includes the same general obligations as those contemplated in the other US FTAs mentioned. However, in addition to the obligation of non-discrimination, Singapore commits to ensure that any government enterprise 'acts solely in accordance with commercial considerations in its purchase or sale of goods or services' (Article 12.3.2(d)), and that its government does not 'directly or indirectly, . . . influence or direct decisions of its government enterprises' (Article 12.3.2(e)). Singapore also undertakes extra obligations on transparency. For example, it is required to publish an annual report to make available information on government ownership and voting rights of covered entities, their annual revenue or total assets and officials on the board of directors and to provide such information on a non-covered entity when requested by the US (Article 12.3.2(g)).

The US–Singapore FTA also offers a definition of the key terms. 'Government enterprises' cover any enterprise in which the Singaporean government has an 'effective influence'. Such influence exists where 'the government and its government enterprises, alone or

---

[17] Trade Agreement between the European Union and its Member States, of the One Part, and Colombia and Peru, of the Other Part, provisionally applied 1 March 2013 (Peru) and 1 August 2013 (Colombia) (EU–Colombia–Peru FTA). Ecuador joined the agreement on 1 January 2017. More information and the agreement available at: https://ec.europa.eu/trade/policy/countries-and-regions/regions/andean-community/.
[18] See EU–South Korea FTA, n. 16, chapter 11; EU–Colombia–Peru FTA, n. 17, Article 263.
[19] See EU–South Korea FTA, n. 16, Article 2.13; EU–Colombia–Peru FTA, n. 17, Article 27.
[20] A survey of 283 FTAs concluded before the CPTPP also shows that most of the FTAs were focused on tackling anti-competitive and discriminatory conducts of SOEs: see L. Rubini and T. Wang, 'State-Owned Enterprises', in Aaditya Mattoo, Nadia Rocha and Michelle Ruta (eds.) *Handbook of Deep Trade Agreements* (Washington, DC, World Bank, 2020), 481–2.
[21] United States–Singapore Free Trade Agreement, effective on 1 January 2004 (US–Singapore FTA), available at: https://ustr.gov/trade-agreements/free-trade-agreements/singapore-fta/final-text.

in combination' (a) 'own more that (sic) 50 percent of the voting rights of an entity', or (b) 'have the ability to exercise substantial influence over the composition of the board of directors or any other managing body of an entity, *to determine the outcome of decisions on the strategic, financial, or operating policies or plans of an entity, or otherwise to exercise substantial influence over the management or operation of an entity*' (emphasis added). The emphasised text addresses situations of de facto influence in the absence of a majority voting right or substantial influence on the composition of the board. Moreover, where the voting securities held by the government and/or government enterprises are between 20–50 per cent, 'there is a rebuttable presumption that effective influence exists' (Article 12.8(5)). 'Covered entities' include government enterprises whose annual revenue and total assets are both greater than SGD 50 million and in which the Singaporean government 'owns a special voting share with veto rights relating to' several major corporate matters (Article 12.8(1)). Excluded from the 'covered entities' are Temasek Holdings (Pte) Ltd, Singapore's state-owned investment company, and government enterprises operating solely for the purpose of investing the government's reserves in foreign markets. 'Commercial considerations' means 'normal business practices of privately-held enterprises in the relevant business or industry' (Article 12.8(8)).

Although the SOE rules in the US–Singapore FTA were not adopted in the pre-CPTPP FTAs of the United States and the EU, they provided the basis for the development of the CPTPP SOE chapter which has in turn influenced the SOE rules under post-CPTPP FTAs of the United States and the EU, as will be discussed in Section 6.4.

In sharp contrast, China has consistently resisted the regulation of SOEs in its FTAs. No existing Chinese FTAs have included specific rules on SOEs. Although China has become increasingly amenable to competition rules in recent FTAs such as the China–South Korea FTA (2015),[22] the China–Singapore FTA Upgrade (2018)[23] and the Regional Comprehensive Economic Partnership (2020) (RCEP),[24] these rules are

---

[22] China–Korea Free Trade Agreement, effective on 20 December 2015, available at: http://fta.mofcom.gov.cn/topic/enkorea.shtml.

[23] China–Singapore Free Trade Agreement, effective on 1 January 2009, amended on 16 October 2019, available at: www.enterprisesg.gov.sg/non-financial-assistance/for-singapore-companies/free-trade-agreements/ftas/singapore-ftas/csfta.

[24] Regional Comprehensive Economic Partnership, signed on 15 November 2020, available at: www.dfat.gov.au/trade/agreements/not-yet-in-force/rcep/rcep-text-and-associated-documents.

primarily focused on ensuring the implementation and enforcement of competition policies and do not provide any rules that directly regulate the behaviour and conduct of SOEs.

6.3 The CPTPP SOE Chapter

Despite the United States' withdrawal from the negotiations of the Trans-Pacific Partnership (TPP) – the predecessor of the CPTPP – in January 2017, the other eleven states carried on the cooperation and brought the CPTPP into force in December 2018. The United States was the key architect of the TPP SOE rules which remain unchanged under the CPTPP.

It is widely observed that chapter 17 of the CPTPP, titled 'State-Owned Enterprises and Designated Monopolies', has developed SOE rules in significant and innovative ways.[25] However, the extent to which the CPTPP rules actually extend beyond those under China's WTO accession instruments warrants a detailed study which is lacking in the existing literature. Indeed, some have observed that the SOE rules in the US–Singapore FTA are based on China's WTO-plus obligations[26] and are more rigorous than the CPTPP SOE chapter in certain aspects.[27] Yet, even in a very recent work by Mavroidis and Sapir who suggested the use of CPTPP rules as a blueprint for the development of multilateral rules on SOEs, there is little consideration of the China-specific rules under the WTO.[28] To fill this significant gap, this section offers a critical analysis of five major elements of the CPTPP SOE chapter: (1) definition of SOEs; (2) substantive obligations; (3) non-commercial assistance (NCA); (4) transparency; and (5) exceptions and non-conforming measures (NCMs).

6.3.1 Definition of SOE

Article 17.1 of the CPTPP defines an SOE as an entity 'that is principally engaged in commercial activities' and in which the government

---

[25] See generally Fleury and Marcoux, 'US Shaping of State-Owned Enterprise Disciplines', n. 2; Miner, 'Commitments on State-Owned Enterprises', n. 2, 91.
[26] See Hufbauer and Cimino-Isaacs, 'How Will TPP and TTIP Change the WTO System?', n. 2, 685.
[27] See e.g. Willemyns, 'Disciplines on State-Owned Enterprises in International Economic Law', n. 2, 666; Kim, 'Regulating the Visible Hands', n. 2, 244.
[28] See Petros C. Mavroidis and Andre Sapir, *China and the WTO: Why Multilateralism Still Matters* (Princeton: Princeton University Press, 2021) 182–6.

(a) directly owns more than 50 per cent of the share capital;
(b) controls, through ownership interests, the exercise of more than 50 per cent of the voting rights; or
(c) holds the power to appoint a majority of members of the board of directors or any other equivalent management body.

This definition is narrower than the one in the US–Singapore FTA in two important aspects: (1) it is limited to SOEs that mainly undertake commercial activities; and (2) it does not explicitly cover entities over which the government has de facto 'effective influence'.

As regards the first aspect, 'commercial activities' refer to the production and sale/supply of goods and services for profits (Article 17.1). Some have observed that the limitation of SOEs to those principally engaged in commercial activities was intended to exclude 'regulatory agencies and other entities that merely grant licenses or permits'.[29] However, this limitation tends to be far broader because it excludes SOEs 'which operates on a not-for-profit basis or on a cost-recovery basis' (footnote 1 of Article 17.1). Where such an SOE also undertakes profit-making activities, it is still excluded from the coverage of the CPTPP as long as most of its activities[30] are not-for-profit.

Generally, this limitation fails to address market distortions caused by non-profit entities.[31] As far as China is concerned, it creates a wide loophole in dealing with Chinese SOEs. Recall that China's current SOE reform maintains a classification of Public Welfare SOEs, Special Commercial SOEs and General Commercial SOEs.[32] The CPTPP definition is unlikely to capture Public Welfare SOEs which supply public goods and services and Special Commercial SOEs that are principally engaged in projects or tasks designated by the Chinese government. Moreover, the lack of a clear definition and scope of the three types of SOEs provides the flexibility for the Chinese government to categorise an SOE as a not-for-profit entity exercising government functions. For example, to avoid the CPTPP rules, China may direct a state entity to undertake production and sale/supply of goods and services – such as SOEs in the major upstream industries (e.g. steel, aluminium, raw

---

[29] See Miner, 'Commitments on State-Owned Enterprises', n. 2, 92.
[30] The term 'principally' means 'for the most part', 'chiefly', 'largely', 'mostly', 'predominantly': see Merriam-Webster Dictionary Online, 'Principally Synonyms, Principally Antonyms': www.merriam-webster.com/thesaurus/principally.
[31] See Matsushita and Lim, 'Taming Leviathan as Merchant', n. 2, 415–6.
[32] See Chapter 2.

materials and rare earths) and state banks – on a not-for-profit or cost-recovery basis so as to support industrial policies and strategic goals. However, as shown in previous chapters, the activities of these SOEs, and many others of the kind, constitute a major cause of market distortions and attract considerable international concerns.

With respect to the second limitation, some commentators have proposed that the CPTPP SOE definition be construed in a broad manner so as to capture entities in which the government has a de facto 'effective influence'. However, the lack of an explicit reference to such 'effective influence' suggests that there was a compromise among the CPTPP governments to avoid a broader definition.[33]

Matsushita and Lim suggested that subparagraph (b) of Article 17.1 'could have a very broad reach ... to encompass indirect ownership interests' and '*de facto* control'.[34] A major issue, as Matsushita and Lim also pointed out, concerns the difficulties in collecting evidence to show '*de facto* control of the exercise of over 50% of voting rights'.[35] In other words, any broad interpretation of subparagraph (b) would be constrained by the requirement of 'the exercise of 50% of voting rights'. In reality, a government does not need to control a majority of voting rights to effectively influence the decision-making of state entities. China's current SOE reform offers a perfect illustration. As discussed in Chapter 2, the corporatisation of Chinese SOEs has led to the creation of a Party Committee in state entities so as to maintain the leadership role of the Party. While this could constitute strong evidence of de facto influence, it would be difficult to show that the committee, its secretary or any of its members control, directly or indirectly, a majority of voting rights in the entities, especially in the listed ones.

Miner argued that subparagraph (c) 'provides reasonable scope for encompassing enterprises ... where the state owns no shares or has no equity voting rights but controls hiring of the top management ... [and] firms that are highly dependent on regulatory approval or public funds

---

[33] See Ian F. Fergusson, Mark A. McMinimy and Brock R. Williams, 'The Trans-Pacific Partnership (TPP) Negotiations and Issues for Congress', Congressional Research Service, 20 March 2015, 43–4; Ian F. Fergusson and Brock R. Williams, 'The Trans-Pacific Partnership (TPP): Key Provisions and Issues for Congress', Congressional Research Service, 14 June 2016, 67 (noting that the CPTPP definition is narrower than the one in the US–Singapore FTA due to the lack of reference to 'effective influence').

[34] See Matsushita and Lim, 'Taming Leviathan as Merchant', n. 2, 413, 422.

[35] Ibid., 413.

and the government effectively selects the board'.[36] While this broad interpretation is plausible, it overlooks the implications of the reference to 'the power to appoint a majority of members of the board of directors'. For example, the Party Committee in a state entity can have sufficient influence on the entity's decision-making without needing to have the power to appoint a majority of the board. While the presence of a Party Committee and the involvement of its secretary in the board of directors may be used to establish a prima facie case of de facto influence, it would be difficult to adduce evidence to show the state/Party has the power to appoint a majority of the board.

The main point of comparison under China's WTO-plus obligations is paragraph 46 of the Report of the Working Party on the Accession of China[37] (Working Party Report or WPR) which is reproduced here:

> *The representative of China further confirmed that China would ensure that all state-owned and state-invested enterprises would make purchases and sales based solely on commercial considerations, e.g. price, quality, marketability and availability, and that the enterprises of other WTO Members would have an adequate opportunity to compete for sales to and purchases from these enterprises on non-discriminatory terms and conditions.* In addition, the Government of China would not influence, directly or indirectly, commercial decisions on the part of state-owned or state-invested enterprises, including on the quantity, value or country of origin of any goods purchased or sold, except in a manner consistent with the WTO Agreement. (emphasis added)

As discussed in Chapter 5, the first sentence of this provision requires that '*all* [Chinese] SOEs and state-invested enterprises [(SIEs)] ... make purchases and sales based solely on commercial considerations' and on a non-discriminatory basis. This coverage of entities is potentially much broader than the CPTPP definition of SOEs precisely in the two aspects discussed in this section. Specifically, the first sentence can be read broadly to cover state entities in which the Chinese government holds, directly or indirectly, a majority or minority interest regardless of whether their activities are for profit or not. More importantly, it can be argued that this obligation is not even conditional upon the state/Party having an 'effective influence' on the entities. Instead, there seems to be an assumption that such an influence exists as long as the SOEs or SIEs

---

[36] See Miner, 'Commitments on State-Owned Enterprises', n. 2, 92–3.
[37] Report of the Working Party on the Accession of China, WT/ACC/CHN/49, 1 October 2001 (Working Party Report or WPR).

concerned fail to fulfil the substantive obligations. This argument is supported by the fact that only the second sentence makes an explicit reference to direct or indirect influence of the Chinese government on SOEs and SIEs. Therefore, the obligations relating to 'commercial considerations' and 'non-discrimination', which are also the major obligations under the CPTPP, apply to all SOEs and SIEs regardless of whether the Chinese government has a majority ownership, controls a majority of voting rights, or otherwise has an effective influence. In short, China's WTO-plus obligations have a wide coverage of state entities, whereas some of the major Chinese SOEs involved in commercial activities in the domestic and global markets may well escape the CPTPP rules. This broader coverage necessarily extends the substantive obligations under paragraph 46 and the other relevant China-specific rules beyond the equivalent CPTPP rules.

6.3.2 Substantive Obligations: Non-discrimination and Commercial Considerations

Article 17.4.1 of the CPTPP sets out two substantive obligations requiring governments to ensure an SOE, when engaging in commercial activities and in its purchase or sale of a good or service, (1) acts in accordance with 'commercial considerations', and (2) accords both national treatment (NT) and most-favoured-nation (MFN) treatment to a good or service supplied by an enterprise of another Party.[38] This provision addresses the limitations of GATT Article XVII:1 by clarifying that the non-discrimination requirement includes both MFN and NT and the 'commercial considerations' requirement is independent from and additional to non-discrimination.[39] However, compared to China's WTO-plus obligations, this provision does not create more rigid or workable rules.

Consider the 'commercial considerations' requirement first. This term is defined under Article 17.1 as follows:

> price, quality, availability, marketability, transportation, and other terms and conditions of purchase or sale, or other factors that would normally be taken into account in the commercial decisions of a privately owned enterprise in the relevant business industry.

---

[38] Article 17.4.2 imposes the same obligations on designated monopolies.
[39] See discussions of GATT Article XVII:1 in Chapter 4. Also see Matsushita and Lim, 'Taming Leviathan as Merchant', n. 2, 408.

Compared to the US–Singapore FTA, this definition merely adds an illustrative list of factors that privately-owned enterprises (POEs) may consider in commercial transactions. However, these factors are already contemplated under GATT Article XVII:1(b) and paragraph 46 of the WPR. Although neither GATT Article XVII:1(b) nor paragraph 46 of the WPR refer to 'the commercial decisions of POEs in the relevant business industry', this reference does not further clarify the standard of 'commercial considerations' or the factors to be considered which are at the heart of this obligation. In contrast, as discussed in Chapter 5, the WTO tribunals in *Canada – Wheat* have provided more guidance on the scope of this obligation and the factors that may be considered in determining whether a decision is made on a commercial basis. While more guidance will need to and can be developed by case law, it is clear that the CPTPP rule on 'commercial considerations' does not extend beyond paragraph 46 of the WPR. Nor does it provide further guidance for the application of this rule compared to the existing WTO jurisprudence.

Turning to the non-discrimination requirement, the CPTPP does set out more specific rules to clarify that (1) both MFN and NT are required in an SOE's purchase or sale of goods or services and (2) this requirement also applies to the purchase/sale of goods or services from/to foreign-invested enterprises (FIEs) in the territory of the host country.[40] While paragraph 46 of the WPR does not offer such level of detail, its intended scope is clearly as broad as the CPTPP rule. Specifically, China's obligations under paragraph 46 were designed to address WTO Members' concerns set out in paragraph 44 of the WPR, which states:

> In light of the role that state-owned and state-invested enterprises played in China's economy, some members of the Working Party expressed concerns about the continuing governmental influence and guidance of the decisions and activities of such enterprises *relating to the purchase and sale of goods and services*. Such purchases and sales should be based solely on commercial considerations, without any governmental influence or application of discriminatory measures. (emphasis added)

In response, China made the following statement in paragraph 45:

> The representative of China emphasized the evolving nature of China's economy and *the significant role of FIEs and the private sector in the economy*. Given the increasing need and desirability of competing with

---

[40] This obligation applies to 'covered investment' which, as defined under Article 1.3, means 'with respect to a Party, an investment in its territory of an investor of another Party in existence as of the date of entry into force of this Agreement for those Parties or established, acquired, or expanded thereafter'.

private enterprises in the market, decisions by state-owned and state-invested enterprises had to be based on commercial considerations as provided in the WTO Agreement. (emphasis added)

While paragraphs 44 and 45 do not create additional commitments,[41] they provide important context for the interpretation of the commitments under paragraph 46. They show that the 'commercial considerations' and non-discrimination rules under paragraph 46 were drafted based on a clear understanding that the rules shall cover the purchase/sale of both goods and services by SOEs and SIEs including from or to FIEs. Accordingly, there is a (con)textual basis to support an interpretation of paragraph 46 at least as broadly as the equivalent CPTPP substantive obligations on SOEs.

Finally, it is worth noting that the 'commercial considerations' and non-discrimination rules under the CPTPP do not apply to 'the purchase or sale of shares, stocks or other forms of equity by a state-owned enterprise as a means of its equity participation in another enterprise' (footnote 13 of chapter 17). Arguably, paragraph 46 does not apply to equity investment either because shares/stocks cannot be treated as goods or services. This exemption is significant because equity infusion is one of the major ways in which Chinese SOEs are used as a vehicle to subsidise entities in strategic sectors.[42] However, as discussed in Chapter 5, the existing WTO rules on subsidies and China's WTO-plus obligations can be employed to address such subsidies. In contrast, as will be discussed in Section 6.3.3, some subsidies of this kind may fall outside of the CPTPP discipline on NCA.

6.3.3 Non-commercial Assistance

Article 17.6.1 of the CPTPP prohibits the provision of NCA by any Party, directly or indirectly, to its SOEs if such assistance causes 'adverse effects to the interests of another Party'. This rule also applies to the provision of NCA by an SOE to another SOE (Article 17.6.2).

Similar to the definition and scope of 'financial contributions' under Article 1 of the WTO Agreement on Subsidies and Countervailing Measures (SCM Agreement), NCA covers (1) 'direct transfers of funds or potential direct transfers of funds or liabilities' such as grants, debt

---

[41] See WPR, n. 37, para. 342.
[42] See Chapter 5.

forgiveness and preferential loans, guarantees and equity investment and (2) the supply of goods or services on terms more favourable than those commercially available (Article 17.1). Furthermore, the scope of NCA is limited to 'assistance to a state-owned enterprise by virtue of that state-owned enterprise's government ownership or control'. This in turn refers to such assistance, access to which is limited to, or predominantly or disproportionately used by, SOEs. This limitation essentially creates a requirement of specificity similar to Article 2 of the SCM Agreement and Section 10.2 of China's Accession Protocol (Accession Protocol or AP).[43] Finally, the requirement of 'adverse effect' is also based on Articles 5 and 6 of the SCM Agreement, although it remains debatable as to whether Article 17.7 of the CPTPP has provided more guidance for the assessment of 'adverse effects'.[44] Accordingly, despite the lack of reference to the SCM Agreement, the NCA section largely incorporates the existing WTO rules on actionable subsidies, including the specificity rule tailored to China.[45]

However, the CPTPP NCA rules are more limited than the existing WTO rules in at least two aspects. One relates to the CPTPP's limited coverage of SOEs which would exclude some major Chinese SOEs from the NCA rules. The other concerns the limited focus of the NCA rules on subsidies provided to SOEs only. While this focus is aimed at removing the preferential treatment and competitive advantages that SOEs receive beyond those enjoyed by POEs (i.e. competitive neutrality),[46] it leaves NCA provided to POEs unregulated. As discussed in Chapters 2 and 5, China's mixed ownership reform is leading to growing investment of state capital in POEs in strategic industries such as the high-tech sector. Where such equity infusion is based on preferential terms and conditions

---

[43] Protocol on the Accession of the People's Republic of China, WT/L/432, 23 November 2001 (Accession Protocol or AP). For a discussion of the specificity requirement including the China-specific rule, see Chapter 5.

[44] See Willemyns, 'Disciplines on State-Owned Enterprises in International Economic Law', n. 2, 671 (noting the CPTPP elaborates on the concept of adverse effects); Miner, 'Commitments on State-Owned Enterprises', n. 2, 94 (observing that while the CPTPP lays out very specific instances in which adverse effects may occur, these conditions are more narrow than those under the SCM Agreement); Matsushita and Lim, 'Taming Leviathan as Merchant', n. 2, 409 (observing that the CPTPP sets a relatively high threshold for showing adverse effects similar to the definition of 'serious prejudice' under the SCM Agreement).

[45] See our detailed discussion of the WTO subsidy rules in Chapter 5.

[46] See Fergusson et al., 'Trans-Pacific Partnership (TPP) Negotiations and Issues for Congress', n. 33, 44; Fergusson and Williams, 'Trans-Pacific Partnership (TPP)', n. 33, 68.

for policy or other non-commercial reasons, it constitutes a 'financial contribution' under the SCM Agreement but is not captured by the CPTPP NCA rules because it is provided to POEs, nor is it captured by the rules on commercial considerations and non-discrimination.

The CPTPP's major breakthrough is the inclusion of specific discipline on subsidies adversely affecting trade in services which are subject to further negotiations under the WTO's General Agreement on Trade in Services (GATS).[47] Currently, this additional discipline only applies to the supply of services via mode 1 (cross-border supply) and mode 3 (commercial presence)[48] and excludes the provision of services within the territory of the subsidising party (Article 17.6.4).[49] This exclusion means that the NCA rules do not protect the competitive condition of foreign services suppliers/firms vis-à-vis SOEs in the home market.

Overall, other than the discipline on services subsidies, the CPTPP does not develop the existing WTO rules in any substantive manner. Due to the limited coverage of the NCA rules, the WTO rules remain the only source of discipline that may be applied to tackle some major trade-distorting subsidies granted to or by Chinese SOEs.

6.3.4 Transparency

Article 17.10 of the CPTPP sets out an extensive list of transparency obligations mandating each Party to provide, *inter alia*,

(1) 'to the other Parties or otherwise make publicly available on an official website a list of its state-owned enterprises' and to 'update the list annually';

and upon request of another Party,

---

[47] General Agreement on Trade in Services, Marrakesh Agreement Establishing the World Trade Organization, Marrakesh, 15 April 1994, in force 1 January 1995, 1869 UNTS 183, (1994) 33 ILM 1167, Annex 1B, Article XV (GATS). Also see Willemyns, 'Disciplines on State-Owned Enterprises in International Economic Law', n. 2, 671; Matsushita and Lim, 'Taming Leviathan as Merchant', n. 2, 409. It is also worth noting that only a small number of FTAs before the CPTPP regulate subsidies in services: see L. Rubini, 'Subsidies', in Aaditya Mattoo, Nadia Rocha and Michelle Ruta (eds.) *Handbook of Deep Trade Agreements* (Washington, DC: World Bank, 2020), 450.
[48] GATS, n. 47, Article I.2; CPTPP, n. 1, Articles 17.6.1 (b)–(c), 17.6.2 (b)–(c).
[49] Annex 17-C(b) of the CPTPP sets out a mandate for the parties to review this exclusion within five years.

(2) a range of information on SOEs including the equity interest, special shares or voting rights of the government or its SOEs in the entities, the government position of any government official on the board, the entities' annual revenue and total assets over the past three years, exemptions and immunities that the Party's law grants to the entities; and
(3) information regarding any policy or programme that provides for NCA including the form, the names of the providers, the legal basis and underlying policy objective, the amount and related budget, the duration, and statistical data for assessment of the effects of the NCA.

Before the CPTPP, most FTAs that had transparency rules on SOEs did not cover such a wide range of information.[50] In this respect, the CPTPP does advance international SOE rules in a positive direction by creating a mechanism for governments to collect evidence necessary to monitor and constrain the market-distorting behaviour and practices of state entities.

It is worth noting that China's accession instruments have also included extensive transparency obligations, including, *inter alia*, obligations to publish all 'laws, regulations and other measures pertaining to or affecting trade in goods, services, TRIPS ... before such measures are implemented or enforced'[51] and to 'establish or designate an enquiry point' to provide all such information 'upon request of any individual, enterprise or WTO Member'.[52] These obligations were designed to address WTO Members' concerns about 'the difficulty in finding and obtaining copies of regulations and other measures undertaken by various ministries as well as those taken by provincial and other local authorities' and 'to ensure that information from all government bodies at all levels could be assembled in one place and made readily available'.[53] These obligations extend significantly beyond the general WTO transparency rules[54] and can be applied to subsidies or NCA, although it

---

[50] See Rubini and Wang, 'State-Owned Enterprises', n. 20, 496–8.
[51] See AP, n. 43, Section 2(C).1.
[52] Ibid., Section 2(C).3.
[53] See WPR, n. 37, para. 324.
[54] See Julia Ya Qin, '"WTO-Plus" Obligations and Their Implications for the World Trade Organization Legal System' (2003) 37(3) *Journal of World Trade* 483, 491–5. For a more detailed analysis of China's transparency obligations and implementation, see Henry Gao, 'The WTO's Transparency Obligations and China' (2017) 12(2) *Journal of Comparative Law* 329–40.

would be hard to construe the reference to 'laws, regulations and other measures' in a way that covers the same detailed information of SOEs as envisaged under the CPTPP. However, as will be discussed further in Section 6.3.5, sub-central SOEs may be exempted from the transparency obligations.[55] In this regard, China's WTO-plus obligations have a wider coverage.

Despite the positive development of transparency rules in the CPTPP, the efficacy of the rules hinges on implementation. Here, the same challenges, faced by the WTO in coaxing Members into fulfilling their transparency commitments, may well arise. As noted in Chapter 4, the WTO's Trade Policy Review Mechanism (TPRM) and notification mechanisms have been largely ineffective in inducing China (as well as other Members) to provide information on SOEs and subsidies. While China has taken a range of actions to implement its WTO-plus transparency obligations, there are notable deficiencies, such as the lack of publication of sub-central governmental measures, insufficient responses by certain enquiry points and a general lack of implementation by local governments.[56] The CPTPP does not seem to have a more effective mechanism to address these implementation challenges.[57]

Notably, Annex 17-B of the CPTPP sets out a detailed process to facilitate information-gathering for the resolution of disputes, including empowering a CPTPP panel to 'draw adverse inferences from instances of non-cooperation by a disputing Party' (paragraph 9). However, this process applies to disputes relating to the 'commercial considerations' and non-discrimination requirements and NCA only (paragraph 1), explicitly excluding the enforcement of the transparency rules from its coverage. In contrast, one should note that Article 13.1 of WTO's *Understanding on Rules and Procedures Governing the Settlement of Disputes*[58] applies to all WTO's multilateral agreements including the general and China-specific transparency requirements except for the TPRM. Article 13.1 provides:

---

[55] CPTPP, n. 1, Annex 17-D.
[56] See Gao, 'The WTO's Transparency Obligations and China', n. 54, 340–55.
[57] The WTO's transparency mechanisms have been plagued by similar issues for years: see Robert Wolfe, 'Sunshine over Shanghai: Can the WTO Illuminate the Murky World of Chinese SOEs?' (2017) 16(4) *World Trade Review* 713, 725.
[58] Understanding on Rules and Procedures Governing the Settlement of Disputes, Marrakesh Agreement Establishing the World Trade Organization, Marrakesh, 15 April 1994, in force 1 January 1995, 1869 UNTS 401, (1994) 33 ILM 1226, Annex 2.

> Each panel shall have the right to seek information and technical advice from any individual or body which it deems appropriate. However, before a panel seeks such information or advice from any individual or body within the jurisdiction of a Member it shall inform the authorities of that Member. A Member should respond promptly and fully to any request by a panel for such information as the panel considers necessary and appropriate. Confidential information which is provided shall not be revealed without formal authorization from the individual, body, or authorities of the Member providing the information.

This provision gives a WTO panel 'ample and extensive discretionary authority' to seek necessary information from disputing parties[59] and requires the parties to provide the requested information promptly and fully. When one party is unable to obtain relevant information, it may ask the panel to request the information from the other party. In such circumstances, the panel will do so to ensure 'the proceedings are fairly conducted' and the requesting party is 'afforded ... a fair opportunity to produce evidence necessary to make out its *prima facie* case'.[60] This is especially the case where the information concerned is 'in the exclusive possession of the other party' and the requesting party has tried but failed to obtain the information through reasonable means.[61] Thus, the WTO dispute settlement rules also provide a process to facilitate information-gathering. Moreover, one may argue that the WTO process also provides scope for the panel to draw an adverse inference if requested information is not provided. Therefore, the CPTPP rules are not necessarily more advanced or effective in inducing implementation of transparency obligations.

In addition, the narrow definition of SOEs under the CPTPP is likely to create uncertainties about the scope of the transparency obligations (i.e. what entities and NCA should be notified), thereby further reducing the efficacy of the rules.[62] In short, while the CPTPP should be praised for setting new and higher standards of transparency, it does not resolve

---

[59] Appellate Body Report, *Canada – Measures Affecting the Export of Civilian Aircraft*, WT/DS70/AB/R, adopted 20 August 1999, para. 192.

[60] Appellate Body Report, *United States – Measures Affecting Trade in Large Civil Aircraft (Second Complaint)*, WT/DS353/AB/R, adopted 23 March 2012, paras. 1143–5.

[61] See Panel Report, *Australia – Certain Measures Concerning Trademarks, Geographical Indications and Other Plain Packaging Requirements Applicable to Tobacco Products and Packaging*, WT/DS435/R, WT/DS441/R, WT/DS458/R, WT/DS467/R, adopted 29 June 2020, para. 1.82. (*Australia – Tobacco Plain Packaging*).

[62] The WTO's transparency mechanisms have been plagued by similar issues for years: see Wolfe, 'Sunshine over Shanghai', n. 57, 720–4.

the longstanding problem of enforcement – the most challenging issue under the WTO's transparency regime.

6.3.5 Exceptions and Non-conforming Measures

The key compromise to the 'strengthened' disciplines on SOEs in the CPTPP is the inclusion of wide-ranging exceptions.[63] Indeed, most pre-CPTPP FTAs that have SOE rules also provide exceptions, particularly for public services and strategic sectors.[64] However, the exemptions in the CPTPP are so extensive as to further reduce the rigour of the obligations just discussed.[65] The main exempted entities/activities include sovereign wealth funds, central banks and financial regulatory bodies exercising regulatory or supervisory authority, independent pension funds, government procurement, the supply of goods or services by SOEs in the exercise of government functions, the supply of financial services pursuant to a government mandate, and smaller SOEs whose annual revenue from commercial activities in any of the past three years was below 200 million Special Drawing Rights (approximately USD 287 million).[66] Furthermore, as flagged in Section 6.3.4, sub-central SOEs are largely not subject to the substantive obligations, the NCA rules and the transparency requirement under Article 17.10.1, that is, the obligation to publish a list of SOEs. Vietnam, Malaysia and Mexico, who have the largest state sectors among CPTPP members, are exempted from the transparency requirements entirely for their sub-central SOEs.[67] In addition, CPTPP members are allowed to maintain a schedule of NCMs reserving the right for select SOEs to undertake the scheduled activities without being subject to the disciplines on 'commercial considerations', non-discrimination and NCA (Article 17.9.1 and Annex IV). These broad exceptions reflect the interests and needs of all CPTPP members,

---

[63] See Willemyns, 'Disciplines on State-Owned Enterprises in International Economic Law', n. 2, 673.
[64] See Rubini and Wang, 'State-Owned Enterprises', n. 40, 495–6.
[65] See Kirk Haywood, 'The Treatment of State Enterprises in the WTO & Plurilateral Trade Agreements', The Commonwealth Secretariat Emerging Issues Briefing Note (3), March 2016, 1, 8 (observing that the extensive exclusions, 'when combined with questions around the overall trade distorting impact of SOEs, raises questions as to the commercial rationale for this Chapter').
[66] CPTPP, n. 1, Articles 17.2, 17.13; ibid., Annex 17-A; International Monetary Fund, 'SDR Valuation', 16 May 2021, available at: www.imf.org/external/np/fin/data/rms_sdrv.aspx.
[67] CPTPP, n. 1, Article 17.9, Annex 17-D. See also Miner, 'Commitments on State-Owned Enterprises', n. 2, 96–7.

not merely those with a more significant state sector. Notably, while actively advocating more rigorous disciplines on SOEs, the United States was also keen to ensure the CPTPP leaves sufficient room for SOEs to exercise public functions, particularly financial institutions, and excludes sub-central SOEs from the substantive obligations.[68]

Instead of discussing all the exceptions, we consider the implications of the exemption of sub-central SOEs and NCMs. As noted in Chapter 2, China has been consolidating the state sector through restructuring and reorganisation to create world-class multinational companies. By May 2021, the consolidation has reduced the number of central SOEs to ninety-seven, a list of which is already published on the website of the State-Owned Assets Supervision and Administration Commission (SASAC).[69] This list satisfies the requirement under Article 17.10.1 of the CPTPP as no existing CPTPP members are required to publish a list of sub-central SOEs. In reality, however, sub-central SOEs continue to flourish in China, reaching a total of 242,000 by the end of 2018.[70] Moreover, while the central SOEs are typically considerably larger and stronger players domestically and globally, local SOEs are actively involved in a much wider range of industries or operations of commercial significance and have become increasingly important actors.[71] In 2020, the revenue of local SOEs accounted for almost half (i.e. 44.2 per cent) of the total annual revenue of all Chinese SOEs.[72] As

---

[68] See Fleury and Marcoux, 'US Shaping of State-Owned Enterprise Disciplines', n. 2, 460–1; Miner, 'Commitments on State-Owned Enterprises', n. 2, 96; Willemyns, 'Disciplines on State-Owned Enterprises in International Economic Law', n. 2, 674–5.

[69] See State-Owned Assets Supervision and Administration Commission of the State Council, 'List of Central State-Owned Enterprises', 10 May 2021, available at: www.sasac.gov.cn/n4422011/n14158800/n14158998/c14159097/content.html.

[70] This is the latest data from China's National Bureau of Statistics: see National Bureau of Statistics, 'Incorporated Entities Enter into a Fast-Growing Stage', 11 January 2020, available at: www.stats.gov.cn/tjsj/sjjd/202001/t20200122_1724483.html#:~:text=%E5%9B%BD%E6%9C%89%E4%BC%81%E4%B8%9A%E7%BB%A7%E7%BB%AD%E5%8F%91%E6%8C%A5%E6%94%AF%E6%9F%B1,%E4%B8%87%E4%B8%AA%EF%BC%8C%E5%A2%9E%E9%95%BF10.9%25%E3%80%82.

[71] See Wendy Leutert, 'State-Owned Enterprises in Contemporary China', in Luc Bernier, Massimo Florio and Philippe Bance (eds.), *The Routledge Handbook of State-Owned Enterprises* (London: Routledge, 2020), 202–3; OECD, 'Report on China's Shipping Industry and Policies Affecting it', OECD Science, Technology and Industry Policy Papers No. 105, April 2021, 51, available at: www.oecd-ilibrary.org/science-and-technology/report-on-china-s-shipbuilding-industry-and-policies-affecting-it_bb222c73-en.

[72] See State-Owned Assets Supervision and Administration Commission of the State Council, 'Financial Performance of All State-Owned Enterprises and State-Controlled Enterprises between January and December 2020', 27 January 2021, available at: www.sasac.gov.cn/n16582853/n16582888/c17476557/content.html.

central SOEs increasingly concentrate into strategic sectors, local SOEs' influence on commercial activities will continue to grow. Thus, the lack of discipline on sub-central SOEs considerably limits the efficacy of the CPTPP in addressing market distortions that Chinese SOEs may generate. Apparently, it falls short of the existing WTO norms, particularly Section 2(A)(1) of China's AP under which WTO rules, including the China-specific ones, 'shall apply to the entire customs territory of China', and Section 2(A)(2), under which China must apply and administer all central and local trade-related measures 'in a uniform, impartial and reasonable manner'.[73] These China-specific rules clearly apply to sub-central SOEs and the relevant trade-distortive measures and practices.

While the CPTPP permits NCMs, the scope of scheduled exceptions varies among the members. For example, Singapore and Japan do not have a schedule for NCMs. Australia has only one NCM, relating to the purchase of goods and services by Indigenous persons and organisations.[74] In contrast, Mexico and Vietnam have the most extensive NCMs. Mexico's NCMs cover exemptions of certain entities in specific activities/sectors such as supply of electricity and gas, exploration and production of oil, finance of infrastructure and public services and other essential financial services for the banking sector and national and regional economic development more broadly.[75] Vietnam's NCMs are even broader, encompassing all SOEs and designated monopolies in a range of activities such as any financing necessary to the restructuring of these entities, production, sale and purchase of public goods or any goods for economic stability and the use of these entities to promote and facilitate the economic development of remote and certain other areas as well as small and medium-sized enterprises.[76] If the CPTPP were employed as a model for future negotiations of SOE rules, undoubtedly China would push very hard for an extensive list of NCMs that are not available under its WTO commitments so as to maintain the strategic role of SOEs for economic development, global competition and other policy goals. Such exceptions, however, do not exist in the current WTO rules.[77]

---

[73] For more discussions of these China-specific rules, see Qin, '"WTO-Plus" Obligations and Their Implications for the World Trade Organization Legal System', n. 54, 497–99.
[74] CPTPP, n. 1, Annex IV Schedule of Australia.
[75] Ibid., Annex IV Schedule of Mexico.
[76] Ibid., Annex IV Schedule of Viet Nam.
[77] Recall our discussions of the non-applicability of GATT exceptions to China's WTO-plus obligations under paragraph 46 of the WPR and Section 9.1 of the AP in Chapter 5.

6.4 Development of SOE Rules in Post-CPTPP Free Trade Agreements

This section briefly reviews the recent development of SOE rules in several major US/EU FTAs after the CPTPP, including the United States–Mexico–Canada Agreement (2020) (USMCA),[78] the EU–Japan FTA (2019)[79] and the EU–Vietnam FTA (2020).[80] Generally speaking, these FTAs are largely based on the CPTPP SOE chapter. While they also sought to address some deficiencies of the CPTPP SOE chapter as discussed in Section 6.3 and expanded the rules on SOEs and subsidies, they did not address all the deficiencies and counterbalanced the expanded rules by including extensive exceptions.

For example, all three FTAs extended the definition of SOEs to cover situations of de facto control/influence.[81] The two EU FTAs took a further step to remove the limitation to SOEs 'principally' engaged in commercial activities so as to capture all commercial activities of SOEs.[82] However, the limitation to profit-making SOEs remained unchanged and no further development of the 'commercial considerations' rule was made.

Furthermore, all three FTAs expanded the NCA/subsidy rules to cover subsidies granted to POEs. Specifically, the USMCA's definition of NCA is no longer confined to SOEs but is expanded to cover assistance provided to 'certain enterprises' which include POEs (Article 22.1). The two EU FTAs have a separate chapter on subsidies which refers to the SCM Agreement, essentially incorporating the WTO rules on actionable subsidies.[83] At the same time, the subsidy chapters set out a range of exceptions, including GATT/GATS exceptions, to provide space for

---

[78] United States–Mexico–Canada Agreement, effective on 1 July 2020 (USMCA), available at: https://ustr.gov/trade-agreements/free-trade-agreements/united-states-mexico-canada-agreement.

[79] Agreement between the European Union and Japan for An Economic Partnership, effective on 1 February 2019 (EU–Japan FTA). More information and the agreement available at: https://ec.europa.eu/trade/policy/in-focus/eu-japan-economic-partnership-agreement/.

[80] Free Trade Agreement between the European Union and The Socialist Republic of Viet Nam, effective on 1 August 2020 (EU–Vietnam FTA). More information and the agreement available at: https://ec.europa.eu/trade/policy/countries-and-regions/countries/vietnam/.

[81] USMCA, n. 78, Article 22.1; EU–Japan FTA, n. 79, Article 13.1(h)(iv); EU–Vietnam FTA, n. 80, Article 11.1(g)(iii).

[82] EU–Japan FTA, n. 79, Article 13.2.1; EU–Vietnam FTA, n. 80, Article 11.2.2.

[83] EU–Japan FTA, n. 79, chapter 12; EU–Vietnam FTA, n. 80, chapter 10.B.

governments to use subsidies for legitimate policy objectives. The GATT/GATS exceptions, for example, are arguably not available under the SCM Agreement[84] or China's accession instruments.

Finally, all three FTAs added two types of 'prohibited subsidies': (1) loans or loan guarantees provided to an uncreditworthy SOE and (2) NCA provided to an SOE who 'is insolvent or on the brink of insolvency, without a credible restructuring plan'.[85] This addition incorporates some of the proposals put forward in the US–EU–Japan joint statements for the reform of WTO rules on industrial subsidies and expands the scope of prohibited subsidies contemplated in the SCM Agreement.[86] Under the USMCA, the new subsidies are prohibited only when they are granted to SOEs 'primarily engaged in the production or sale of goods other than electricity', thereby limiting these subsidies to trade in goods. This limitation is removed under the two EU FTAs which expand the application of the subsidies to trade in services.

While expanding the rules on SOEs and subsidies, all three FTAs maintained the various types of exceptions envisaged in the CPTPP SOE chapter. The two EU FTAs sought to remove the exemption of sub-central SOEs from the substantive rules.[87] However, they also expanded the exceptions by confining the rules to the parties' specific commitments under their schedules on trade in services and investment.[88] In addition, the EU–Vietnam FTA allows Vietnam to maintain a list of NCMs (Article 11.2.8). The EU–Japan FTA incorporates the GATT/GATS general exceptions (Article 13.8).

As of this writing, the three FTAs represent the latest development of international regulation of SOEs and have influenced the negotiation of SOE rules in other FTAs. For example, the Peru–Australia FTA (2020)[89]

---

[84] See Steve Charnovitz, 'Green Subsidies and the WTO', World Bank Policy Research Working Paper 7060, October 2014, 18, available at: https://openknowledge.worldbank.org/handle/10986/20500; Robert Howse, 'Making the WTO (Not So) Great Again: The Case against Responding to the Trump Trade Agenda through Reform of WTO Rules on Subsidies and State Enterprises' (2020) 23(2) *Journal of International Economic Law* 371, 374.

[85] USMCA, n. 78, Article 22.6; EU–Japan FTA, n. 79, Article 12.7; EU–Vietnam FTA, n. 80, Article 10.9.

[86] See n. 3.

[87] EU–Japan FTA, n. 79, Article 13.2.2; EU–Vietnam FTA, n. 80, Article 11.2.4.

[88] EU–Japan FTA, n. 79, Article 13.2.8; EU–Vietnam FTA, n. 80, Article 11.4.4.

[89] Peru–Australia Free Trade Agreement, effective on 11 February 2020. More information and the agreement available at: www.dfat.gov.au/trade/agreements/in-force/pafta/Pages/peru-australia-fta.

combines the approaches adopted in the US/EU FTAs by expanding SOE rules and exceptions in a similar manner (chapter 16). Overall, other than the inclusion of services subsidies and the additional types of prohibited subsidies, these post-CPTPP FTAs do not extend beyond China's WTO-plus obligations. To the extent that they leave some deficiencies in the CPTPP SOE chapter unaddressed and maintain the extensive exceptions, they are not as rigorous as the existing WTO rules tailored to China.

Finally, it is worth noting that in the EU–China Comprehensive Agreement on Investment (CAI),[90] China agreed to some rules on SOEs for the first time. Interestingly, the terms 'State-Owned Enterprises' and 'SOEs' never formally appear in the CAI. Instead, it is referred to in the agreement as a 'covered entity', a seemingly innocuous expression probably chosen carefully to avoid the controversies surrounding SOEs. Moreover, by using 'covered entity', the CAI is also able to expand the coverage from just those owned by the government (either through majority share or majority voting rights) to entities in which the government has the power to influence or control the board or the decisions of the enterprises or 'to legally direct the actions or otherwise exercise an equivalent level of control in accordance with its laws and regulations'.[91] This is consistent with the Appellate Body's function/authority-based approach to determining whether an entity is a 'public body' under the SCM Agreement, which is discussed in Chapter 5. In addition, 'covered entities' also cover cases of monopoly and duopoly, where ownership by the state is not required. With such a broad definition, the CAI extends beyond the scope of SOEs under the CPTPP to cover most situations where the competitive environment is undermined due to government ownership or control or monopolistic power of the enterprise.

The CAI sets out two major obligations for covered entities. The first is the obligation to act in accordance with commercial considerations and provide non-discriminatory treatment in their purchases or sales of goods or services. The EU regards this as a significant achievement and

---

[90] EU–China Comprehensive Agreement on Investment, Agreement in Principle, concluded on 30 December 2020 (CAI), available at: https://trade.ec.europa.eu/doclib/press/index.cfm?id=2237.
[91] Ibid., Article 3bis.1(b).

calls the CAI 'the first agreement to deliver on obligations for the behavior of state-owned enterprises'.[92] But this is nothing new and simply repeats what was already in China's WTO accession package and the existing rules in recent FTAs. The other is the transparency obligation, which grants the right to a Party to request the other Party to 'supply information about the operations of [a covered] entity related to the carrying out of the provisions of [the Article on SOEs]'.[93] This includes information on ownership and the voting structure, special shares and voting rights, organisational and management structures, annual revenue or total assets, exemptions, immunities and equivalent measures, and government authorities responsible for exercising the ownership function and regulatory power. This list of information also largely reproduces the transparency requirements in the CPTPP and the post-CPTPP FTAs discussed. In any event, the transparency rules will confront the same issues of enforcement, and the CAI does not seem to provide a solution to such issues.

Despite its promises, the CAI is unlikely to be ratified in the short term due to ongoing tensions between the two sides.[94] As per EU internal procedure, the text of the agreement shall first go through the necessary legal and technical review, before it is approved by the European Council and translated into all official languages.[95] Then it will be referred to the European Parliament, which will decide with a majority vote within a year.[96] Unfortunately, the European Parliament is not really known for being friendly towards China. Instead, it has for years been criticising China over allegations ranging from human rights violations to economic aggression.[97] Such an approach is clearly reflected in the EU's December 2020 'Resolution on forced labor and the situation of the

---

[92] European Commission, 'Key Elements of the EU-China Comprehensive Agreement on Investment', Press Release, 30 December 2020, available at: https://ec.europa.eu/commission/presscorner/detail/en/IP_20_2542.

[93] See CAI, n 90, Article 3bis.4(a).

[94] European Parliament, 'European Parliament Resolution of 20 May 2021 on Chinese Countersanctions on EU Entities and MEPs and MPs', P9_TA(2021)0255, 20 May 2021, available at: www.europarl.europa.eu/doceo/document/TA-9-2021-0255_EN.pdf.

[95] The Diplomat, 'Will the EU–China Investment Agreement Survive Parliament's Scrutiny?', 27 January 2021, available at: https://thediplomat.com/2021/01/will-the-eu-china-investment-agreement-survive-parliaments-scrutiny/.

[96] Ibid.

[97] Ibid.

Uyghurs in the Xinjiang Uyghur Autonomous Region'.[98] In response, on 22 March 2021, China imposed sanctions on ten EU individuals, which included five Members of the European Parliament.[99] In protest, the European Parliament cancelled a meeting to review the CAI and the Chairman of the Parliament's Trade Committee reportedly said that '[t]here has to be a solution of these sanctions before we come back to ordinary business on this'.[100] Thus, before China lifts its sanctions on the five parliamentarians, the CAI will not even enter the ratification process. Even if this hurdle is cleared, the aftertaste of such a foul play would probably cast a shadow over the minds of many Members of the European Parliament. Trying to persuade 700+ parliamentarians will prove to be a much harder task than the dozens of officials in the Directorate General for Trade, especially as these parliamentarians see their roles as much broader than the narrow confines of trade and investment interests.

Overall, the CAI largely follows the approaches of the post-CPTPP FTAs by incorporating the CPTPP's 'commercial considerations' and non-discrimination requirements and the wider definition of SOEs.[101] Moreover, given its (limited) focus on investment liberalisation, these rules do not apply to trade in goods or services 'other than through establishment of an enterprise and operation of a covered investment'.[102] In addition, both parties maintain a long list of exceptions or NCMs.[103] Thus, the CAI does not seem to break new ground compared to the CPTPP-based rules on SOEs, although its text is subject to further modifications. Nevertheless, the CAI signals China's growing openness to negotiations of international regulation of SOEs.

---

[98] European Parliament, 'Resolution of 17 December 2020 on Forced Labour and the Situation of the Uyghurs in the Xinjiang Uyghur Autonomous Region', 17 December 2020, available at: www.europarl.europa.eu/doceo/document/TA-9-2020-0375_EN.html.

[99] Yew Lun Tian, Tom Daly and Toby Chopra, 'China Hits Back at EU with Sanctions on 10 People, Four Entities over Xinjiang', Reuters, 23 March 2021, available at: www.reuters.com/article/us-eu-china-sanctions-ministry-idUSKBN2BE1WB.

[100] Philip Blenkinsop, 'EU–China Deal Grinds into Reverse after Tit-for-Tat Sanctions', Reuters, 24 March 2021, available at: www.reuters.com/article/us-eu-china-trade-idUSKBN2BF276.

[101] See CAI, n. 90, Section II, Article 3bis.

[102] Ibid., Section II Article 3bis para. 3, footnote 8.

[103] Ibid., China's Schedule of Commitments and Reservations; ibid., EU's Schedule of Commitments and Reservations.

6.5 Conclusion

While the CPTPP SOE chapter was developed with China as a major target,[104] this chapter has shown its lack of development and deficiencies when compared to China's WTO-plus obligations. Specifically, the CPTPP does not provide more rigorous or workable SOE rules but rather has narrower application and more carve-outs. More recent development of SOE rules in major US/EU FTAs after the CPTPP is largely based on the CPTPP SOE chapter. While these FTAs also seek to address some deficiencies in the CPTPP SOE chapter and gradually expand the rules on subsidies and SOEs, the expanded rules are balanced by the inclusion of extensive exceptions. Our discussions and observations challenge the mainstream view that the CPTPP and its subsequent developments have advanced international regulation of SOEs in significant ways. Thus, it remains debatable whether the CPTPP provides an ideal model for the reform of WTO rules if the major goal is to strengthen the discipline on Chinese SOEs.

---

[104] Raj Bhala, 'TPP, American National Security and Chinese SOEs' (2017) 16(4) *World Trade Review* 655, 661; Daniel C. K. Chow, 'How the United States Uses the Trans-Pacific Partnership to Contain China in International Trade' (2016) 17(2) *Chicago Journal of International Law* 370, 398–9.

7

Tackling China's State Capitalism
WTO Litigation and Trade Negotiation

7.1 Introduction

As we have shown in Chapter 5, existing WTO rules, especially coupled with the China-specific provisions, do hold great potential in tackling China's state capitalism. Thus, the next logical step is actually using these rules to bring WTO cases against China. However, there have been few such cases in the WTO. In this chapter, we analyse some possible reasons for the lack of WTO litigation and discuss ways to address these concerns. At the same time, we also recognise that some WTO Members regard the existing WTO rules as being insufficient to deal with China's state capitalism and have been engaging in efforts to update the rulebook of the WTO. Thus, we also discuss these proposed new rules and suggest how these rules might be finetuned to make their negotiation more productive.

7.2 WTO Litigation

Since its WTO accession, China has been one of the most frequent litigants in the WTO. As of 1 October 2021, China has been a complainant in twenty-two cases and the respondent in forty-seven cases.[1] Most cases were brought against it by major players such as the United States, the EU, Japan, Canada, Brazil and Mexico, while almost all of the cases brought by China targeted the United States and the EU (including its member states), with the exception of one recent case against Australia.

When China first acceded to the WTO, it took a rather cautious approach towards WTO litigation due to its lack of familiarity with

---

[1] WTO, Disputes by member, available at: www.wto.org/english/tratop_e/dispu_e/dispu_by_country_e.htm.

WTO legal rules and the political importance it attached to international disputes.[2] Trying very hard to avoid being dragged to court, it usually settled disputes quickly with the complainants even when it had strong defences.[3] As it gradually learned the rules of the game by participating in numerous cases as a third party, however, China was able to overcome its fear of WTO disputes.[4] With its newly-acquired confidence in its ability to participate, China began to aggressively defend itself in WTO disputes, starting with the 2006 case of *China – Auto Parts*,[5] as well as bring cases against the major players. In both circumstances, China's new strategy involved extensive substantive arguments and sophisticated use of procedural objections. The most successful example of this new strategy is the *US – Anti-Dumping and Countervailing Duties (China)* case of 2008,[6] in which the Appellate Body (AB) sided with China by rejecting the 'ownership-based' approach advocated by the United States, thus freeing state-owned enterprises (SOEs) from the concerns that they would be automatically deemed 'public bodies' for the purpose of determining whether a subsidy exists under the Agreement on Subsidies and Countervailing Measures (SCM Agreement).

The loss of the United States in this case also led many to believe that the existing WTO rules are inadequate to deal with China's state capitalism. Using this case and China's non-market economy (NME) status in anti-dumping (AD) cases post-2016 as examples, Mark Wu argued in his seminal article 'China Inc.' that they are 'emerging points of tension' that the existing WTO law is ill-equipped to address.[7] In their new book, Mavroidis and Sapir also deemed the WTO rules inefficient and argued

---

[2] Henry Gao, 'Aggressive Legalism: The East Asian Experience and Lessons for China', in Henry Gao and Donald Lewis (eds.), *China's Participation in the WTO* (London: Cameron May, 2005) 315–51.

[3] Henry Gao, 'China's Ascent in Global Trade Governance: From Rule Taker to Rule Shaker, and Maybe Rule Maker?', in Carolyn Deere-Birkbeck (ed), *Making Global Trade Governance Work for Development: Perspectives and Priorities from Developing Countries* (Cambridge: Cambridge University Press, 2011) 153, 168.

[4] Ibid., 168–70.

[5] Panel Report, *China – Measures Affecting Imports of Automobile Parts*, WT/DS339/R, WT/DS340/R, WT/DS342/R, adopted 12 January 2009; Appellate Body Report, *China – Measures Affecting Imports of Automobile Parts*, WT/DS339/AB/R, WT/DS340/AB/R, WT/DS342/AB/R, adopted 12 January 2009.

[6] Appellate Body Report, *United States – Definitive Anti-Dumping and Countervailing Duties on Certain Products from China*, WT/DS379/AB/R, adopted 25 March 2011 (*US – Anti-Dumping and Countervailing Duties (China)*).

[7] Mark Wu, 'The "China, Inc." Challenge to Global Trade Governance' (2016) 57(2) *Harvard International Law Journal* 261, 299–308.

instead for 'amending the law'.[8] This view also influenced the US government, with the United States Trade Representative (USTR) lamenting that the WTO 'is not effective in addressing a trade regime that broadly conflicts with the fundamental underpinning of the WTO system'.[9]

7.2.1 Does WTO Litigation Work?

More specifically, the concern over the futility of WTO litigation can be separated into three different but related assertions: first, existing WTO rules do not cover China's trade practices; second, even if there are such rules, they will not be interpreted with sufficient rigour in WTO cases to obtain favourable rulings against China; and third, even if the complainants managed to win such cases, China will just comply with the ruling on paper but not in substance.[10] However, closer examination reveals that none of these really holds true.

First, as discussed in Chapter 4, existing WTO rules, especially those on state trading enterprises, transparency and AD indeed do not provide sufficient disciplines for the regulation of Chinese SOEs. Nonetheless, WTO Members were aware of the potential problems that could be created by China's state capitalism and used China's accession negotiation to craft new rules. As discussed in Chapter 3, however, the Members did not regard China's unique economic model to be problematic per se. Instead, they identified specific features of the Chinese system which were inconsistent with WTO rules and negotiated China-specific rules to address these issues, especially those on the role of SOEs in the economy, pricing policies, industrial policy and subsidies, trading rights, and dumping and AD. In other words, the special rules in China's accession instruments were not designed to mandate or cause a systemic overhaul of the Chinese economic model but to make sure that the Chinese system will not run into conflict with specific obligations in the WTO system. Therefore, as discussed in Chapter 5, existing WTO rules, particularly the rules on subsidies and the relevant China-specific

---

[8] Petros C. Mavroidis and Andre Sapir, *China and the WTO: Why Multilateralism Still Matters* (Princeton: Princeton University Press, 2021) 82–100, 174–92.

[9] United States Trade Representative, '2017 USTR Report to Congress on China's WTO Compliance', January 2018, 5, available at: https://ustr.gov/sites/default/files/files/Press/Reports/China%202017%20WTO%20Report.pdf.

[10] Timothy Webster, 'Paper Compliance: How China Implements WTO Decisions' (2014) 35(3) *Michigan Journal of International Law* 525.

obligations, do hold great potential in reigning in China's state capitalism.

Second, in response to complaints that WTO rules have been diluted by the AB's interpretation of the term 'public body' under the SCM Agreement, we have discussed how the problem has been ameliorated both by the further refining of the jurisprudence on the issue and the shift of course in China's SOE reform. To start, the adoption of an 'authority-based approach' by the AB in *US – Anti-Dumping and Countervailing Duties (China)* does not necessarily mean that it is impossible to make a positive finding on the term 'public body' in all cases involving SOEs. Instead, as the AB made clear in the decision, 'the absence of an express statutory delegation of authority' does not necessarily preclude a positive determination.[11] Moreover, barriers to the application of the 'authority-based approach' have been eased significantly in the more recent decision of *US – Countervailing Measures (China) (Article 21.5)*,[12] as we have discussed in detail in Chapter 5. By rejecting China's argument for a 'conduct-based' approach and opting for an 'entity-based' approach, the AB has greatly reduced the evidentiary burden for investigating authorities. This means that they only need to make one positive finding of 'public body' for each entity under investigation, and then all conduct of this entity will be 'directly attributable to' the subsidising government.[13] At the same time, China's own SOE reform has made it easier to infer the government's 'meaningful control' of SOEs, especially with the new rules mandating deeper involvement by the Party in the management and decision-making of SOEs.

Third, the criticism that China does not comply with unfavourable rulings of WTO tribunals is also unfounded. As discussed in detail elsewhere, China has maintained an impressive record of compliance, comparing more favourably with the record of compliance of the other key players in the system.[14] As mentioned, China has been a respondent in forty-seven disputes involving a total of thirty-four matters. Among

---

[11] Appellate Body Report, *US – Anti-Dumping and Countervailing Duties (China)*, n 6, para. 318.

[12] Appellate Body Report, *United States – Countervailing Duty Measures on Certain Products from China – Resources to Article 21.5 of the DSU by China*, WT/DS437/AB/RW, adopted 15 August 2019, paras. 5.65, 5.77–5.78 (*US – Countervailing Measures (Article 21.5 – China)*).

[13] Ibid., para. 5.103.

[14] See generally Weihuan Zhou, *China's Implementation of the Rulings of the World Trade Organization* (Oxford: Hart Publishing, 2019).

the thirty-four cases, twenty-four have been completed either through a mutually agreed solution (twelve cases) or China's implementation of WTO rulings (twelve cases).[15] In all twelve cases in which China was found to have breached WTO rules, China implemented the adverse findings by repealing or modifying a wide range of measures in all areas of trade such as internal taxes, AD or countervailing duties, export restraints, regulatory restrictions on foreign services suppliers and inadequate protection of intellectual property rights (IPRs). The only circumstance in which China failed to change the measures involved related to those restricting the right to import films in the *China – Publications and Audiovisual Products* case. Nevertheless, China entered into a memorandum of understanding with the United States granting more market access to US films, a step toward further liberalisation of the relevant Chinese market.[16] China's record of compliance is strong evidence of the effectiveness of the WTO's dispute settlement system. Overall, the system has caused not only changes to specific policy instruments but also systematic adjustments of China's complex regulatory regime in an incremental manner.

7.2.2 Which Cases?

In an article written in early 2018, we discussed the potential of using the WTO dispute settlement system to tackle China's state capitalism.[17] Even though our paper challenged the conventional wisdom at the time, over the years more and more scholars have been persuaded. For example, Bacchus, Lester and Zhu have suggested bringing cases against systemic Chinese violations of US IPRs including trade secrets, forced technology

---

[15] As regards the other ten cases, nine remain in the litigation process and one has lapsed as the panel's work was suspended for more than twelve months under Article 12.12 of the *Understanding on Rules and Procedures Governing the Settlement of Dispute* (DSU). See Marrakesh Agreement Establishing the World Trade Organization, opened for signature 15 April 1994, 1867 UNTS 3 (entered into force 1 January 1995), Annex 2 (Understanding on Rules and Procedures Governing the Settlement of Disputes) 1869 UNTS 401.

[16] WTO, *China – Measures Affecting Trading Rights and Distribution Services for Certain Publications and Audiovisual Entertainment Products, Joint Communication from China and the United States*, WT/DS363/19, 11 May 2012.

[17] Weihuan Zhou, Henry Gao and Xue Bai, 'Building a Market Economy through WTO-Inspired Reform of State-Owned Enterprises in China' (2019) 68(4) *International and Comparative Law Quarterly* 977.

transfer practices and subsidies.[18] Similarly, Hillman has also suggested recourse to 'a big, bold case' against a wide range of issues such as technology transfer, discriminatory licensing restrictions, outward investment regimes and the Made in China 2025 plan, cyber intrusions, inward investment restrictions, subsidies, export promotion measures, standards requirements, sanitary and phytosanitary (SPS) measures, China's breach of its services and transparency commitments and a non-violation claim for failing to have 'open, market-oriented policies'.[19] More recently, it has also been reported that the US government is considering another Section 301 investigation on Chinese subsidies, to be followed by coordinated action with its allies in the WTO.[20]

Besides the general strategy on greater utilisation of WTO litigation to discipline China's state capitalism, the cases must be chosen carefully to make the strategy work. In particular, we would caution against the inclination to throw everything into the kitchen sink and try to attack the economic system of China as a whole. Instead, as we have outlined in Chapter 3, we should focus on those specific concerns which were raised during China's WTO accession process, especially its WTO-plus commitments on the behaviour and conduct of SOEs, price distortions and industrial subsidies. It is unclear why these commitments should be left un-enforced while new rules are being developed. As discussed in Chapter 5, we believe these commitments provide sufficient tools for WTO Members to address market distortions caused by China's state capitalism.

In particular, WTO litigation on three of these commitments would be particularly fruitful. The first commitment concerns the behaviour and conduct of SOEs, which states:

> China would ensure that all state-owned and state-invested enterprises would make purchases and sales based solely on commercial

---

[18] James Bacchus, Simon Lester and Huan Zhu, 'Disciplining China's Trade Practices at the WTO: How WTO Complaints Can Help Make China More Market-Oriented', Cato Institute Policy Analysis No. 856, 15 November 2018, 1, 20–9.

[19] Testimony of Jennifer Hillman, United States–China Economic and Security Review Commission Hearing on U.S. Tools to Address Chinese Market Distortions, 8 June 2018, 3–11, available at: www.uscc.gov/sites/default/files/Hillman%20Testimony%20US%20China%20Comm%20w%20Appendix%20A.pdf.

[20] Matthew Dalton, 'Chinese Manufacturers Sidestep Trade Barriers by Buying Factories Overseas', *The Wall Street Journal*, 6 May 2021, available at: www.wsj.com/articles/chinese-manufacturers-sidestep-trade-barriers-by-buying-factories-overseas-11620314120?mod=article_inline.

considerations, e.g., price, quality, marketability and availability, and that the enterprises of other WTO Members would have an adequate opportunity to compete for sales to and purchases from these enterprises on non-discriminatory terms and conditions. In addition, the Government of China would not influence, directly or indirectly, commercial decisions on the part of state-owned or state-invested enterprises, including on the quantity, value or country of origin of any goods purchased or sold, except in a manner consistent with the WTO Agreement.[21]

Essentially, this obligation is about making sure that the decisions of SOEs are made independently based on commercial considerations and are not subject to the influence of the Chinese government directly or indirectly. The problem though is that the nature of business decisions is such that it is often hard to untangle the actors and factors that go into the decision-making process, especially as the Chinese economic reform has reached an advanced stage where the government rarely makes direct intervention in the economy, if at all. However, the problem has now been largely solved with China's aggressive new drive for 'Party-building'. The role of the Party in the state and economy has been gaining increasing attention among other WTO Members in the past few years. For example, in 2017, the EU issued a staff working document on how to determine significant distortions in trade defence investigations involving China. This document noted that 'the [Chinese Communist Party] ("CCP") and State [are] practically indistinguishable'.[22] In particular, it noted the significant role played by the Party not only in the appointments of key positions in the SOEs, but also other key management decisions.[23] Over the next few years, the EU applied the methodology in a few cases,[24] but they were mainly focused on the CCP membership of the

---

[21] Report of the Working Party on the Accession of China, WT/ACC/CHN/49, 1 October 2001, para. 46.
[22] European Commission, 'Commission Staff Working Document on Significant Distortions in the Economy of the People's Republic of China for the Purposes of Trade Defence Investigations' SWD(2017) 483 final/2, 20 December 2017, 25, available at: https://trade.ec.europa.eu/doclib/docs/2017/december/tradoc_156474.pdf.
[23] Ibid., 27–30.
[24] See e.g. Commission Implementing Regulation (EU) 2019/915 of 4 June 2019 imposing a definitive anti-dumping duty on imports of certain aluminium foil in rolls originating in the People's Republic of China following an expiry review under Article 11(2) of Regulation (EU) 2016/1036 of the European Parliament and of the Council (*Official Journal of the European Union*, L 146/63, 5.6.2019); Commission Implementing Regulation (EU) 2019/687 of 2 May 2019 imposing a definitive anti-dumping duty on imports of certain organic coated steel products originating in the People's Republic of

senior management and did not really go into the details of the CCP influence in decision-making. In a recent case concerning the imposition of AD duties on imports of aluminium flat-rolled products from China, however, the European Commission discussed the role of the Party in the decision-making of firms at great length. It started by noting that:

> CCP cells in enterprises, state owned and private alike, represent another important channel through which the State can interfere with business decisions. According to the Chinese company law, a CCP organisation is to be established in every company (with at least three CCP members as specified in the CCP Constitution) and the company shall provide the necessary conditions for the activities of the party organisation. In the past, this requirement appears not to have always been followed or strictly enforced. However, since at least 2016 the CCP has reinforced its claims to control business decisions in SOEs as a matter of political principle. The CCP is also reported to exercise pressure on private companies to put 'patriotism' first and to follow party discipline. In 2017, it was reported that party cells existed in 70% of some 1,86 million privately owned companies, with growing pressure for the CCP organisations to have a final say over the business decisions within their respective companies.[25]

This general observation was followed by a detailed examination of the role of the Party in the exporters under investigation, where the Commission referred to the firms' Articles of Association, annual reports, and news stories to illustrate the significant roles played by the Party in the decision-making of the firms.

In response, Xiamen Xiashun, a private firm under investigation, opposed the findings by explaining that:

> the fact that there are party members in the company, does not mean that they are controlling the company. Xiamen Xiashun observed that it is legally obliged to allow the party members to organise party building activities, but it does not mean the party members have any influence over the company. It added that every person is allowed to belong to a religion or political party of its choice and it has no bearing on the decision making in the company. Furthermore, it underlined that the fact that there are party building activities organised in the company, does not

---

China following an expiry review pursuant to Article 11(2) of Regulation (EU) 2016/1036 of the European Parliament and of the Council (Official Journal of the European Union, L 116/5, 3.5.2019).

[25] Commission Implementing Regulation (EU) 2021/582 of 9 April 2021 imposing a provisional anti-dumping duty on imports of aluminium flat-rolled products originating in the People's Republic of China (*Official Journal of the European Union*, L 124/40, 12.4.2021), para. 138.

mean that there are CCP members among the management of the company. Finally, Xiamen Xiashun explained that Commission's translation of the 'party building' is wrong and that the CCP's members' activities within the company are mainly those related to the studying of government policies, providing their opinion and advice to their party organisation, or sometimes even some entertainment activities. It added that there was nothing in the record indicating that the CCP is controlling the respondent companies.[26]

In the final determination, the Commission reviewed and rejected these explanations based on the view that

the presence of CCP members in the company and the fact that the company facilitates party building activities and involvement thereof into 'decision making' is a clear indicator ... that the company is not independent from the state, and is liable to be acting in accordance with CCP policy rather than market forces.[27]

This case provides an instructive approach on how to make China's commitments on SOEs operational. While it is hard to prove the direct intervention by the government in the decision-making of SOEs, the confluence of the Party and state in China, and the heightened demands on 'Party building' in firms, especially SOEs, do provide an easy way to prove state influence. If it can be proved that Xiamen Xiashun, a wholly foreign-owned firm,[28] is subject to state influence through Party cells, it would not be hard to find state influence in SOEs, all of whom have their senior executives directly appointed by the Party.

As discussed in Chapter 5, an even broader commitment is set out in Section 9.1 of China's Accession Protocol mandating the Chinese government to ensure 'prices for traded goods and services in every sector to be determined by market forces'. This obligation goes beyond regulation of the behaviour and conduct of SOEs to cover all potential state intervention in the market that causes price distortion. Here, it is worth noting that the EU's assessment of the Party's influence on commercial

---

[26] Ibid., para. 280.
[27] Commission Implementing Regulation (EU) 2021/2170 of 7 December 2021 imposing a definitive anti-dumping duty on imports of aluminium converter foil originating in the People's Republic of China (*Official Journal of the European Union*, L 438/46, 8.12.2021), para. 62.
[28] 厦门厦顺铝箔有限公司 [Xiamen Xiashun Aluminium Foil Company Limited] available at: http://act.chinatt315.org.cn/hy/tthy/2014/0906/13763.html, which notes that Xiamen Xiashun is a foreign-invested firm wholly owned by Daching Enterprise Limited based in Hong Kong.

decisions of Chinese firms in recent AD investigations constitutes only part of its overall assessment of whether significant distortions exist in the Chinese market. Adopted in the overhaul of the EU's AD regime in December 2017, the new methodology based on an assessment of 'significant distortions' is aimed at maintaining the rigour of the EU's trade defence regime against NMEs.[29] Thus, to facilitate positive findings of such distortions, the European Commission prepared a 446-page long report providing a detailed analysis of market distortions in China based on a wide range of evidence concerning not only SOEs and Party/state influence on firms but also distortions in wage costs, preferential access to finance, public policies and discrimination against foreign firms and the lack of enforcement of certain laws.[30] Such evidence is highly useful for WTO litigation under Section 9.1 of the Accession Protocol to show that prices are distorted and are not determined by market forces in China.[31]

The final commitment addresses China's industrial policies, especially subsidies. As we have discussed extensively in Chapter 5, the SCM Agreement, coupled with the China-specific commitments, does provide sufficient defence against the encroachment of Chinese SOEs beyond its own shores. While there have been some concerns over the established jurisprudence, especially the AB's interpretation of 'public body', the alleged shortcomings have been balanced by the more recent AB decision in *US – Countervailing Measures (China) (Article 21.5)*, which rejected the 'conduct-based' approach in favour of the 'entity-based' approach. To the extent that there are still difficulties in establishing some elements of subsidies under the SCM Agreement, they are inherent problems in the framework of the SCM Agreement and not specific to China.

---

[29] Regulation (EU) 2017/2321 of 12 December 2017 amending Regulation (EU) 2016/1036 on protection against dumped imports from countries not members of the European Union and Regulation 2016/1037 on protection against subsidized imports from countries not members of the European Union (*Official Journal of the European Union*, L 338/1, 19.12.2017). For a discussion of the EU's amendment of its trade defence regime in 2017, see Andrei Suse, 'Old Wine in a New Bottle: The EU's Response to the Expiry of Section 15(a)(ii) of China's WTO Protocol of Accession' (2017) 20(4) *Journal of International Economic Law* 951.

[30] European Commission, 'Commission Staff Working Document on Significant Distortions in the Economy of the People's Republic of China for the Purposes of Trade Defence Investigations', n. 22.

[31] For discussions of how the European Commission has applied such evidence in AD investigations, see e.g. Stephanie Noel and Weihuan Zhou, 'EU's New Anti-Dumping Methodology and the End of the Non-Market Economy Dispute?' (2019) 14(9) *Global Trade and Customs Journal* 417.

As the SCM Agreement allows both domestic countervailing measures and multilateral litigation against subsidies, we would suggest that WTO Members not only bring WTO disputes but also countervailing investigations at the domestic level. In response to concerns that countervailing actions are impossible without sufficient information on the subsidy programmes in China, we would note that this problem can be remedied by the open-ended language of 'special difficulties' in Section 15(b) of China's Accession Protocol. This clause allows investigating authorities of the importing countries to use alternative methodologies for identifying and measuring subsidy benefits, especially when information on subsidies is lacking, insufficient, or otherwise difficult to obtain.

In addition, we would recommend greater utilisation of the rules on subsidies rather than those on other trade remedies measures, such as the NME rule in AD, for the following reasons.

First of all, the WTO AD rules are designed mainly to deal with the micro practices of businesses or firms, rather than to address market distortions stemming from state interventions at the macro level. Thus, countervailing measures provide better remedy against China's state capitalism as they target the source of the distortions created by government interventions.

Second, in practice, AD measures usually affect private Chinese firms, while countervailing measures by definition tend to target SOEs or firms on which special rights or privileges have been conferred. Thus, more frequent use of countervailing measures would place more restraints on SOEs or privileged firms while expanding the space for the growth of private firms, which are the main driving forces in a market economy. Such cases would also send the signal that the other WTO Members are genuinely interested in pushing for market-oriented reforms in China and help to steer China on the path of market economy in the long run.

Third, the (ab)use of AD measures to address market distortions in so-called NMEs like China is likely to attract retaliation. As shown in Chapter 4, the latest development of WTO case law in *Australia - A4 Copy Paper* has created flexibilities for investigating authorities to consider market distortions caused by state intervention in determining whether an external benchmark should be used in the calculation of normal values.[32] Such flexibilities can be utilised by all WTO Members; therefore, the effect of the decision is to open the door for WTO

---

[32] Panel Report, *Australia - Anti-Dumping Measures on A4 Copy Paper*, WT/DS529/R, adopted 27 January 2020. For a detailed analysis of the panel decision, see Weihuan Zhou

Members to treat each other as having an NME situation, which tends to remove the distinction between market economies and NMEs that has been long and widely adopted in AD practices.[33] In recent AD investigations, China has already utilised the flexibilities under the AD Agreement to retaliate against other countries' continued treatment of it as an NME. Notably, in a series of cases since 2017, China has found that a particular market situation (PMS) existed in a range of the United States' energy and resources industries based on evidence showing US government intervention in these industries through industrial policies, laws and regulations, subsidies at both federal and state levels, import and export restrictions and price controls.[34] These findings provided a basis for Chinese authorities to disregard the relevant prices in the US market and use benchmarks for the calculation of normal values. Most recently, China also found that a PMS existed in Australia's wine industry.[35] It is true that there is no hard evidence to show that China's increasing use of the PMS approach in recent AD investigations against the United States and Australia was motivated by retaliation. However, there is abundant literature to show that AD has become a convenient tool that China regularly uses in retaliation for others' AD measures[36]

---

and Delei Peng, 'Australia – Anti-Dumping Measures on A4 Copy Paper' (2021) 115(1) *American Journal of International Law* 94.

[33] See generally James Nedumpara and Weihuan Zhou, *Non-Market Economies in the Global Trading System: The Special Case of China* (Singapore: Springer, 2018).

[34] See e.g. 《关于原产于韩国、台湾地区和美国的进口苯乙烯反倾销调查最终裁定的公告》 [Notice of Ministry of Commerce on the Final Determination of an Anti-Dumping Investigation into Styrene Exported from South Korea, Taiwan and the United States] (People's Republic of China) Ministry of Commerce, Notice No 43, 22 June 2018, 46–71, available at: www.mofcom.gov.cn/article/b/e/201806/20180602758088.shtml; 《关于对原产于美国、韩国和欧盟的进口三元乙丙橡胶反倾销调查最终裁定的公告》 [Notice of Ministry of Commerce on the Final Determination of an Anti-Dumping Investigation into Ethylene-Propylene-Non-conjugated Diene Rubber Exported from the United States, South Korea and the European Union] (People's Republic of China) Ministry of Commerce, Notice No 60, 18 December 2020, 15–43, available at: www.mofcom.gov.cn/article/b/c/202012/20201203024350.shtml.

[35] See 《关于对原产于澳大利亚的进口相关葡萄酒反倾销调查最终裁定的公告》 [Notice of Ministry of Commerce on the Final Determination of an Anti-Dumping Investigation into Wine Exported from Australia] (People's Republic of China) Ministry of Commerce [hereinafter 'Wine Final Determination'], Notice No 6, 26 March 2021, 21–37, available at: www.mofcom.gov.cn/article/b/c/202103/20210303047613.shtml.

[36] See generally Mark Wu, 'Antidumping in Asia's Emerging Giants' (2012) 53(1) *Harvard International Law Journal* 102; Weihuan Zhou and Shu Zhang, 'Anti-Dumping and China's Implementation of WTO Rulings' (2017) 230 *The China Quarterly* 512.

and even as a weapon in economic or political conflicts.[37] Coupled with the fact that China reproduced the ways in which Australia and the United States have applied the PMS approach, particularly by relying on a very similar set of evidence,[38] it is reasonable to observe that China's recourse to the PMS method is essentially responsive to AD practices in the other countries. China's tit-for-tat use of the PMS approach against the United States and Australia sends a strong signal that it can treat other countries as NMEs when needed. If the trend continues, the AD system could also be rendered practically useless.

7.2.3 Is There Enough Evidence?

Another frequently-cited difficulty with WTO litigation against China is the lack of concrete information and evidence, especially given its poor record of transparency.[39] However, as discussed, this is not much of a problem as Section 15(b) of China's WTO Accession Protocol allows investigating authorities to resort to external benchmarks so long as they encounter 'special difficulties' in the application of the normal rules of the SCM Agreement. On state intervention in SOEs, more information becomes available on the role of the Party in the firms' decision-making process as the Party steps up its 'Party building' campaign in SOEs. For example, both the State-owned Assets Supervision and Administration Commission[40] (SASAC) and the

---

[37] See generally Weihuan Zhou and James Laurenceson, 'Demystifying Australia – China Trade Tensions' (2022) 56(1) *Journal of World Trade* 56.

[38] For a discussion of Australia's approach to the PMS method, see Weihuan Zhou, 'Australia's Anti-Dumping and Countervailing Law and Practice: An Analysis of Current Issues Incompatible with Free Trade with China' (2015) 49(6) *Journal of World Trade* 975, 980–7. For an example of the United States' practices, see United States Department of Commerce, Issues and Decision Memorandum for the Final Results of the 2014–2015 Administrative Review of the Anti-Dumping Duty Order on Certain Oil Country Tubular Goods from the Republic of Korea, 10 April 2017, 40–1, available at: http://enforcement.trade.gov/frn/summary/korea-south/2017-07684-1.pdf. See also Daniel Ikenson, 'Tariffs by Fiat: The Widening Chasm between U.S. Antidumping Policy and the Rule of Law', Cato Institute Policy Analysis No. 896, 16 July 2020, available at: www.cato.org/sites/cato.org/files/2020-07/pa-896-updated.pdf.

[39] For a comprehensive overview of China's compliance with the transparency obligations, see Henry Gao, 'The WTO Transparency Obligations and China' (2018) 12(2) *Journal of Comparative Law* 329.

[40] 国务院国有资产监督管理委员会 [State-owned Assets Supervision and Administration Commission], '国企党建 [Party building in SOEs]' available at: www.sasac.gov.cn/n2588030/n2588919/index.html.

People's Daily[41] have dedicated microsites on SOE 'Party building' efforts, which include troves of information on many SOEs. Interestingly, they also include information on some private and foreign-invested firms, such as an article on Xiamen Xiashun in 2015, where the Board Chairman of the company proudly stated that 'Party organization and party members have played a vital role in ensuring our impressive performance'.[42]

Moreover, as noted by Hillman and Bacchus, there has already been plenty of evidence as the USTR 'and other U.S. government agencies, along with numerous business and industry groups'[43] have been 'gathering evidence of questionable Chinese trade practices for years',[44] which are contained in 'the extraordinarily comprehensive and well-documented Section 301 Report, the annual reports of the [US–China Economic and Review Security Commission], and the annual USTR report to Congress on China's WTO compliance'.[45] If one adds to that 'the work done in the EU, Japan, Canada and others, and at the OECD along with other multilateral institutions, . . . it becomes clear that there is more than sufficient evidence to demonstrate that China's economy is operating in ways that undermine the WTO's rules-based, market-based system'.[46]

7.2.4 How to Bring Them?

In her testimony before the US–China Economic and Review Security Commission, Hillman suggested the United States bring a broad collective case along with a group of like-minded countries for the following reasons:[47] to muster the political power to achieve 'sustained pressure at the highest levels on China'; to test 'the most likely applicable provisions'; to provide a shield against potential retaliation from China against

---

[41] 人民网 [People's Daily Online], '国企党建 [Party building in SOEs]' available at: http://dangjian.people.com.cn/gq/.
[42] 人民网 [People's Daily Online], '叫声朋友，一起走—福建厦门海沧非公党建为企业插上腾飞的翅膀 [Friends, Let's Go Together – Party Building in Non-State Owned Firms at Fujian Xiamen Haicang helps enterprise taking off]', 21 April 2015, available at: http://dangjian.people.com.cn/n/2015/0421/c117092-26880305.html.
[43] Testimony of Jennifer Hillman, n. 19, 12.
[44] Bacchus et al., 'Disciplining China's Trade Practices at the WTO', n. 18, 7.
[45] Testimony of Jennifer Hillman, n. 19, 12.
[46] Ibid.
[47] Ibid., 11–12.

coalition partners and the companies behind; to pool the evidence on China's violations; and to 'provoke a more systemic response from China'.

We agree that a coalition case is a good way to bring such cases, as illustrated by many successful examples such as the *China – Raw Materials*[48] case, which was brought by the United States along with the EU and Mexico.[49] Through coordinated action among allies, the export restrictions on raw materials from China were removed. Yet, this case also illustrated two potential pitfalls that should be addressed in future coalition cases.

First, if the scope of the products covered in a case is too narrow, such as certain raw materials, then China could simply remove the measures on those products without making systemic changes to its export control system. This is what happened in the *Raw Materials* case, which prompted another joint case by the United States along with the EU and Japan on the same types of export restrictions on rare earths.[50] To avoid such repetitive breaches, the complainants in a coalition case need to make sure that the scope of the case is broad enough. In this regard, we would suggest that the scope of such disputes should focus on general practices rather than specific products, so that the whole process does not need to be repeated for every possible product. Our proposed approach, while rare, is not unprecedented in the WTO system. A good example is the case of *US – Section 301 Trade Act*,[51] where the panel essentially decided that the US Section 301 legislation, to the extent that it authorises unilateral action without authorisation of the WTO, could be

---

[48] Panel Report, *China – Measures Related to the Exportation of Various Raw Materials*, WT/DS394/R, WT/DS395/R, WT/DS398/R, adopted 22 February 2012; Appellate Body Report, *China – Measures Related to the Exportation of Various Raw Materials*, WT/DS394/AB/R, WT/DS395/AB/R, WT/DS398/AB/R, adopted 22 February 2012.

[49] Interestingly, the lead counsel of the United States in the case was Katherine Tai, the current USTR, see Howard Schneider, 'At WTO, U.S. Racks up Wins against China, but the Benefit Is Less Than Certain', *Washington Post*, 6 August 2012, available at: www.washingtonpost.com/business/economy/at-the-wto-a-growing-us-record-of-wins-against-china-but-a-less-than-certain-benefit/2012/08/06/345fc5a2-d285-11e1-adf2-d56eb210cdcd_story.html.

[50] Panel Report, *China – Measures Related to the Exportation of Rare Earths, Tungsten and Molybdenum*, WT/DS431/R, WT/DS432/R, WT/DS433/R, adopted 29 August 2014; Appellate Body Report, *China – Measures Related to the Exportation of Rare Earths, Tungsten and Molybdenum*, WT/DS431/AB/R, WT/DS432/AB/R, WT/DS433/AB/R, adopted 29 August 2014.

[51] Panel Report, *United States – Sections 301–10 of the Trade Act of 1974*, WT/DS152/R, adopted 27 January 2000.

WTO-inconsistent. However, based on 'the US undertakings articulated in the Statement of Administrative Action approved by the US Congress at the time it implemented the Uruguay Round agreements and confirmed and amplified in the statements by the US to this Panel',[52] the panel made a conditional finding of consistency. More specifically, to make sure that the United States would not go back on its words, the panel emphatically stated at the end of its report that 'should [such undertakings] be repudiated or in any other way removed by the US Administration or another branch of the US Government, the findings of conformity contained in these conclusions would no longer be warranted'.[53] We believe that a similar case could be brought against China's various laws and policies which mandate state/Party intervention in the decision-making of SOEs, guarantee government support to SOEs through subsidies, etc., as illustrated by the Xiamen Xiashun case. The aim of the case would not be just to prevent the government from intervening in a specific case, but to prevent government intervention with commercial considerations in all such cases, so that the market economy commitments could be upheld.

Second, even with a focus on problematic trade practices, there is still the possibility that China may just make minor tweaks to its measures to achieve 'paper compliance'.[54] Of course, this problem is not limited to China and many other WTO Members have resorted to similar tactics. To deal with this problem, the complainants should try to push for rulings with systemic implications. One good example is the recent case of *US – Safeguard Measure on PV Products*, where the United States was able to obtain confirmation from the panel that China's 'industrial policies, five-year plans, and other government support programs ... resulted in a massive and unforeseen increase in Chinese production capacity for CSPV products'[55] and thus constitute 'unforeseen development'.[56] Such decisions help to shape the jurisprudence, which can provide useful guidance to future cases even though, strictly speaking,

---

[52] Ibid., para. 8.1. The United States' undertakings and statements were essentially a commitment to not take actions under Sections 301–10 prior to exhaustion of DSU proceeding which effectively curtailed the relevant discretion of US authorities.
[53] Ibid.
[54] Webster, 'Paper Compliance', n. 10.
[55] Panel report, *United States –Safeguard Measure on Imports of Crystalline Silicon Photovoltaic Products*, WT/DS562, circulated 2 September 2021, 7.24.
[56] Ibid., 7.26–7.28.

the WTO does not have a formal system of binding precedents.[57] Of course, to make such a strategy work, we need to first bring back the AB,[58] which ironically has been paralysed by the United States itself. In addition, such decisions could also create the consensus necessary to bring about changes to WTO rules, which provides a more systemic solution to the challenges created by China's state capitalism, as we will discuss next.

7.3 Trade Negotiation

While we would prefer to use WTO litigation to deal with the challenges created by China's state capitalism, we also understand that this view is not shared by everyone and there have been ongoing efforts to tackle the problem through trade negotiation. In this section, we will review these efforts at both the bilateral and multilateral levels, which complement the rules in regional trade agreements as we have discussed in Chapter 6.

7.3.1 Bilateral Negotiation

As many of the concerns over China's economic system are systemic, the most ideal venue for negotiating new rules would be multilateral fora such as the WTO. However, this does not mean that bilateral negotiation is not an option. Instead, some major WTO Members have already tried this approach.

7.3.1.1 US–China Phase One Deal

The first such attempt is the Phase One trade deal,[59] which was signed by the United States with China on 15 January 2020 after a roller-coaster ride spanning the better part of two years. At ninety-six pages, the agreement includes seven chapters on the following issues: (1) intellectual

---

[57] On whether the WTO has a system of stare decisis, see Henry Gao, 'Dictum on Dicta: Obiter Dicta in WTO Disputes' (2018) 17(3) *World Trade Review* 509.
[58] On how to bring back the AB, see Henry Gao, 'Finding a Rule-based Solution to the Appellate Body Crisis: Looking Beyond the Multiparty Interim Appeal Arbitration Arrangement' (2021) 24(3) *Journal of International Economic Law* 534.
[59] Office of the United States Trade Representative, Economic and Trade Agreement between the Government of the United States of America and the Government of the People's Republic of China, 15 January 2020, available at: https://ustr.gov/sites/default/files/files/agreements/phase%20one%20agreement/Economic_And_Trade_Agreement_Between_The_United_States_And_China_Text.pdf.

property, (2) technology transfer, (3) trade in food and agricultural products, (4) financial services, (5) macroeconomic policies and exchange rate matters and transparency, (6) trade expansion, and (7) dispute resolution. Most of the chapters cover rules or regulatory issues, with chapter 6 setting out detailed market access commitments by spelling out in dollar values China's additional import targets for the next two years. The purchase commitments are supposed to solve the trade imbalance problem, which is what prompted President Trump to launch the US–China trade war in the first place,[60] through the imposition of tariffs on a massive list of Chinese goods.[61] Technically speaking, however, all the trade war tariffs imposed by the United States over the past two years were triggered by the rules issues, as elaborated in the USTR's Section 301 Report into China's Acts, Policies and Practices Related to Technology Transfer, Intellectual Property and Innovation.[62] While the Phase One deal helped to avoid further escalation of the trade war, it has left most existing retaliatory tariffs intact[63] and institutionalised the unilateral and confrontational approach to resolving disputes, which could reignite the bilateral trade tensions.[64] Moreover, the deal fails to address the more significant and systemic issues, such as China's SOEs and industrial policies and subsidies. Instead, these issues are expected to be addressed by the two parties in their Phase Two negotiations.[65]

---

[60] Benn Steil and Benjamin Della Rocca, 'Tariffs and the Trade Balance: How Trump Validated His Critics', Blog Post, Council on Foreign Relations, 21 April 2021, available at: www.cfr.org/blog/tariffs-and-trade-balance-how-trump-validated-his-critics, which mentioned that Trump tweeted '[W]e have a Trade Deficit of $500 billion per year', and 'We cannot let this continue!' right before the trade war.

[61] For more on the background on the trade war, see Henry Gao, 'WTO Reform and China: Defining or Defiling the Multilateral Trading System?' (2021) 62 *Harvard International Law Journal* 1, 26–30.

[62] Office of the United States Trade Representative, 'Findings of the Investigation into China's Acts, Policies, and Practices Related to Technology Transfer, Intellectual Property, and Innovation under Section 301 of the Trade Act of 1974', 22 March 2018, available at: https://ustr.gov/sites/default/files/Section%20301%20FINAL.PDF.

[63] Chad Bown, 'US–China Trade War Tariffs: An Up-to-Date Chart', Peterson Institute for International Economics, 16 March 2021, available at: www.piie.com/research/piie-charts/us-china-trade-war-tariffs-date-chart.

[64] Weihuan Zhou, 'WTO Dispute Settlement Mechanism without the Appellate Body: Some Observations on the US–China Trade Deal' (2020) 9(2) *Journal of International Trade and Arbitration Law* 443, 451–3.

[65] United States Trade Representative, '2019 USTR Report to Congress on China's WTO Compliance', March 2020, 30, available at: https://ustr.gov/sites/default/files/2019_Report_on_China%E2%80%99s_WTO_Compliance.pdf.

7.3.1.2 EU–China Comprehensive Agreement on Investment

As discussed in Chapter 6, the EU–China Comprehensive Agreement on Investment[66] (CAI) also includes some rules on SOEs, although these rules do not really add much new. Nevertheless, the fact that such issues can be included does signal China's growing openness to negotiations on SOE issues, which is confirmed by President Xi's recent statement, as discussed next.

7.3.2 Multilateral Negotiation

At the eleventh WTO Ministerial Conference in Buenos Aires, the United States, the EU and Japan issued a joint statement[67] condemning 'severe excess capacity in key sectors exacerbated by government-financed and supported capacity expansion, unfair competitive conditions caused by large market-distorting subsidies and state owned enterprises, forced technology transfer, and local content requirements and preferences' as 'serious concerns for the proper functioning of international trade, the creation of innovative technologies and the sustainable growth of the global economy'. To 'address this critical concern', they vowed to 'enhance trilateral cooperation in the WTO and in other forums'.

At the same conference, the United States also set the agenda on the substance of the negotiation and strived to control how the negotiations should be conducted. At the conclusion of the conference, the USTR Robert Lighthizer stated that 'MC11 will be remembered as the moment when the impasse at the WTO was broken. Many members recognized that the WTO must pursue a fresh start in key areas so that like-minded WTO Members and their constituents are not held back by the few Members that are not ready to act'.[68] In other words, instead of trying

---

[66] EU–China Comprehensive Agreement on Investment, Agreement in Principle, concluded on 30 December 2020, available at: https://trade.ec.europa.eu/doclib/press/index.cfm?id=2237.

[67] Office of the United States Trade Representative, 'Joint Statement by the United States, European Union and Japan at MC11', 12 December 2017, available at: https://ustr.gov/about-us/policy-offices/press-office/press-releases/2017/december/joint-statement-united-states.

[68] Office of the United States Trade Representative, 'USTR Robert Lighthizer Statement on the Conclusion of the WTO Ministerial Conference', 14 December 2017, available at: https://ustr.gov/about-us/policy-offices/press-office/press-releases/2017/december/ustr-robert-lighthizer-statement.

to seek a consensus among all WTO Members like it did in the past, the United States would now work with the 'coalition of the willing' and move at its own speed.

Since then, the trilateral group has intensified its work with several more joint statements. In turn, these statements have morphed into WTO reform proposals, with the key players all chipping in.

Among the major players, the EU was the first to issue a comprehensive concept paper. Released on 18 September 2018, it is entitled 'WTO Modernisation: Introduction to future EU proposals'[69] and covers three aspects: rule-making and development, regular work and transparency and dispute settlement. Three days later, Canada followed with its own discussion paper on 'Strengthening and Modernizing the WTO', which also includes three aspects: '(1) improve the efficiency and effectiveness of the monitoring function; (2) safeguard and strengthen the dispute settlement system; and, (3) lay the foundation for modernizing the substantive trade rules when the time is right'.[70] In addition to the two comprehensive papers, both the EU and Canada have also tabled various more specific proposals.[71] The United States has not issued any comprehensive proposal, but prefers to address the specific issues directly through stand-alone proposals.[72] In addition, Canada also convened a series of meetings with a group of like-minded countries. Informally referred to as the Ottawa Group, the group includes most of the key players in the WTO except the United States, China and India.[73] The

---

[69] European Commission, 'WTO Modernisation: Introduction to Future EU Proposals', 18 September 2018, available at: https://trade.ec.europa.eu/doclib/docs/2018/september/tradoc_157331.pdf.

[70] WTO, General Council, Strengthening and Modernizing the WTO: Discussion Paper – Communication from Canada, JOB/GC/201, 24 September 2018.

[71] See e.g. WTO, General Council, Communication from The European Union, China, Canada, India, Norway, New Zealand, Switzerland, Australia, Republic of Korea, Iceland, Singapore, Mexico, Costa Rica and Montenegro, WT/GC/W/752/Rev.2, 11 December 2018 (Multiparty Proposal); WTO, Strengthening the Deliberative Function of the WTO – Discussion paper – Communication from Canada, JOB/GC/211, 14 December 2018 (Canada Proposal).

[72] See e.g. WTO, General Council, An Undifferentiated WTO: Self-Declared Development Status Risks Institutional Irrelevance – Communication from the United States, WT/GC/W/757/REV.1, 14 February 2019; WTO, Council for Trade in Goods, Procedures to Enhance Transparency and Strengthen Notification Requirements under WTO Agreements – Communication from Argentina, Costa Rica, the European Union, Japan, and the United States, JOB/GC/204, 1 November 2018.

[73] The members include Australia, Brazil, Canada, Chile, European Union, Japan, Kenya, Korea, Mexico, New Zealand, Norway, Singapore and Switzerland.

proposals by the EU, the United States, Canada and the Ottawa Group share a lot of commonalities, especially on the following groups of issues, which are of particular relevance to China.

The first concerns the need to update the substantive rules of the WTO, such as clarifying the application of 'public body' rules to SOEs, expanding the rules on forced technology transfer and addressing barriers to digital trade.[74] All of these are long-standing issues which have been litigated in the WTO.[75] They each reflect a major concern over China's trade and economic systems, which employ measures that are perceived as unfair trade practices. The first relates to China's unique state-led development model, which emphasises the role of SOEs in the Chinese economy, often without a clear boundary between the state and the firm. The second refers to China's over-zealous drive to obtain and absorb foreign IPRs, where foreign firms are met with explicit or implicit demands to trade their technologies for markets. The third touches on the core of the authoritarian regime in China, where the government maintains tight control over information and the Internet.[76]

The second group addresses the procedural issue of boosting the efficiency and effectiveness of the WTO's monitoring function, especially the rules relating to compliance with the WTO's notification requirements, with subsidies as the leading example.[77] While no WTO Member may claim a perfect record in subsidy notifications, China's failure in

---

[74] See Multiparty Proposal, n. 71, 4–6; Canada Proposal, n. 71, 5; European Commission, Concept Paper on WTO Reform: WTO Modernisation – Introduction to Future EU Proposals, 18 September 2018, available at: https://trade.ec.europa.eu/doclib/docs/2018/september/tradoc_157331.pdf.

[75] On 'public body', see *US – Anti-Dumping and Countervailing Duties (China)*, n. 6; *US – Countervailing Measures (Article 21.5 – China)*, n. 12. On 'forced technology transfer', see *China – Certain Measures Concerning the Protection of Intellectual Property Rights, Request for Consultations by the United States*, WT/DS542/1, 26 March 2018; *China – Certain Measures on the Transfer of Technology, Request for Consultations by the European Union*, WT/DS549/1, 6 June 2018; on digital trade barrier, see Appellate Body Report, *China – Measures Affecting Trading Rights and Distribution Services for Certain Publications and Audiovisual Entertainment Products*, WT/DS363/AB/R, adopted 19 January 2010. See also the potential WTO case when Google pulled out of China, which was discussed in Henry Gao, 'Google's China Problem: A Case Study on Trade, Technology and Human Rights Under the GATS' (2011) 6 *Asian Journal of WTO and International Health Law and Policy* 347.

[76] For an overview of China's data regulation framework, see Henry Gao, 'Data Regulation with Chinese Characteristics', in Mira Burri (ed), *Big Data and Global Trade Law* (Cambridge: Cambridge University Press, 2021) 245.

[77] See Multiparty Proposal, n. 71, 9–11; Canada Proposal, n. 71, 2.

fulfilling that obligation seems to be particularly egregious. This seems to be a perennial problem, which the USTR has been complaining about ever since China's accession to the WTO.[78] After much nudging from the United States, China finally submitted its first subsidies notification in April 2006, nearly five years behind schedule.[79] However, even that remained incomplete as China did not notify subsidies by sub-central governments, which took China another ten years to report.[80] Moreover, the next notification took China four more years to submit. Frustrated over the slow progress, the United States invoked Article 25.10 of the SCM Agreement to file a 'counter notification' in October 2011, which identified more than 200 unreported subsidy measures.[81] To address the problem, the joint draft proposal by the United States, the EU, Japan and Canada on strengthening the notification requirements put forward some rather drastic measures, such as naming and shaming the delinquent Member by designating it as 'a Member with notification delay'; curtailing its right to make interventions in WTO meetings and nominations to chair WTO bodies, and even levying a fine at the rate of 5 per cent of its annual contribution.[82]

The last significant issue is development, another longstanding issue stemming from the call of the United States and the EU for greater 'differentiation' among WTO Members. The underlying rationale is that, while developed countries are willing to extend special and differential treatment to smaller developing countries, they are rather reluctant to extend the same treatment to large developing countries such as China which have already become economic powerhouses in their own right. Thus, in their proposals, the EU and Canada called for the rejection of 'blanket flexibilities'[83] for all WTO Members, which are to be replaced by

---

[78] United States Trade Representative, '2002 USTR Report to Congress on China's WTO Compliance', 1 December 2002, 22–3, available at: https://china.usc.edu/sites/default/files/article/attachments/2002-report-chinas-wto-compliance.pdf.
[79] United States Trade Representative, '2018 USTR Report to Congress on China's WTO Compliance', February 2019, 75, available at: https://ustr.gov/sites/default/files/2018-USTR-Report-to-Congress-on-China%27s-WTO-Compliance.pdf.
[80] Ibid.
[81] Ibid., 76.
[82] WTO, Council for Trade in Goods, Procedures to Enhance Transparency and Strengthen Notification Requirements under WTO Agreements – Communication from Argentina, Australia, Canada, Costa Rica, the European Union, Israel, Japan, New Zealand, the Separate Customs Territory of Taiwan, Penghu, Kinmen and Matsu, and the United States – Revision, JOB/GC/204/Rev.3, 5 March 2020, 3–4.
[83] Multiparty Proposal, n. 71, 6.

'a needs-driven and evidence-based approach'[84] that 'recognizes the need for flexibility for development purposes while acknowledging that not all countries need or should benefit from the same level of flexibility'.[85] The US proposal is more radical by proposing the automatic termination of special and differential treatment for Members which fall into one of the following four categories: OECD members; G20 members; classification as 'high income' by the World Bank; or a share of at least 0.5 per cent of global goods trade.[86] Such a classification system would strip many WTO Members of their developing countries status, including China, as it meets two criteria, that is, G20 membership and a large trade share.

Realising that it has become the unspoken target of WTO reform, China quickly responded with two documents. The first was a November 2018 position paper setting out China's three principles and five suggestions on WTO reform.[87] In May 2019, China submitted a formal proposal on WTO reform, which further elaborated the main issues of concern to China, as well as the specific actions that need to be taken.[88] While many of the suggestions directly respond to the China-related reform proposals, China is also trying to turn the tables by launching its own offensives. For example, China suggests that the first priority should be solving the existential issues facing the WTO, such as the impasse over the AB member appointment process, the abuse of the national security exception and the resort to unilateral measures.[89] Of course, given the mounting pressure, most of the Chinese proposals directly address the three groups of issues mentioned.

First, with regard to the new substantive issues being proposed, while China expresses willingness to consider some of the issues, such as electronic commerce and investment facilitation, it objects to many proposals. For example, one of the five suggestions in China's position paper is the need to 'respect members' development models', which means that China 'opposes special and discriminatory disciplines against

---

[84] Ibid., 7.
[85] Canada Proposal, n. 71, 5.
[86] WTO, Draft General Council Decision – Procedures to Strengthen the Negotiating Function of the WTO, WT/GC/W/764, 15 February 2019, 1–2.
[87] Ministry of Commerce of China (MOFCOM), 'China's Position Paper on WTO Reform', 20 December 2018, available at: http://english.mofcom.gov.cn/article/newsrelease/counselorsoffice/westernasiaandafricareport/201812/20181202818679.shtml.
[88] WTO, General Council, China's Proposal on WTO Reform – Communication from China, WT/GC/W/773, 13 May 2019.
[89] Ibid., para. 2.1–2.10.

state-owned-enterprises in the name of WTO reform'.[90] This is duly reiterated in China's reform proposal under the heading of 'Adhering to the Principle of Fair Competition in Trade and Investment'.[91] While some Western commentators might be puzzled by such an adamant position on the SOE issue, this is not surprising at all as SOEs relate to two of the three 'core interests' of China, as famously defined by State Councillor Dai Binguo in 2009.[92] Due to its unhappy experience with the discriminatory provisions in its WTO accession package, China resents being singled out in WTO negotiations. Because these proposals clearly target China, it is no surprise that China would react so strongly. Moreover, even in respect of issues on which China seems to agree with other WTO Members, the Chinese position sometimes comes with a twist. Electronic commerce is one such example, with the Chinese proposal focusing on 'cross-border trade in goods enabled by the Internet, as well as on such related services as payment and logistics services'.[93] As discussed elsewhere, this is very different from the position taken by the United States, which emphasises digital transmissions and the associated issue of free flow of data.[94]

Second, on the procedural issue of subsidy notifications, China adopts a dual-track approach. On the defensive side, China proposes that developing countries only comply with the notification obligations on a best-endeavour basis, and should receive more technical assistance for that purpose.[95] On the offensive side, China throws the ball into the court of developed countries by calling them to 'lead by example in submitting comprehensive, timely and accurate notifications' and 'improve the quality of their counter-notifications'.[96]

---

[90] MOFCOM, 'China's Position Paper on WTO Reform', n. 87.
[91] WTO, 'China's Proposal on WTO Reform', n. 88, section 2.4.2.
[92] The three core interests are: preserving China's basic state system and national security, national sovereignty and territorial integrity, and the continued stable development of China's economy and society. See Michael D. Swaine, 'China's Assertive Behavior: Part One: On "Core Interests"', China Leadership Monitor No. 34 (15 November 2010), available at: https://carnegieendowment.org/files/CLM34MS_FINAL.pdf. State-owned economy is the basic economic system according to Articles 6 and 7 of the Chinese Constitution, which also state that public ownership and state-owned economy shall be the leading force in the economy.
[93] WTO, 'China's Proposal on WTO Reform', n. 88, para. 2.22.
[94] Henry Gao, 'Digital or Trade? The Contrasting Approaches of China and US to Digital Trade' (2018) 21(2) *Journal of International Economic Law* 297, 308–10.
[95] WTO, 'China's Proposal on WTO Reform', n. 88, para. 2.28.
[96] Ibid.

Third, with regard to development, China is taking a flexible approach. As a matter of principle, it made clear that special and differential treatment is an 'entitlement' that China 'will never agree to be deprived of'.[97] At the same time, it also indicated its willingness to 'take up commitments commensurate with its level of development and economic capability'.[98] Such an approach is not new but is actually consistent with what China has been doing for some time. For example, when trade facilitation was first brought within the scope of WTO negotiations as one of the four 'Singapore Issues', most developing country Members were unwilling to participate as they believed that the benefits would mostly accrue to developed countries with large trade volumes while developing countries would need to foot the bill for modernising their customs processes.[99] China, however, took a different position because it realised that it, as one of the world's largest and most diversified traders, stood to benefit greatly from such an initiative. Thus, China actively participated in the negotiations and became one of the first developing countries to ratify the agreement upon conclusion. Moreover, China did not designate any Category C measures[100] and agreed to implement 94.5 per cent of the measures immediately upon ratification.[101] All of its Category B measures had been fully implemented by January 2020.[102]

Interestingly, China's position on WTO reforms may continue to evolve. A major policy shift was first announced in President Xi's speech at China's Fourth Import Expo in November 2021. After reiterating that '[t]he multilateral trading regime with the WTO at its core is the cornerstone of international trade', President Xi went on to state that 'China will take an active and open attitude in negotiations on issues such as the digital economy, trade and the environment, industrial subsidies and state-owned enterprises.'[103] This seems to contradict China's earlier

---

[97] MOFCOM, 'China's Position Paper on WTO Reform', n. 87.
[98] Ibid.
[99] Third World Network, 'Many Developing Countries against Trade Facilitation Rules in WTO', 28 June 2003, available at: www.twn.my/title/twninfo35.htm.
[100] The Trade Facilitation Agreement designates three categories of measures, with those in category A to be implemented immediately upon the entry into force of the Agreement, those in category B to be implemented after a transition period and those in category C to be implemented after receiving the necessary technical assistance.
[101] WTO, Trade Facilitation Agreement Database, Status of Implementation Commitments – China, available at: https://tfadatabase.org/members/china.
[102] Ibid.
[103] 'Full Text: Keynote Speech by Chinese President Xi Jinping at the Opening Ceremony of the 4th China International Import Expo', XinhuaNet, 4 November 2021, available at: www.news.cn/english/2021-11/04/c_1310290787.htm.

position, which explicitly stated that 'during discussions on subsidy disciplines, no special or discriminatory disciplines should be instituted on state-owned enterprises in the name of WTO reform'.[104]

While it is encouraging to see that China is now more receptive to reform discussions in the multilateral context, such willingness to negotiate does not necessarily mean that China will regard all issues as negotiable, let alone accept the results of such negotiations. Notwithstanding this cautious note, negotiations with China could still be fruitful if the following principles of engagement are observed.

The first principle is non-discrimination. China regarded the period between the Opium War and the founding of the People's Republic as the 'century of humiliation', when 'unequal treaties' were forced upon China by the imperialist powers.[105] Such experience made China very sensitive to discriminatory gestures. For example, when a key negotiation held in July 2008 on the Doha Round ran into an impasse due to India's refusal to make concessions on special agricultural safeguards, the United States pressured China to make additional concessions in certain sectors to make the results commercially meaningful for American businesses. China rejected the request because no such demands were made of the other emerging economies. In response to the United States complaint that China had failed to contribute to the round even though it was given 'a seat at the big kids' table'[106] as requested, China's Ambassador to the WTO, Sun Zhenyu, gave a diatribe at the informal Trade Negotiations Committee meeting held afterwards.[107] Sun outlined China's contributions across all areas of agricultural and non-agricultural market access and services, and blasted the United States and other developed countries for pressuring China while protecting their own sensitive areas. To have a productive negotiation, such mistakes should not be repeated. Instead, any proposed rules, be it on SOEs, subsidies or competition, should be

---

[104] WTO, 'China's Proposal on WTO Reform', n. 88.
[105] Michael Zhou, 'For China, the History that Matters Is Still the "Century of Humiliation"', *South China Morning Post*, 28 September 2021, available at: www.scmp.com/comment/opinion/article/3150233/china-history-matters-still-century-humiliation.
[106] See Paul Blustein, *Misadventures of the Most Favored Nations: Clashing Egos, Inflated Ambitions, and the Great Shambles of the World Trade System*, 1st ed. (New York: Public Affairs, 2009) 274.
[107] Henry Gao, 'China's Contributions in the DDA – from Ambassador Sun Zhenyu', Blog Post, Blogspot.com, 26 August 2008, available at: http://wtoandchina.blogspot.com/2008/08/chinas-contributions-in-dda-from.html.

neutral, at least on their face, so that they would not be deemed as China-specific or discriminatory against China. Otherwise, proposed reforms could well be perceived by China as a 'tailor-made straightjacket' and rejected.[108]

The second principle is reciprocity. It is too tempting to just fill the negotiation document with a long list of demands on China. The primary example for such an approach is the US–China Phase One deal, which contains ninety-seven references to 'China shall', while only three references to 'the United States shall'. Given the one-sided nature of the deal, it is no surprise that China has no incentive to implement it.[109] Anyone with any level of familiarity with the Chinese culture would understand the importance of 'saving face' to the Chinese. Thus, it is hard to imagine that China would be willing to engage unless it is offered something in return, even if just as a token. This point is also proven by China's warm reactions to President Biden's announcement that the United States will not try to change China's economic system. But this is just the starting point and more substantive gestures of good will would be needed before concrete results could be achieved. Such gestures could include discontinuing practices such as the NME methodology in AD investigations against China, the WTO-inconsistent trade war tariffs and the deprivation of China's right to invoke the general exceptions clause to justify its export restrictions on raw materials and rare earth.[110]

The third principle is understanding China's own priorities. As stated by Sun Tzu: 'If you know both yourself and your enemy, you can win numerous battles'.[111] In particular, a good understanding of China's own reform goals and policy movements is crucial as it provides important insights on what China may agree to. President Xi's recent announcement on SOEs and subsidies noted above is a good example, as it signals

---

[108] The Permanent Mission to the World Trade Organization, 'On the Reform of the WTO Intervention by H. E. Ambassador Zhang Xiangchen at the Luncheon in Paris Workshop', 20 November 2018, available at: http://wto.mofcom.gov.cn/article/meetingsandstatements/201811/20181102808197.shtml.

[109] Chad Bown, 'China Bought None of the Extra $200 Billion of US Exports in Trump's Trade Deal', Peterson Institute for International Economics, 8 February 2022, available at: www.piie.com/blogs/realtime-economic-issues-watch/china-bought-none-extra-200-billion-us-exports-trumps-trade.

[110] Henry Gao, 'China's Changing Perspective on the WTO: From Aspiration, Assimilation to Alienation', 8 November 2021, available at: https://papers.ssrn.com/sol3/papers.cfm?abstract_id=3958510.

[111] The Internet Classics Archive, 'The Art of War by Sun Tzu', available at: http://classics.mit.edu/Tzu/artwar.html.

that China is now willing to discuss these issues. But a seasoned China observer could feel the wind of change long before this formal announcement just by reading other moves made by China, such as its agreement to commitments[112] on SOEs and subsidies in the CAI and its recent application to join the Comprehensive and Progressive Agreement for Trans-Pacific Partnership (CPTPP).[113]

On industrial subsidies, the ongoing COVID-19 pandemic, ironically, might facilitate negotiations in the WTO for the following reasons:

First, during the pandemic, it has become popular for governments around the world to inject capital into firms, both public and private.[114] This raises an interesting issue on the definition of SOEs. Does government equity infusion make these firms state owned and, more importantly, qualify them as 'public bodies' under the SCM Agreement? So far, the United States and the EU have been arguing that the determination of 'public bodies' shall be based primarily on governmental ownership instead of the exercise of governmental functions. As the pandemic made more and more firms in the West reliant on government equity infusions, the ownership-based argument has become less and less relevant in the policy debate. Instead, WTO Members need to find ways to differentiate among firms based on what they do and the effects of such actions on the market rather than who contributes the capital.

Second, unlike most crises in human history, the COVID-19 pandemic is different in that its effect is economy-wide rather than just limited to specific sectors. This also raises difficult issues of how to ascertain the market benchmark, which is a key issue in determining the 'benefit conferred' on recipients of subsidies under the SCM Agreement. When

---

[112] Henry Gao, 'The EU–China Comprehensive Agreement on Investment: Strategic Opportunity Meets Strategic Autonomy', 1 May 2021, available at: https://papers.ssrn.com/sol3/papers.cfm?abstract_id=3843434.

[113] Henry Gao and Weihuan Zhou, 'China's Entry to CPTPP Trade Pact Is Closer Than You Think', Nikkei Asia, 20 September 2021, available at: https://asia.nikkei.com/Opinion/China-s-entry-to-CPTPP-trade-pact-is-closer-than-you-think.

[114] For a detailed review of subsidies (and other measures) provided by major economies during the COVID-19 pandemic, see Jan Bohanes, 'An Overview of Trade-Related Measures Taken by WTO Members during the COVID-19 Pandemic and a Few Reflections Thereon', in Amrita Bahri, Weihuan Zhou and Daria Boklan (eds.), *Rethinking, Repackaging, and Rescuing World Trade Law in the Post-Pandemic Era* (Oxford: Hart Publishing, 2021), chapter 2; Ru Ding, 'Time to Reform the Non-actionable Subsidy Rules in the WTO: The COVID-19 Subsidies and Beyond', in Amrita Bahri, Weihuan Zhou and Daria Boklan (eds.), *Rethinking, Repackaging, and Rescuing World Trade Law in the Post-Pandemic Era* (Oxford: Hart Publishing, 2021), chapter 4.

the whole market is distorted by a pandemic, the usual benchmarks would not be of much use in the determination of benefits. In a way, we have seen such problems before in the so-called NMEs, where the whole market is usually treated as being distorted, thereby providing no reliable benchmarks. This problem has traditionally been solved with the use of alternative benchmarks from surrogate countries, but now, with the pandemic sweeping the whole globe, it is extremely hard, if not impossible, to find such an imaginary surrogate country that could provide the necessary benchmarks. This might force WTO Members to rethink the surrogate price model and come up with new methodologies which better capture the distortions.

Third, the pandemic also provides a unique opportunity for reviving non-actionable subsidies, a category that existed under the original SCM Agreement, including certain subsidies for research and development (R&D), environmental protection and regional development, which were permitted and exempted from countervailing actions on a provisional basis for five years.[115] However, this category lapsed at the turn of the century due to the lack of consensus for its renewal among WTO Members.[116] Many countries are subsidising the research on and development of COVID-19 vaccines and many more countries will probably justify the various COVID-19 subsides they have introduced as necessary for protecting human life or health or to avoid devastating effects on the economy. However, the existing WTO framework does not provide sufficient policy space to shield these subsidies from WTO challenges. It would be good to have such flexibilities re-introduced into the SCM Agreement.

Last, unlike before the pandemic, many of the COVID-related subsidies have been provided by the United States and EU countries, rather than just China, the country which many deemed to be the worst offender on subsidies before the pandemic.[117] This is probably due to

---

[115] Agreement on Subsidies and Countervailing Measures, Marrakesh Agreement Establishing the World Trade Organization, Marrakesh, 15 April 1994, in force 1 January 1995, 1869 UNTS 14, Articles 8 and 31.

[116] WTO, Committee on Subsidies and Countervailing Measures, Minutes of the Special Meeting Held on 20 December 1999, G/SCM/M/22, 17 February 2000.

[117] Simon Evenett and Johannes Fritz, 'Subsidies and Market Access: New Data and Findings from the Global Trade Alert', Voxeu.org, 25 October 2021, available at: https://voxeu.org/article/subsidies-and-market-access-new-data-and-findings-global-trade-alert; Ding, 'Time to Reform the Non-Actionable Subsidy Rules in the WTO', n. 114.

the fact that, despite it being the first country hit with COVID-19, China was able to control the pandemic rather quickly while most of the West are still fighting the pandemic. In a way, this could turn the tables on subsidies discussions and usher in a new set of negotiating dynamics, as the United States and the EU now find themselves to be more on the defensive side. Now that everyone has become sinners, it could be easier to negotiate subsidies disciplines, especially if the WTO Members could agree on the types of subsidies which are necessary to combat the pandemic and aid the recovery.

7.4 Conclusion

To conclude, we believe that the current WTO framework does provide great potential to tackle China's state capitalism. These include actions both through WTO litigation, WTO-consistent unilateral measures and trade negotiation. First, contrary to the conventional view that the existing rules are insufficient to deal with China's SOEs and subsidies, we have illustrated how the WTO dispute settlement system may be used to address relevant problems in a creative manner. In particular, we have argued that the cases need to be selected strategically with an aim to addressing systemic issues and WTO-illegal trade practices generally and to causing changes to relevant WTO jurisprudence that would facilitate future actions against China's state-led market distortions via WTO litigation and trade remedies. Between subsidy-countervailing and AD actions, we suggest resorting more to the former as they directly address the effect of market distortions created by China's state capitalism. In addition, it must be noted that bad cases could create bad jurisprudence, which could backfire in cases like the NME issue for AD measures. Second, on trade negotiation, we do not believe that bilateral negotiations would be successful, as illustrated by China's recently-concluded Phase One deal with the United States and the CAI with the EU. Instead, we believe that there is great potential through multilateral negotiations, especially in view of President Xi's recent announcement that China would be willing to address issues relating to SOEs and subsidies at a multilateral level. At the same time, we also caution against the plurilateral approach such as the trilateral negotiation and suggest rules of engagement which could make the negotiations more conducive. We also note how the COVID-19 pandemic could help with the reform discussion on subsidies, especially in view of the massive subsidies provided by Western governments which are equally as problematic as China's subsidies. Hopefully, our suggestions will be picked up to facilitate both the utilisation of existing rules and the development of new rules to tackle China's state capitalism.

8

Conclusion

The Potential of Multilateralism

Twenty years after its accession to the WTO, China has emerged as one of the most important Members. China's growing strength and influence, however, has also aggravated the longstanding concerns about its behaviour and practices in global economic activities. Observers such as former United States Trade Representative (USTR) Robert Lighthizer, for example, called China an 'existential'[1] threat to the multilateral trading system, arguing that China's system of state capitalism is inherently incompatible with the liberal world trading order.

How to deal with the China challenge? For people like Robert Lighthizer and Donald Trump, the answer was obvious: unilateral measures. Believing that '[t]rade wars are good, and easy to win',[2] Trump tried to attack China's state capitalism practices through Section 301 measures and unilateral tariffs.[3] Such an approach could be effective in the short term, as the additional tariffs disrupted and even temporarily paused the bilateral trade flow. However, this approach does not address systemic issues related to China's pervasive use of state-owned enterprises (SOEs), subsidies and other government support in the pursuit of ambitious industrial policies. These are the true problems with the Chinese model

---

[1] Office of the United States Trade Representative, 'Opening Statement of USTR Robert Lighthizer to the House Ways and Means Committee', 27 February 2019, available at: https://ustr.gov/about-us/policy-offices/press-office/press-releases/2019/february/opening-statement-ustr-robert.

[2] Jacob M. Schlesinger, '"Trade Wars Are Good," Trump Tweets', *The Wall Street Journal*, 2 March 2018, available at: www.wsj.com/articles/trade-wars-are-good-trump-tweets-1519996161.

[3] Office of the United States Trade Representative, 'Findings of the Investigation into China's Acts, Policies, and Practices Related to Technology Transfer, Intellectual Property, and Innovation Under Section 301 of the Trade Act of 1974', 22 March 2018, available at: https://ustr.gov/sites/default/files/Section%20301%20FINAL.PDF; Office of the United States Trade Representative, 'China Section 301-Tariff Actions and Exclusion Process', available at: https://ustr.gov/issue-areas/enforcement/section–investigations/tariff-actions.

which tend to undermine the condition of competition that WTO rules are designed to protect. These problems have been intensified by China's current SOE reform which has further strengthened the role and influence of the Party/state in state entities and created even more powerful SOEs to engage in domestic and global economic activities, often for strategic purposes. Moreover, as a big economy, China does not capitulate easily and may instead (as it actually did) retaliate in kind by imposing its own tariffs, resulting in a no-win situation. Thus, the US–China trade war has effectively dissipated any hope that unilateral measures could still force changes in China.

It can be argued, however, that unilateral measures are not meant to be effective on their own, but must be understood as part of a bigger campaign to force China to the negotiating table and enter into bilateral deals that address systemic issues, which is exactly what Trump has done in the trade war. The problem, however, is that this strategy is also more wishful thinking than reality. For example, the US–China Phase One deal was largely focused on purchase commitments and barely touched upon the systemic issues.[4] Moreover, as our analysis of the EU–China Comprehensive Agreement on Investment shows, even if a bilateral deal sets out to address some of the systemic issues, it is unlikely to provide much beyond what China has already committed to under the WTO. This is not necessarily a fault of the negotiators. Instead, it simply reflects the limits of bilateral agreements.

Similar observations can be made of the various plurilateral deals, with the Comprehensive and Progressive Agreement for Trans-Pacific Partnership (CPTPP) as the leading example. As we have shown in Chapter 6, despite its ambitions, the CPTPP does not really add much new beyond existing WTO disciplines on China's state capitalism. But that is not the most challenging aspect of plurilateral agreements. Rather, even if any such agreements do ultimately include more meaningful rules, it could prove difficult to persuade China to accept such rules, as such agreements may not provide sufficient market access incentives for China to agree to the new rules. This is why we have always advocated the multilateral approach.

---

[4] For a detailed analysis of the Phase One agreement, see Weihuan Zhou and Henry Gao, 'US–China Phase One Deal: A Brief Account', Regulating for Globalization: Trade, Labor and EU Law Perspectives (22 January 2020), available at: http://regulatingforglobalization.com/2020/01/22/us-china-phase-one-deal-a-brief-account/.

CONCLUSION: THE POTENTIAL OF MULTILATERALISM

This book is premised on the potential of multilateralism. As we have documented, it was the desire to normalise its trade relations within the multilateral framework that prompted China's initial decision to return to the multilateral trading system.[5] During its accession process, China made a conscious effort to reform its economic system in line with the requirements of the GATT and WTO. The period also coincided with China's domestic economic reform, with a major component being the reform of its SOEs. On the other hand, the GATT/WTO Members were also well aware of potential inconsistencies between the rules of the GATT/WTO and China's economic and trade system. To address these problems, they carefully crafted special rules in China's accession package to help the Chinese economy become more market-oriented.

While China did pursue unprecedented market-oriented reform, the potential of the multilateral rules to tame China's state capitalism has not been fully unleashed since China's accession. This is partly due to the reversal of China's own SOE reform process and partly due to the lack of utilisation of China-specific rules in its accession package, as discussed in detail in this book. While the Appellate Body (AB)'s rulings in some earlier cases have made it difficult to apply some of the general WTO rules, these obstacles have largely been removed by later developments in both WTO jurisprudence and China's SOE reform. Thus, it is time to return to multilateralism by challenging China's policies, laws and practices at the WTO dispute settlement system based on China's existing WTO-plus obligations.

Of course, recognising the potential of multilateralism does not mean that multilateralism is perfect. Instead, we believe that multilateralism is the most promising compared with unilateral measures and the bilateral and plurilateral negotiations previously outlined. In addition to making fuller use of the existing rules under the WTO, this book has also put forward some approaches for the negotiation of new rules at the multilateral level where such rules are needed. In particular, we call for the major players to resist the temptation to agree on rules in small circles and then force them upon China as fait accompli. Such tactics not only do not work, but more likely will backfire and destroy China's faith in multilateralism, which is already waning amidst suspicions of

---

[5] See Henry Gao, 'China's Changing Perspective on the WTO: From Aspiration, Assimilation to Alienation', (2022) 21(3) *World Trade Review* 342, 343–344.

double-standards by major Western powers.⁶ Instead, the major powers should set a good example for China by following the rules-based system in settling their differences, even in hard times.

Unfortunately, with the demise of the AB, WTO litigation against China can be less effective than it used to be, at least in the short term, as China may appeal unfavourable rulings into the void.⁷ On the other hand, China has consistently presented itself as a staunch defender of the multilateral trading system,⁸ advocated the appointment of new AB members⁹ and signed on to the so-called multi-party interim appeal arbitration arrangement (MPIA) as a temporary replacement for the AB.¹⁰ Thus, it can be argued that China is unlikely to abuse the right of appeal to avoid unfavourable rulings in disputes involving MPIA parties. This is evidenced by the ongoing China–Australia dispute over China's anti-dumping action against barley imported from Australia in which the two parties agreed to use the MPIA process if needed.¹¹ However, even in these disputes, it remains to be seen whether China will maintain its good record of compliance as before.¹² In contrast, in another recent dispute with the United States (which is not a MPIA party), China did just the opposite by appealing into the void after the panel found in favour of the United States' imposition of safeguard measures on certain Chinese crystalline silicon photovoltaic products.¹³ China's different approaches suggest that it is likely to continue to block

---

⁶ Ibid.
⁷ Joost Pauwelyn, 'WTO Dispute Settlement Post 2019: What to Expect?' (2019) 22(3) *Journal of International Economic Law* 297.
⁸ The State Council Information Office of the People's Republic of China, '《中国与世界贸易组织》白皮书 [The China and the WTO White Paper]', 28 June 2018, available at: www.scio.gov.cn/zfbps/ndhf/37884/Document/1632379/1632379.htm.
⁹ WTO, General Council, 'China's Proposal on WTO Reform – Communication from China', WT/GC/W/773, 13 May 2019, 3.
¹⁰ European Commission, 'The WTO Multi-party Interim Appeal Arrangement Gets Operational', 3 August 2020, available at: https://trade.ec.europa.eu/doclib/press/index.cfm?id=2176.
¹¹ WTO, *China – Anti-Dumping and Countervailing Duty Measures on Barley from Australia*, Agreed Procedure for Arbitration under Article 25 of the DSU, WT/DS598/5, 20 August 2021.
¹² Weihuan Zhou, *China's Implementation of the Rulings of the World Trade Organization* (Oxford: Hart Publishing, 2019).
¹³ WTO, *United States – Safeguard Measure on Imports of Crystalline Silicon Photovoltaic Products*, Notification of An Appeal by China under Article 16 of the Understanding on Rules and Procedures Governing the Settlement of Disputes, WT/DS562/12, 20 September 2021.

the adoption of unfavourable panel reports in future disputes with the United States and probably with other non-MPIA parties as well. This reveals a deep flaw in the US complaints against China's trade practices: if the United States really regards them as serious problems in violation of WTO rules, why would the United States undermine its ability to challenge such practices in the WTO by destroying the very institution created to enforce these rules? Thus, unless the United States discontinues its blockage of the appointments of AB members, it is unlikely to succeed in its own campaign to make new rules against China, as the other Members will doubt the seriousness of the United States in making new rules without a proper enforcement mechanism in place. Moreover, the lawless actions of the United States will teach China that WTO rules and institutions are disposable, a bad example that China will surely follow at some point.

We hope that we have demonstrated, through our modest work in this book, the potential of multilateralism to tackle China's state capitalism. But we would also caution that such potential could not be realised without positive actions affirming the commitment to international rule of law. In particular, we have advised a course of action for the major players in the WTO including the following:

First, actively utilising existing rules in the WTO framework, especially those rules on subsidies and market economy principles, to show that they are serious in bringing China's state capitalism practices in compliance with WTO rules;

Second, restoring the proper functioning of the WTO dispute settlement system by starting the selection process for AB members, either through the ending of the blockage by the United States or, failing that, by forcing the vote on appointments of AB members through the General Council of the WTO;[14]

Third, engaging China constructively in the reform discussions by taking advantage of China's recent announcement that they are open to discuss issues on SOEs and subsidies.[15]

---

[14] Henry Gao, 'Finding a Rule-Based Solution to the Appellate Body Crisis: Looking Beyond the Multiparty Interim Appeal Arbitration Arrangement' (2021) 24(3) *Journal of International Economic Law* 534.

[15] 'Keynote Speech by Chinese President Xi Jinping at the opening ceremony of the 4th China International Import Expo', XinhuaNet, 4 November 2021, available at: www.news.cn/english/2021-11/04/c_1310290787.htm.

Contrary to those who see China as an 'existential' threat to the multilateral trading system, we believe that the China-related challenges provide an opportunity for the WTO to once again prove its raison d'être, that is, to 'develop an integrated, more viable and durable multilateral trading system ... by entering into reciprocal and mutually advantageous arrangements directed to the substantial reduction of tariffs and other barriers to trade and to the elimination of discriminatory treatment in international trade relations'.[16] Thus, for WTO Members which are keen to improve and strengthen the rules on SOEs and industrial subsidies, it is crucial that any negotiations must be conducted on a reciprocal and non-discriminatory basis. This means that, instead of targeting China, future negotiations must target the problems and must consider China's position and needs on these issues. As many economies maintain a significant state sector and almost all major economies increasingly resort to subsidies, the fundamental challenge for negotiations is how to strike a proper balance between the regulation of SOEs and subsidies and the need to leave sufficient policy space for governments to use SOEs and subsidies for legitimate policy objectives. With its WTO-plus obligations, China is already subject to remarkably more rigorous disciplines and has less such policy space compared to other WTO Members. It would be difficult, if not impossible, to push China to accept more rules that target it, such as those contemplated in the US–EU–Japan joint proposals on industrial subsidies. As far as SOE rules are concerned, it is true that some of the disciplines developed under the CPTPP and some post-CPTPP trade and investment treaties provide a solution for how transparency may be enhanced and how services subsidies may be regulated. It is also true that the CPTPP offers a more balanced approach (compared with China's rigid WTO-plus obligations) by allowing governments the flexibility to develop preferred exceptions to counterbalance gradually expanded disciplines. In these respects, the CPTPP does provide a model for future negotiations at the multilateral level. China's recent request to join the CPTPP[17] also suggests that the CPTPP SOE rules are acceptable

---

[16] *Marrakesh Agreement Establishing the World Trade Organization*, 15 April 1994, 1867 UNTS 154, 33 I.L.M. 1144 (1994), chapeau.

[17] Ministry of Commerce of China, 'China Officially Applies to Join the Comprehensive and Progressive Agreement for Trans-Pacific Partnership (CPTPP)', 18 September 2021, available at: http://english.mofcom.gov.cn/article/newsrelease/significantnews/202109/20210903201113.shtml.

to it. However, due to the various deficiencies of the CPTPP SOE rules in dealing with Chinese SOEs, especially when compared with China's WTO-plus obligations, WTO Members need to ensure that negotiations of SOE rules based on the CPTPP model would not provide an opportunity for China to soften its existing obligations by seeking to, for example, limit the coverage of state entities and create a range of exceptions or non-conforming measures that are not available to it under the current WTO rules.

Toward this end, scholars, negotiators and policymakers will need to carry on the unfinished business in this book. For academic research, some of the remaining questions are concerned with whether there is an existing theoretical framework that can be applied or whether a new framework needs to be developed to guide the negotiations and design of SOE rules in a way that can effectively address real-world problems. Moreover, more research is also needed to explore the ways to enhance harmonisation of competition policy, especially competitive neutrality, at the global level as part of the solution to the problems caused by SOEs. For negotiators and policymakers, some of the major tasks going forward involve re-conceptualising and rethinking world trade rules in general so that they can be applied and further developed to accommodate different economic models and, more specifically, developing feasible modalities for the negotiations of more advanced rules on SOEs and industrial subsidies. It is our hope that this book offers a valuable source for researchers, lawyers, policymakers and negotiators to deal with the mounting challenges posed by state capitalism.

INDEX

accession to WTO. *see* WTO accession
adequate opportunity requirement, 71, 75–6, 98, 136, 160
adoption of corporatisation strategies. *see* commercialisation and modernisation of SOEs
Agreement on Subsidies and Countervailing Measures (SCM Agreement), 11, 61–4, 125
  'benefit conferred' test, 115
  direct transfer of funds, 103–4
  duty and tax exemptions, 107–8
  provision of goods or services/purchase of goods, 104–7
  public bodies categorisation, 155, 157
  revenue foregone, 104
  specificity requirement, 119
Agreement on Trade-Related Aspects of Intellectual Property Rights (TRIPs), 82
Agreement on Trade-Related Investment Measures (TRIMS), 83
anti-dumping (AD) investigations, 10, 59–61, 87–9
  AD Agreement, 89–91
  China-specific rule, 89–90
  'ordinary course of trade' test, 91–2
  'particular market situation' test, 92–3, 164–6
  'reasonably reflecting' test, 93–4
  special rules facilitating investigations, 59
  US–China bilateral negotiations, 60–1
anti-dumping (AD) measures. *see* anti-dumping (AD) investigations

Appellate Body (AB) of WTO, 10
  anti-dumping measures, 88–92, 157
  commercial considerations requirement, 99–100
  external benchmarks, 115–18
  multi-party interim appeal arbitration arrangement, 188–9
  non-discrimination principle, 74–6
  public body categorisation, 111–14, 155, 163
  revenue foregone, 104
  systematic subsidy programmes, 122–3

barriers to digital trade, 174
behaviour and conduct requirement, 7–8, 54–6, 159–62
'benefit conferred' test
  adjustments to benchmarks, 116–19
  China-specific obligations, 114–19
  external benchmarks, application of, 115–19
  SCM Agreement, 115
  subsidy rules, 115–19
bilateral agreements
  limitations, 186
  see also China–EU Comprehensive Agreement on Investment; EC–China bilateral negotiations; US–China bilateral negotiations
bound goods
  exports, 110
  import monopolies, 77–9
  import tariffs, 56, 77

carve-outs
  SOEs
    CPTPP rules, 11, 153

192

INDEX

GATT rules, 56–7
China's WTO Accession Protocol, 11, 52–3, 166
China's WTO-plus obligations, 3
  behaviour and conduct requirement, 159–62
  commercial considerations requirement, 97–100
  duty and tax exemptions, 110
  import purchasing procedures, 97–100
  price controls, 100–1, 111
  price distortions, 162–3
  subsidies, 102–10, 118, 124, 139, 150, 163–6
    direct transfer of funds, 103–4
    indirect subsidies, 109–10
    provision of goods or services/ puchase of goods, 104–9
    revenue foregone, 104
  transparency obligations, 86, 143
  see also China-specific obligations
China/Biden administration, relationship between, 1, 180
China/EU, relationship between, 2
China/Trump administration, relationship between, 1, 186
China/WTO, relationship between, 1–2
China–EU Comprehensive Agreement on Investment (CAI), 3, 8, 11, 172, 186
  commercial considerations requirement, 150, 152
  non-discrimination requirement, 150
  SOE rules, 150–2
  transparency obligation, 151
China-specific obligations, 125
  anti-dumping investigations, 89–90
  subsidy rules, 102
    'authority-based' test, 111–14
    'benefit conferred' test, 114–19
    direct transfer of funds, 103–4
    indirect subsidies, 109–10
    provision of goods or services/ purchase of goods, 104–9
    public body categorisation, 111–14
    revenue foregone, 104

specificity requirement, 119–24
WTO-plus obligations on SOEs
  import purchasing procedures, 97–100
  price controls, 100–1
  see also China's WTO-plus obligations
Civil War, 43–5
commercial considerations requirement, 55–6, 75–6, 97–100, 124, 160–1
CAI, 150, 152
CPTPP, 137–8
EU–Japan FTA, 148
EU–Vietnam FTA, 148
commercialisation and modernisation of SOEs, 9, 17–19
  corporate governance, 26–9
  ownership diversification, 29–33
  restructuring and reorganisation, 34–8
Communist Party of China (CPC)
  SOEs, influence on, 6, 160–2
Company Law 1994, 18, 161
competitive neutrality, 2–7, 140, 191
compliance with unfavourable rulings, 157–8
Comprehensive and Progressive Agreement for Trans-Pacific Partnership (CPTPP), 3, 8, 11, 127, 186
  SOE rules, 153
    commercial considerations requirement, 137–8
    exceptions, 145–7
    non-commercial assistance, 139–41
    non-conforming measures, 147, 190
    non-discrimination requirement, 138–9
    SOEs defined, 133–7
    specificity requirement, 140
    sub-central SOEs, 146–7
    subsidy rules, 139–41
    transparency obligations, 141–5
contract responsibility system, 15–16
coronavirus

coronavirus (cont.)
  economy-wide impact, 181–2
  public bodies categorisation, impact on, 181
  subsidies argument, impact on, 182–3
corporate governance, 18
  commercialisation and modernisation of SOEs, 26–7, 29
  Communist Party of China involvement, 27–9

disclosure rules, 8, 84
  insufficient disclosure, 119
discrimination against China in negotiations, 179–80, 190
Doha Round, 1, 53, 179
duty and tax exemptions, 110
  SCM Agreement, 107–9

EC–China bilateral negotiations, 53
enforcement challenges, 7, 11, 163, 189
  transparency rules, 143, 145, 151
EU–Japan FTA (2019), 11
  commercial considerations requirement, 148
  non-commercial assistance, 148
  prohibited subsidies, 149
  subsidy rules, 148
EU–Vietnam FTA (2020), 11
  commercial considerations requirement, 148
  non-commercial assistance, 148
  prohibited subsidies, 149
  subsidy rules, 148
European Community (EC)
  China's contracting party status, concerns over, 46
  see also EC–China bilateral negotiations
European Union (EU), 125
  anti-dumping investigations, 89, 162
  concerns over state-capitalist model, 2
  FTAs, 128–31
  litigation against China, 154, 168
  significant distortions in trade defense investigations, 160
  WTO modernisation, 173
  'differentiation' among WTO members, 175
  notification requirements, 175
  see also China–EU Comprehensive Agreement on Investment; EU–Japan FTA; EU–Vietnam FTA
exemptions, 6, 8, 111, 147
  CPTPP rules, 11, 139, 145, 149
  duty and tax exemptions, 107–10
  non-discrimination obligation, 100

forced technology transfer, 159, 172, 174
Foreign Trade Law 2004, 66
free trade agreements (FTAs)
  EU–China cooperation, 128–9
    pre-CPTPP, 130–1
  US–China cooperation, 128–9
    pre-CPTPP, 129–30
  US–Singapore FTA, 131–3
  see also Comprehensive and Progressive Agreement for Trans-Pacific Partnership; EU–Japan FTA; EU–Vietnam FTA; United States–Mexico–Canada Agreement

General Agreement on Tariffs and Trade (GATT), 10
  China's return to, 2–3, 45–6
  contracting party status, 46–52
  contracting party status
    US reservations, 46
  limitations. see limitations of GATT/WTO rules
  market economy concept, 48–50
  non-discrimination. see non-discrimination obligation
  People's Republic of China, 43–5
    withdrawal from GATT, 44
  Republic of China, 42–3
  subsidy exceptions, 148–9
  Uruguay Round negotiations, 51
  US–China bilateral negotiations, 47–9, 53
General Agreement on Trade in Services (GATS), 82, 141

subsidy exceptions, 148–9
General Commercial SOEs, 24–5, 114, 134
    non-discrimination obligation, 73
    ownership diversification, 29
    privately-owned enterprises, 25
growth of the private sector, 5–7, 18, 21, 40

horizontal mergers, 34

import monopolies, 77
    profit margins, 78
Industrial Enterprises Law 1988, 16–17
industries critical to national security, 20, 25, 34, 176
intellectual property rights, 51, 82, 158, 174
    US–China Phase One Deal, 170
    see also Agreement on Trade-Related Aspects of Intellectual Property Rights
International Trade Organization (ITO), 42, 81

limitations of GATT/WTO rules, 69–71
    see also China-specific obligations
    anti-dumping, 87–95
    see also anti-dumping (AD) investigations
    import monopolies, 77–9
    see also import monopolies
    non-discrimination principle, 71–6
    see also non-discrimination obligation
    quotas, 79–80
    see also quotas
    transparency obligations, 80–7
    see also transparency obligation
litigation
    China as complainant, 154
    China as respondent, 154, 188
    coordinated action against China, 168
        broadness of scope, 168–9
        non-/limited compliance, 169–70
    inadequacy of WTO rules, 155, 183–4
    China's compliance, 156–8

China's trade practices, 156
    insufficiently rigorous interpretion, 156
    insufficiency of evidence, 166–7
    ownership disputes, 155

Made in China 2025 plan, 24, 120, 159
managerial and operational autonomy of SOEs, 9, 13, 15, 27, 57, 65
    Industrial Enterprises Law, 16–17
    ownership and management of SOEs, separation of, 15–17
market economy principles, 189
market-distortive behaviours of SOEs, 5, 10, 95, 97, 101, 116–18, 134–5, 183–4
    anti-dumping investigations, 10, 59–61, 69, 95, 164–6
    'ordinary course of trade' test, 91–2
    'particular market situation' test, 92–3
    CPTPP, 147
    European Commission report, 163
    SCM Agreement, 109
mergers, 6, 35
    horizontal mergers, 34
    vertical mergers, 37
mixed ownership, 18
    see also ownership diversification
mixed ownership reform opinions, 30, 32
modern enterprise system, 21
    professional management, 18
    property rights, 17
    regulatory versus business functions, 18, 23
    rights and responsibilities of SOEs, 18
most-favoured-nation (MFN) treatment, 43
    CPTPP, 137
    GATT rules, 44–5, 73
    non-discrimination principle, 71, 73–4
    anti-circumvention function, 74–5
    see also non-discrimination obligation
multilateralism
    China's market-orientated reforms, 187

multilateralism (cont.)
  CPTPP, 186
  SOE reforms, 186–7
multi-party interim appeal arbitration arrangement (MPIA), 188–9

national champions, 9, 23
  State-Owned Assets Supervision and Administration Commission, 19–22
National Development and Reform Commission (NDRC), 21
national treatment (NT) rule
  CPTPP, 137
  non-discrimination principle, 71, 73–4
    anti-circumvention function, 74–5
  see also non-discrimination obligation
new WTO rules, 4, 8, 11
  see also China–EU Comprehensive Agreement on Investment; Comprehensive and Progressive Agreement for Trans-Pacific Partnership
non-commercial assistance, 139–41
  EU–Japan FTA, 148
  EU–Vietnam FTA, 148
  USMCA, 148
non-discrimination obligation, 71
  anti-circumvention function
    MFN treatment, 74–5
    NT rule, 74–5
  CAI, 150
  China's commitments to WTO members, 55–6, 97–100
  CPTPP, 138–9
  limitations, 76
  MFN treatment, 71, 73–4
  NT rule, 71, 73–4
  scope of 'exclusive or special rights or privileges', 72–3
  state trading enterprises, 71–6
  types of enterprises covered, 71–2
  see also most-favoured-nation treatment; national treatment rule
non-market economy (NME) status

anti-dumping investigations, 59–61, 87–9, 164
  AD Agreement, 89–91
  China-specific rule, 89–90
  'ordinary course of trade' test, 91–2
  'particular market situation' test, 92–3
'reasonably reflecting' test, 93
notification requirements
  subsidy rules, 174–5, 177
  transparency, 81, 83–6
  WTO reform proposals, 174–5

operational autonomy of SOEs. see managerial and operational autonomy of SOEs
'ordinary course of trade' (OCT)
  anti-dumping measures, 91–2
Organization for Economic Co-operation and Development (OECD)
  SOEs, 5
ownership and management of SOEs, separation of, 15–17
  Industrial Enterprises Law, 16–17
  see also managerial and operational autonomy of SOEs
ownership diversification
  General Commercial SOEs, 29
  permitted ownership diversification, 30
  Public Welfare SOEs, 32
  Special Commercial SOEs, 29–30
  trends, 32–3
'particular market situation' (PMS), 90, 92–4, 165–6

People's Republic of China (PRC), 43
periodic review of trade policies.
  Trade Policy Review documents, 86
  transparency, 81, 85–7
  see also Trade Policy Review Mechanism
preferential regulatory treatment, 6–7, 124
  see also subsidy rules
pricing policies
  anti-protectionism commitment, 58
  price controls, 57–8, 100–1, 162–3

commitment to WTO consistent application, 58–9
transparency commitment, 58
WTO Members' concerns, 59–61
private ownership, 18
privately-owned enterprises (POEs)
  expansion of, 21–2
  General Commercial SOEs, 25
  SOEs, relationship with, 5
privatisation of SOEs, 9, 18, 64
  corruption, 19
prohibited subsidies, 62, 119
  EU–Japan FTA, 149
  EU–Vietnam FTA, 149
  USMCA, 149
public bodies
  AB categorisation, 111–14, 155, 163
  coronavirus, impact of, 181
  SCM Agreement categorisation, 155, 157
  subsidy rules, 111–14, 155, 174
  trade negotiation, 174
public policy objectives, 8
Public Welfare SOEs, 24–5, 134
  non-discrimination obligation, 72
  ownership diversification, 32
publication and administration of trade-related laws
  transparency, 81–3

quantitative restrictions. see quotas
quotas
  disputes, 79
  general prohibition, 79
  'reasonably reflecting' test, 93–4

reciprocity, lack of in negotiations, 180
recognition of companies as legal entities, 18
recognition of limited liability of shareholders, 18
Republic of China
  International Trade Organization, 42
  Taiwan, 43
restrictions to market access
  GATT rules, 45
  SOEs, 6
Restructuring Opinions, 34

right to import and export goods. see trading rights

Sanitary and Phytosanitary (SPS) Measures Agreement, 83, 159
'Socialist Market Economy', 17, 49–53, 57
Special Commercial SOEs, 24–5, 134
  non-discrimination obligation, 72
  ownership diversification, 29
specificity rule
  CPTPP, 140
  de facto specificity, 120, 122–4
  de jure specificity, 120–2
  subsidies, 62–3, 119–21, 140
  regional specificity, 121–2
State Capital Investment and Operation Companies (SCIOs). see State Capital Investment Companies (SCICs), see State Capital Operation Companies (SCOCs)
State Capital Investment Companies (SCICs), 38
  State Capital Operation Companies distinguished, 38–9
State Capital Operation Companies (SCOCs), 38
  State Capital Investment Companies distinguished, 38–9
state capitalism concept, 1–5, 10
state intervention.
  WTO rules, 3
  see also anti-dumping (AD) investigations; subsidy rules
state trading enterprises (STEs), 10
  non-discrimination obligation, 71–6
  quotas, 79–80
state-invested enterprises (SIEs)
  state-invested holding companies, 20
  state-invested joint stock companies, 20
  wholly-SIEs, 20
State-Owned Asset Law 2009, 20
State-Owned Assets Supervision and Administration Commission (SASAC), 9, 38–9
  classification of SOEs, 25

State-Owned Assets Supervision and Administration Commission (SASAC) (cont.)
　Communist Party of China involvement, 21
　mandate, 19–20
state-owned enterprises (SOEs)
　behaviour and conduct, impact of, 54–6
　CAI, 150–2
　calls to strengthen WTO rules, 2–3
　CPTPP rules, 133, 153, 190
　　commercial considerations requirement, 137–8
　　exceptions, 145–7
　　non-commercial assistance, 139–41
　　non-conforming measures, 147
　　non-discrimination requirement, 138–9
　　SOEs defined, 133–7
　　sub-central SOEs, 146–7
　　subsidies, 139–41
　　transparency obligations, 141–5
　FTAs, 128–33
　government procurement carve-outs, 56–7
　market-distortive behaviours. *see* market-distortive behaviours of SOEs
　non-discrimination obligation, 71–6
　privately-owned enterprises, relationship with, 5
　reforms, 2–3, 5, 9–10, 13–14, 41, 186–7
　　classification of SOEs, 24–6
　　commercialisation and modernisation of SOEs, 18
　　corporate governance, 26–9
　　impact of, 39–40
　　managerial autonomy of SOEs, 15–17
　　operational autonomy of SOEs, 15
　　ownership diversification, 29–33
　　restructuring and reorganisation, 34–8
　　state asset management system, 38–9
　　State-Owned Assets Supervision and Administration Commission, 19–23
　　see also commercialisation and modernisation of SOEs
　restricting market access, role in, 6
　role and conduct, 4–5, 8
　subsidies. *see* subsidy rules
subsidy rules, 6, 10–11, 189
　benchmark mechanism, 63–4
　'benefit conferred' test, 114–15
　　adjustments to benchmarks, 116–19
　　external benchmarks, application of, 115–19
　CPTPP, 139–41
　direct transfer of funds, 103–4
　EU–Japan FTA, 131
　EU–Vietnam FTA, 148
　exceptions, 148
　export subsidies, 62
　GATT/GATS exceptions, 149
　import substitution subsidies, 62
　notification requirements, 174–5
　ownership as specificity criterion, 62–3
　prohibited subsidies, 62, 119, 149
　provision of goods or services/ purchase of goods, 104–11
　public bodies categorisation, 155, 174
　　'authority-based' test, 111–14
　revenue foregone, 104
　SCM Agreement, 61–4, 163–6
　specificity rules, 62–3, 119–21
　　de facto specificity, 120, 122–4
　　de jure specificity, 120
　　regional specificity, 121–2

tariff concessions, protection of value of, 45, 56, 77, 95
Technical Barriers to Trade (TBT) Agreement, 82–3
Tiananmen Square protests, 50
trade disputes. *see* litigation
trade negotiations, 12
　bilateral negotiation
　　CAI, 172
　　US–China Phase One Deal, 170–1
　multilateral negotiation
　　China's response, 176–83
　　greater 'differentiation' among WTO Members, 175–6

reform proposals, 172–4
WTO's monitoring function, 174–5
WTO's notification requirements, 174–5
Trade Policy Review Mechanism (TPRM), 81, 143
trading rights
examination and approval system, 64, 66
historical restriction of trading rights, 64
WTO Members' concerns
lack of transparency, 64–5
Trans-Pacific Partnership (TPP), 133
transparency obligation, 8, 10–11
CAI, 151
China's commitments to WTO members, 64–5
CPTPP, 141–3
implementation challenges, 143–5
notification of regulatory measures, 81, 83–6
passive/paper transparency, 83
periodic review of trade policies, 81, 85–7
positive/participatory transparency, 84
pricing policies, 58
publication and administration of trade-related laws, 81–3
trading rights, 64–5

unfair trade practices, 70, 174
state-capitalist model, 2, 129
United States, 11, 148
Biden administration, 1, 180
FTAs
US–China cooperation, 128–30
US–Singapore FTA, 131–3
Trans-Pacific Partnership, 133
Trump administration, 1, 186
see also US–China bilateral negotiations
United States–Mexico–Canada Agreement (USMCA) (2020), non-commercial assistance, 148
prohibited subsidies, 149
Uruguay Round, 51, 169
US–China bilateral negotiations

anti-dumping, 60–1
GATT, 47–9, 53
Phase One Deal, 170–1

vertical mergers, 37

WTO accession
China's commitments to WTO members, 67–8
anti-dumping, 59–61
government procurement, 56–7
non-discrimination commitment, 55–6, 97–100
pricing policies, 57–9
purchases and sales solely based on commercial considerations, 55–6, 97–100
quantitative import commitment, 56
subsidies, 61–4
transparency commitment, 64–5
impact of, 185–6
international concerns about China's economic model, 53–4
industrial policies and subsidies, 61–4
see also subsidy rules
pricing policies and market distortion, 57–61
see also pricing policies
SOEs, role of, 54–7
see also state-owned enterprises
trading rights, 64–7
see also trading rights
market access negotiations, 52–3
see also China's WTO Accession Protocol
WTO dispute settlement system, 188–9
WTO reform proposals, 173–4
China's response
subsidy notification, 177
substantive issues, 177–80
notification requirements, 174–5, 177
updating substantive rules, 174
WTO 'Schedule of Concessions on Goods' (Goods Schedule), 77

For EU product safety concerns, contact us at Calle de José Abascal, 56–1°,
28003 Madrid, Spain or eugpsr@cambridge.org.

www.ingramcontent.com/pod-product-compliance
Ingram Content Group UK Ltd.
Pitfield, Milton Keynes, MK11 3LW, UK
UKHW022246220326
469255UK00019B/379